THE GIRLHOOD OF

QUEEN VICTORIA

A Selection from Her Majesty's Diaries
between the Years 1832 and 1840

Volume II

Elibron Classics
www.elibron.com

Elibron Classics series.

ISBN 978-0-543-67774-7 (paperback)
ISBN 978-0-543-67773-0 (hardcover)

This Elibron Classics Replica Edition is an unabridged facsimile of the edition published in 1912 by John Murray, London.

THE GIRLHOOD OF QUEEN VICTORIA

Emery Walker Ph. sc.

Viscount Melbourne
from a portrait by Sir Edwin Landseer R.A.
in the possession of the Earl of Rosebery

THE GIRLHOOD OF QUEEN VICTORIA

A SELECTION FROM HER MAJESTY'S DIARIES BETWEEN THE YEARS 1832 AND 1840

PUBLISHED BY AUTHORITY OF
HIS MAJESTY THE KING

EDITED BY VISCOUNT ESHER, G.C.B., G.C.V.O.

IN TWO VOLUMES

VOL. II

LONDON
JOHN MURRAY, ALBEMARLE STREET, W.
1912

CONTENTS

VOL. II

CHAPTER XI

September, 1838

CHAPTER XII

October, November, and December, 1838

PAGES

CHAPTER XV

June, July, and August, 1839

LIST OF ILLUSTRATIONS

VOL. II

Note.—Illustrations marked * are taken from the Queen's private portrait albums.

INTRODUCTORY NOTE TO CHAPTER XI

Lord Melbourne had now reached the climax of his career. It is as the tutor, secretary, and guardian of the young Queen that his fame is firmly established among the Prime Ministers of Great Britain. Not that he was in character or intellect below the average of the statesmen who have held that great office. Although sometimes frivolous in speech and unconventional in manner, he was, according to the universal testimony of those who knew him best, firm and earnest of purpose. His shrewd appreciation of men was only equalled by his keen sense of the political requirements of the people he was engaged in governing. He was a convinced but moderate reformer. His Whig training confirmed the traditional instinct for government with which, like so many aristocrats of that day, he appeared to be endowed. His mind was cultured in the broad sense of the term. He was a scholar, but not a pedant. He was a firm believer in the doctrines of Christianity, but not "religious." He elected to call himself a quietest. It was a favourite phrase. He had been described as pensive and solitary. It was not the popular conception of him, but it is probably the true one.

As a Minister he belonged to a caste that, although passing away and depreciated by modern Britons, has done glorious service for our country. He was an aristocrat of a fibre fearless, prompt, and haughty. As of Lord Salisbury in after-years, so of him. He was something different from a "clerk raised to the *n*th."

His task was not an easy one, but he carried the burden of government lightly, and with consummate tact, through those difficult years from 1834 to 1840, when the middle classes, conscious of power, but as yet ignorant of its uses, were initiating the great series of economic changes that in the course of thirty years converted the Kingdom of Great Britain into the British Empire. To that Empire, as we know it to-day, the Monarchy was essential. Awe of the Throne, and respect for its occupant, were elements necessary to the growth of Imperial sentiment and racial unity. When Queen Victoria succeeded her uncle, William IV., the Monarchy had been, for many years, associated with failing powers and with low ideals. That the young Princess when she ascended the Throne should have found Lord Melbourne at her side was a piece of singular good fortune. These Journals prove it; but if any doubt arises, let the reader imagine what might have happened if, during those few impressionable years before her marriage, the Queen had been associated with and controlled by a Minister with the hard precision of a Strafford or the rash timidity of a Bute.

CHAPTER XI

1838

Saturday, 1st September.—Spoke of my going to Bushey and Bagshot which I disliked ; of my hating morning visits ; of the habit I had when a little girl and visited my Aunts, of praising every thing, in order to get it, which made Lord Melbourne laugh very much. Speaking of red-legged partridges, he said to Lady Normanby, " Haven't you any of those red-legged fellows in Italy ? I don't mean Cardinals," he said. Spoke to Lord M. of the former *very* severe etiquette in George III.'s and Queen Charlotte's time, which Lord M. said they introduced very much. The Duchess of Brunswick,[1] he said, used always to lay it to Queen Charlotte's account and used to say indignantly, " For a *petite Princesse* to give herself airs, which my Mother and my Grandmother never did ! " Lord M. said that all the *Ladies* dined with the King and Queen and Family, but no gentlemen, except perhaps on very particular occasions the Archbishop of Canterbury and the Lord Chamberlain. He said that Lady Charlotte Bellasyse,[2] his Cousin, who was Lady to the Duchess of Gloucester—when

[1] Augusta, sister of George III. and daughter of Frederick Lewis, Prince of Wales, and his wife, Princess Augusta of Saxe-Gotha. She married Charles William Frederick, Duke of Brunswick.

[2] See Vol. I., p. 314.

her husband, Mr. Bellasyse, came down, he dined at the Equerries' table and came up after dinner; *she* dined with the King; I said the Princesses were very fond of her; "She was a good creature," said Lord M. Spoke of the Princesses, their high spirits; of the King's not allowing them to marry; upon which Lord M. asked if they ever showed an inclination to marry; "For, that's a thing," he said, "which can't come of itself; you must either let people see one another, or you must negotiate," which is very true.

Sunday, 2nd September.—I gave him Uncle Leopold's letter to read, and when he had done reading it, he said, "It is very kind." Lord M. said he had a letter from Lord John who will be down here on the 12th. Lord M. then said that here was this long Despatch from Durham, which he offered to read to me, and did read. But before he read it, he said that I must know that Canada originally belonged to the French and was only ceded to the English in 1760, when it was taken in an expedition under Wolfe; "A very daring enterprize," he said. Canada was then entirely French, and the British only came afterwards; they divided it into Upper and Lower Canada, and allowed the French to keep their particular rights and Institutions; and in a little while gave the country Executive and Legislative Assemblies like in England. Lord Melbourne explained this very clearly (and much better than I have done) and said a good deal more about it. He then read me Durham's despatch, which is a very long one and took him more than ½ an hour to read. Lord M. read it beautifully with that fine, soft voice of his, and with so much expression, so that it is needless to say I was much interested by it.

Lord M. had intended to ride, but on hearing I meant to walk, *most kindly* gave it up and said he would walk with me. Wrote my journal. Read in Durham's despatch. At 5 I walked out with all my ladies and gentlemen; I had not been out many minutes when Lord Melbourne joined me, and walked near me the whole time. We walked down to Adelaide Cottage. Lord M. asked me if Uncle Leopold was very angry with Mamma; I said Pretty well; upon which Lord M. observed laughing, "I think he's afraid of her," which I fear is the case. I asked Lord M. if he thought I should walk round the Terrace; "I think it would be better," he replied. In going up to the terrace, there is a very steep hill which is a dreadful pull, and Lord M. and I were quite blown in coming up. I then walked round the terrace, crowded to an amazing degree with people, between Lord Melbourne and Lord Torrington,—Lady Normanby just behind me, and also the other ladies; and my 3 other gentlemen in front; it was hot work. We then walked up and down the Terrace (the private part) for a few minutes, listening to the band, and came home at 6.[1] It was a beautiful evening. Read in Durham's despatch.

At a ¼ to 8 we 13 dined. Lord Melbourne led me in, and I sat between him and Lord Torrington. Lord Melbourne said he wasn't tired. Spoke with him of various things; of my tight *sleeves* which he admired; of some excellent red deer we had at dinner; of being able to manage animals by feeding. Lord M. said, "You can do anything almost by feeding, from a man down to a goat or

[1] This custom the Queen adhered to up to the time of the Prince Consort's death.

a deer," which made us laugh much and which I wouldn't allow. Spoke of *Irvingism*; and Lord M. said, "People should be quite sure, when they have any of these revelations, from *what* quarter they come." After dinner, before we sat down, Lord Melbourne, Lord Torrington, Major Keppel,[1] Lady Normanby (and I listening), talked of *rowing*, and Matches; and Lord M. said, "I don't like any pleasure which is *drudgery*"; he thinks rowing very laborious. "Why, you might as well dig."

I asked Lord Melbourne who his paternal grandmother was[2]; a Miss Coke of Melbourne, he replied; she was a great heiress, and through her came all that property. She was the daughter of Thomas Coke, Vice-Chamberlain to George 1st, who was the descendant of a famous Sir John Coke. Her brother died, and all the property came to her. Lord M. never saw her, as she died before his father could remember her; his father was born in 1745, and she died about 1751; "she was very pretty," he added. Spoke of Queen Caroline, and of the feeling for her; "I never saw anything like it in my life," said Lord M.; "it was very alarming; it even spread to the Troops." "George IV. never was popular," Lord M. said. And whatever Queen Caroline did, had no weight with the people, for, they said, it was all his fault at first. Lord M. continued, that it was quite madness his (George IV.) conduct to her; for if he had only separated from her, and let her alone, that wouldn't have signified; but he persecuted her, and "he cared as much

[1] George Thomas Keppel succeeded his brother in 1851 as sixth Earl of Albemarle. He was a groom-in-waiting to the Queen. He served in the 14th Regiment at Waterloo, and lived till 1891.

[2] For Lord Melbourne's ancestry, see the Appendix.

about what she did, as if he had been very much in love with her," which certainly was very odd. "He (George IV.) was a clever man," Lord M. said, but he thinks that he never was honestly advised about Queen Caroline; though, he continued, he very often disliked advice that was contrary to his wishes, and resented it; yet Lord M. thinks one can do anything with clever people, and if he had been properly talked to he might have listened.

We spoke of animals for a long time; Lord M. said a horse was a most powerful and formidable enemy if he were to attack you; and Lord M. said, "his neck is clothed in thunder"; he considers a dog the most courageous animal, and the one that helps man the most; and "he assists you, and will go through thick and thin with you."

Monday, 3rd September.—Lord M. said that Lord North was Minister when we lost the United Provinces, but didn't make the peace. The Marquis of Rockingham [1] came in, but died soon, and was succeeded by Lord Shelburne (Lord Lansdowne's father). Then, Lord M. continued, Mr. Fox and Lord North formed the Coalition and turned out Lord Shelburne; they came in, and were beat upon the India Bill, upon which which Mr. Pitt came in. Lord M. said that after Lord North went out the first time, the Marquis of Rockingham came in; his Government comprised Lord Shelburne and Mr. Fox; and Mr. Fox expected

[1] Charles Watson-Wentworth, second Marquess of Rockingham, during North's Ministry had declared for recognition of the independence of the colonies. In 1782, on the fall of North, he formed a coalition Government with Lord John Cavendish, Shelburne, and Fox.

to come in, Lord M. continued, but Lord Shelburne is supposed to have intrigued very much. "Then Mr. Fox and Lord North, being in the Opposition, formed the famous Coalition, which was extremely unpopular; and they beat him upon the Peace, and they forced themselves in; the King was very unwilling to take them and fought very hard, but however at last he took them; and he took the earliest opportunity to trip them up." It was upon the proposition of the India Bill, which was very like the present Government of India, by Commissioners here (India having been badly managed before, and there having been a great many malversations), but it was considered as taking away from the Prerogative of the Crown; "and the King turned them out; and he received the thanks of the Country, and the House of Commons went with him," Lord M. said. Mr. Pitt came in then, and was Minister for 18 years; till the King turned him out upon the Catholic question. I observed the King did a great deal himself; Lord M. replied, "That's what he is accused of; but he strenuously denies it in these letters; he said he always gave his Minister his confidence." Lord M. thinks he did while they were his Ministers; "If he disliked them, I don't wonder he tried to get rid of them," said Lord M. He couldn't bear Fox, Lord M. said, and he don't know, but he thinks it dates from a very early period; "Mr. Fox was very much in love with Lady Sarah Lennox," and Lord M. thinks that may have had something to do with it.[1] Mr. Pitt, Lord M. said, was a tall, thin man, with a red face; drank amazingly; so did Mr. Fox, Lord M. continued,

[1] See *The Life and Letters of Lady Sarah Lennox*, by Lady Ilchester and Lord Stavordale, *passim*.

and that neither had the slightest restraint over himself; they died the same year; Fox 13th Sept. 1806, aged 54; Pitt aged 47. Lord M. thinks Lord Holland (who is Fox's nephew; the late Lord Holland being Fox's elder brother) very like Fox, both in appearance and character; only that Fox was always very shy, which Lord Holland is not. Lord Melbourne told all this in such a delightful manner. He told me an anecdote of some Officers who saw a man on the banks of the Ganges, put there to die; and one of them had a bottle of lavender water with him; he put it to the man's lips, "who sucked it down"; and having only been accustomed to water and a little rice, this spirit quite revived him, and the man recovered and was taken home. The next day he came to the Officer and said, "You must maintain me, for I've lost my Caste"—by being thus restored to life. Spoke of the custom of burning the Widows, which Lord M. said "is not a good custom" and is very nearly abandoned. Mr. Macaulay went to India in '33, as Counsel; he is 40 years old, and a very clever man, Lord M. says.

We then looked at 2 vols. of portraits of the Characters concerned in the French Revolution, which are very fine and very interesting. It was quite a delight and treat to look at them with Lord Melbourne, for there was hardly one character whom he did not know *everything* about, what they did, who they were; and he has such a charming, agreeable way of telling it all. When we came to Cambacérès,[1] Lord M. said "he was a

[1] Cambacérès and Lebrun were the second and third Consuls in the Constitution of December 1799. In 1804 the former became Arch-chancellor of the Empire and President of the Senate.

great gourmand; and Napoleon used to keep him at the Council while his dinner was spoiling." And one day, Napoleon saw him writing a note, "and he insisted on seeing it; it was to his Cook: 'Sauvez les rôtis; les entremets sont perdus.'" We were about an hour looking at them. Lord M. told me that Sir John Coke (who was father to Col. Coke, who was a good deal engaged in the Revolution and who (Col. Coke) was grandfather to his (Ld.M.'s) grandmother) lived in the time of Charles I. and James I. I said I feared Lord M. must be so bored here, and he answered most kindly, "Oh! I assure you not the least." Spoke of the State rooms here, and we agreed what a pity it was they shouldn't be used.

Tuesday, 4th September.—I returned Lord Melbourne Munster's book which I had read through. I said I liked French books; he observed, "They write shortly and clearly, and very concise, with a great deal of *netteté*." "The English books," he continued, "are so very long; they are apt to be prosing, and one gets to read without attending, and not to know what it's all about," which is most true. He added that long books alarmed one. I said that I couldn't understand the German books; Lord M. mentioned Schiller's *Thirty Years' War* (which he has read the Translation of) as a very good book. "They are apt to be misty and obscure, the Germans,—and cloudy," he said laughing. Spoke of my disliking Ancient History; of my having read many dull books; of my having disliked learning formerly, and particularly Latin, and being naughty at that, and at my Bible-lessons; Lord M. said it was a good thing to know a little Latin, on account of the construction of English; Greek he thinks unnecessary for a woman, as there are many other things more necessary.

Read Despatches. Read in *L'Histoire de la Révolution d'Angleterre*,[1] which is extremely well written and highly interesting. Lord Melbourne rode out at ½ p. 3 with Murray to Cumberland Lodge to see the Prints, and came home at ½ p. 6. He said it was a most splendid collection. There are 37 books of Domenichino's Original Drawings, some of Raphael's, some beautiful Michael Angelos, Lord M. said (all sketches), some of Albert Dürer's, a book of Holbein's drawings, which he told me Horace Walpole routed out in a drawer at Kensington, they having been lost for some reigns. I said I had seen in the afternoon a book of beautiful sketches by Guido, and one of Domenichino's. Lord Melbourne said they were kept in 2 rooms, in cases; that there were every sort of print, and most valuable, and that it was impossible to look at them all; we spoke of all this for some time, and of the use Lord M. said these original drawings would be to Artists; Lord M. said there was a collection of Theatrical Prints, of every sort of Actor and Actress that ever existed; and an account drawn up of each; collected by Sir Hilgrove Turner[2]; "Not the most proper book in the World," said Lord M., "but very entertaining." Every sort of print of Nell Gwynn in every character; I asked if she was a celebrated Actress; in

[1] By Guizot.

[2] General Sir Tomkyns Hilgrove Turner, a distinguished soldier. He was present in 1801 at the capitulation of Alexandria. It fell to his lot to take charge of the famous Rosetta stone, part of the booty, which he conveyed to England. He was an antiquarian, and had a fair knowledge of the mysteries of ancient chivalry and of armour.

some characters, Lord M. replied. Lord M. said she was twice mentioned in Mme. de Sévigné's letters; Nell Gywnn was Mother to the Duke of St. Albans, and a Mrs. Waters to the Duke of Monmouth. Lord Melbourne and I looked at three books of curious, old, and very fine prints—portraits—which came from Cumberland Lodge and which seemed to interest Lord Melbourne. He made his clever observations about each; and thought there were (as there are) a great many Bishops and Monks. Lord Melbourne said George III., though accused of the contrary, was excessively fond of the Arts; he made the greater part of this splendid Collection. He had, Lord M. said, Canaletto and Zucarelli over here, to paint; spoke of portrait painting; of there being so few, or hardly any Portrait Painters now; Lord M. said that it was in human nature to have portraits painted, either from good or bad motives, from vanity or from affection.

Wednesday, 5th September.—I said how civil the Duke of Wellington always was to Uncle Leopold. I observed that I thought the Duke didn't like Uncle's going to Belgium, and Lord M. said: "I don't think he did; but he would be more studiously civil for that." I remained in my habit till a ¼ p. 7 when my beloved Uncle Leopold and Aunt Louise arrived. They are both looking remarkably well and in good spirits, and very kind. I took them to their apartments, and then hastened to dress.

Thursday, 6th September.—Uncle praised my excellent friend Lord Melbourne much to me during dinner; he *really* appreciates his inestimable qualities. Uncle remembers his Mother, as a clever agreeable woman, and his father as a good-natured old man. Lady Caroline he also knew, and says she was very clever, but mad. After dinner I made the *rond des Messieurs*. We were seated as the night before; that is, Uncle part of the evening near me, and then Aunt Louise the greater part, and Lord Melbourne replacing Uncle. Count Erdödy[1] was good enough to play on the piano beautifully; he improviséed *most* beautifully, and played some Valses of his own composition; some of Lanner's and Strauss's, with such a light yet powerful touch. He then came and sat down next Lord Melbourne. He is a very agreeable person, quiet yet lively, and speaks English perfectly. Spoke to Lord Melbourne of various things; he was excessively surprised when Aunt Louise told him that her father had his large carriages made in England (unknown in France), sent to Ostend, and smuggled to Paris by them (Uncle and Aunt). Spoke to Lord Melbourne of Durham; and when we got up I spoke to him and to Lord Palmerston of some curious letters of Lord John Hay's[2] which they had sent me to read in the afternoon, and which proved what a blow this loss at Morella[3] would be to the Queen's cause. I took

[1] Antoine Charles Palffy d'Erdödy, hereditary Count Palatine of Pressburg, born in 1793, was Chamberlain to the Emperor of Austria: from 1821 to 1828 he was Austrian Envoy at the Court of Saxony. In 1803 he married the daughter of Prince Alois Kaunitz.

[2] Rear-Admiral Lord John Hay, third son of George, seventh Marquess of Tweeddale, at this time commanded a small squadron on the north coast of Spain, landing from time to time a command of a naval and marine brigade. He was M.P. for Windsor, and a Lord of the Admiralty in Lord John Russell's Administration of 1846.

[3] In February of this year, Morella, a considerable town in Valencia, fell into the hands of the Carlists. Accordingly, a great attempt to retake it was made in the summer by the Christinos, and it was invested by General Craa; but to the disappointment of the

H. M. Leopold I. King of the Belgians.
from a portrait by Diez 1841.

leave of Prince Schwartzenberg, Prince Windisch Grätz and Count Erdödy, and expressed my hope of seeing them and the Princess again. Stayed up till 20 m. to 12.

Friday, 7th September.—I dressed for riding and at a ¼ to 5 rode out with Lord Melbourne, Lord Palmerston, Miss Anson, Lehzen, Lord Falkland, Lord Portman, Lady Forbes, Col. Wemyss, and the Equerry and Groom. Came home at 7. I rode Tartar who went beautifully. We had two showers when we first went out and had to take shelter under Oak Trees twice; during the last shower Lord Melbourne said, "It is the heaviest rain with the clearest sky I ever saw." We had but little rain afterwards, though the sky looked most gloomy, and it poured at the Castle. We came home at an amazing pace; it was a delightful ride. Lord Melbourne rode near me the whole time, and we talked a good deal together. Lord Palmerston also rode near me on the other side for some little time and admired Tartar very much. When we rode past Cumberland Lodge Lord Melbourne said that he had been staying there at the end of '27; the King had ordered a room for him in the Cottage, but there was some mistake about it, and the King was very angry. He had an immense party staying there then, Lord M. said; Durham and Lord Jersey, who used, he said, at one time to be a very great favourite of the King's. The King paid Lord Jersey's debts once. We spoke of Van de Weyer's marriage to a Miss Bates,[1] a great match in point of money, which Lord Palmerston said was a great thing.

Queen's adherents, all assaults on the town failed, and the siege was raised.

[1] See *ante*, Vol. I., p. 73.

Saturday, 8th September.—Lord M. said he had seen Sir Charles Metcalfe,[1] whom he had never seen before; and that he thinks him an odd-looking, though not an ugly man. "He was next boy to my brother at Eton," said Lord M.; his brother George he meant; he knew him very well. Sir Charles went to India, he told Lord M., in 1800, and came home in '38, never having been home since! He went when he was 15, as a Writer, and is now 53! What a change. "He says he is very happy," continued Lord M., "but that he feels the want of being useful," which Lord M. thinks is a slight hint to be employed. "He remembers me at Eton," said Lord M. Lord M.'s brother George was five years younger than himself, he told me.

We rode round Virginia Water. As I was galloping homewards, before we came to the Long Walk, on the grass and not very fast, Uncle left my side and I went on alone with Lord Melbourne, when something frightened Uxbridge, who was alarmed at being left without his second companion, and he swerved against Lord M.'s horse so much, that I came *off*; I fell on one side sitting, not a bit hurt or put out or frightened, but astonished and amused,—and was up, and laughing, before Col. Cavendish and one of the gentlemen, all greatly alarmed, could come near me, and said, "I'm not hurt." Lord M.'s horse shied away at the same moment mine did; *he* was much frightened and turned quite pale, kind, good man; he said, "Are you sure you're not

[1] Sir Charles Metcalfe, an Indian administrator, who during an interregnum acted as Provisional Governor-General, during which time the heavy restrictions on the Indian press were removed. The Ministry would not give effect to the wish of the East India Company to continue him permanently in the office, but in 1839 he became Governor of Jamaica.

hurt ?" I instantly remounted and cantered home; Lord M. was rather alarmed again and thought Uxbridge was inclined to shy. I sat between Uncle and Lord Melbourne. Uncle talked much, and praised me for my behaviour during my *feat* of falling! Lord Melbourne said most kindly and anxiously, "Are you *really* not the worse ?" He repeated this twice. We spoke of how it happened; he said he didn't *see* me fall, but *heard* me fall; he said it was fortunate his horse jumped away, else I might have been hurt.

Sunday, 9th September.—Sir George Villiers [1] came and sat down near us, when we were just at the end of the Album, looking at some Spanish drawings. Sir George told us that the Spaniards could drink a gallon of wine without stopping, pouring it down as if they didn't swallow; and he spoke of the extreme cruelty of Bull-fights.

Uncle and Sir George then spoke for a long while of Spain and its state, and Lord Melbourne and I listened, and occasionally joined in. Sir George said it was quite dreadful the state of misery in which the poor Nuns and Monks were in who had been turned out of their Monasteries. He said he had supported some Nuns at Madrid, the youngest of whom was 85, and the eldest 91! and these poor people have lived in a convent since they were children, and now they turn them out and tell them they may have their liberty! "It's cruel mockery," said Sir George. The Monks are likewise very badly off; for, Lord M. observed, to men who have been accustomed to pass their lives in Prayer, to be told to dig, is very hard.

[1] Sir George Villiers (afterwards Earl of Clarendon) was British Minister in Spain 1833–9. See Vol. I., p. 229.

Monday, 10th September.—When Uncle came, he praised Sir C. Metcalfe, and Lord Melbourne said, "He is a very able man; the most able we have; he is a very bold man—*he* introduced the freedom of the press in India, which was a very bold step; but didn't do as much harm as we expected. He is extremely liberal," Lord M. continued, he was quite one of Lord William Bentinck's followers; "William Bentinck is a very reckless man, who doesn't mind what follows if he thinks his reason good."

Wednesday, 12th September.—Spoke of Dropmore being such a pretty place, and that we could ride over there one day. "It's a lovely place," Lord M. said. It belongs to Lady Grenville,[1] who he told me was a Miss Pitt, Lord Camelford's sister; he (Lord Camelford), Lord M. told me, was killed in a fatal duel with a Mr. Best. Spoke of Cliveden,[2] on the Thames, *now* Sir George Warrender's, as being also very pretty. "It's the place that belonged to the Duke of Buckingham, which is mentioned in Pope." It belonged to Villiers Duke of Buckingham, Charles II.'s favourite.[3] . . . Uncle and Lord

[1] Lord Grenville was a nephew of Hester, Lady Chatham, wife of the great commoner. He held many high offices of state under the younger Pitt, becoming Foreign Secretary 1791–1801. He was First Lord of the Treasury, February 1806–March 1907. His wife was sister and heir to the second Lord Camelford, and on her death in 1864 devised her estate (including Boconnoc in Cornwall) to the Hon. George Matthew Fortescue.

[2] It was afterwards sold to the Duke of Sutherland, then to the Duke of Westminster, and now belongs to Mr. Waldorf Astor.

[3] Lord Shrewsbury died in 1668 of wounds received in a duel with Buckingham, a duel said to have been concerted between Buckingham and Lady Shrewsbury. This enterprising lady, in the disguise of a page, is said to have held the Duke's horse during the fight. Pope's lines referred to are the following:

"Gallant and gay in Cliveden's proud alcove,
The bower of wanton Shrewsbury and love."

M. spoke of James II., Louis XIV., and then Uncle, Lord John, Lord Melbourne, and Lord Palmerston also joined in, spoke most agreeably about the Sessions of Parliament, and of anecdotes of Tierney,[1] but I've not room or time to record them. They spoke of the fatigue of Sessions; and Lord M. said it was less fatiguing to be obliged to attend than *not* to attend. Lord M. said the hard Sessions began in 1816. Lord M. and Lord John said that formerly there used to be great debates always upon the Estimates, and Lord Palmerston remembers having had 13 nights of it; and whenever a new person came in, who, as Lord M. said, *ought* to have been there before, the Secretary at War had to explain the same thing over again, sometimes 3 or 4 times. Hume used, Lord John said, to make the same speech every year, and so they used to tell him he had been answered the year before. "And now," Lord M. said, "the Estimates are passed, without one word being said; which is very extraordinary." They spoke of Tierney, his speaking so well; and Lord M. said *he* thought him a very honest man; that he used always to say, "such a person told me so and so, by which you may judge that that is the opinion of all the people of that class and calibre"; "This appears to me sound reasoning," said Lord M., but that it had been very much condemned.

Thursday, 13*th September*.—Lord M. said he had seen Lord John, whom he thought in good spirits,

[1] George Tierney (1761–1830), a well-known Parliamentarian. He went into opposition to Pitt, and took pleasure in provoking that Minister to the use of language in debate which led to a duel on Putney Heath. Tierney took office under Addington and later under Canning.

and "He begins to see the great difficulties of a change in the Government very strongly." We agreed the difficulties were very great. I said Lord John had been to see Uncle.

Lord M. said he saw by the papers that the Emperor of Austria had proclaimed a general Amnesty at Milan on the occasion of the Coronation,[1] with permission for those to return who had been obliged to leave the place,—which Lord M. said was very important. Lord M. begged me to get a quiet horse for Lord John to ride, as Lord M. didn't like asking Cavendish about it, after all that had passed. Lord M. said, in speaking of Lord John: "He is very much impressed with the difficulties we shall have to encounter from the Ballot"; that the declaration Lord John made at the beginning of last Session had rather weakened his influence with his followers, and that it would be rather disagreeable if our friends were to vote against us, on that subject.[2]

Uncle Leopold and Lord M. then spoke about the Church; and Lord M. said, "My intention is to stand by the Established Church, but to keep the Church to her own principles as established at the Reformation." Then Lord M. said, "Upon the whole our Church is the best Church, the least meddling"; and speaking of Dissenters, Lord M. said, "The Church is still very strong." He spoke of the various changes which have taken place in it,

[1] The Austrian Emperor, Ferdinand I., was invested at Milan, on September 6th, with the iron crown of Lombardy. See Vol. I., p. 256.

[2] In the course of the debate on the Address at the end of 1837, Lord John had stated that he considered the ballot, the extension of the suffrage, and triennial parliaments "as nothing else but repeal of the Reform Act, and placing the representation on a totally different footing."

and which he would have been content to have done without, but that "the cry for Reform came from the bosom of the Establishment itself." Lord M. spoke of this Sulphur Monopoly,[1] which he repeated would much affect our merchants; and he said they (monopolies) had been given up *here* in Queen Elizabeth's time, for that when she saw there was any difficulty about them, "she with her usual sagacity gave them up." Lord John spoke of Wilberforce's *Life*, which he is reading; and Lord M. said he disliked Wilberforce; though he felt it was ungrateful to say so, "as he liked me very much and was always wanting me to come more forward." Lord John said, in this *Life* there is a letter of Lord M.'s published, to him, about Lord John, which made Lord M. laugh very much. Lord John said, it is also mentioned that Canning had said that Lord Melbourne would have done very well as Speaker; Lord M. said he believed Wilberforce to be a good man, and to be actuated by good motives and opinions; "but they were very uncomfortable opinions for those who acted with him," and he used to leave his friends in difficulties.

Friday, 14th September.—Lord Melbourne spoke of this Treaty with Turkey,[2] which he says is to settle the duties, and to do away with the Monopolies; it's

[1] A monopoly of working the sulphur mines in Sicily was granted to a Frenchman named Taix in August 1838. The abolition of it was demanded by the British Government in 1840, and refused by the Government of the Two Sicilies, but conceded a few months later in response to the mediation of France.

[2] On November 16, 1838, a treaty between Great Britain and Turkey was ratified, whereby the duty on import of British goods was regulated, and a charge was levied on English shipping entering the Dardanelles and the Black Sea. English goods passing through Turkey for exportation were allowed to go free.

to settle the Duties according to the value of the articles. It is a great step, we both agreed. Lord Melbourne had sent me a box full of despatches from Constantinople, which he said I needn't read *all* through; that the private letters and Mr. Bulwer's[1] despatch would show what it was intended to do.

Saturday, 15th September.—Lord Melbourne said he must get Lord Granville to speak to Louis Philippe about this Mexican and Buenos Ayreian business, and explain to him the feeling there is here about it; Lord M. said, "Molé[2] is so touchy and so jealous"; that if there had been Broglie, or any other Minister, they would have accepted the mediation of England. I said to Lord Melbourne I had been rather surprised at Lord John's saying to me, that he should be very sorry to leave the Government, but thought if he was obliged to do so, that another could be found to replace him. Lord Melbourne said, "It's what he said to me; but I think he sees now that wouldn't do." Lord M. continued, that Lord John meant by that, that having lost a good deal of influence by the strong declaration he made in the early part of last Session, if he was to retire from the Government, another leader could be found, who hadn't pledged himself, and "who would regain the confidence of that party." "But I told him," continued Lord Melbourne, "that would never do; it would never do for me to give the Government a more

[1] See *post*, p. 22.

[2] Molé was Louis Philippe's Prime Minister at this time. Somewhat exacting demands having been made upon the Mexican nation by the French Government, followed by the despatch of a blockading squadron, there were protests against the interruption of commerce stimulated by English and American merchants. A naval force was consequently despatched to Mexico to protect British interests. See Vol. I., p. 394.

radical character." Lord M. told him that he need make no declaration now, *before* Parliament meets, but wait till then, and see what course it will be best to pursue. Of course, Lord John don't like if many of our friends vote against him; Lord Melbourne said *50 did,* last session, principally belonging to the Government. "We must put it to them," said Lord Melbourne, "that if they do vote they'll most probably break up the Government; and then see what they'll do."

Spoke then about Canada, and Uncle said that the Boundary Question[1] would give us trouble, which Lord M. said it *already did*; of the number of Troops there—10,000—which Uncle said it would be good to keep there; Lord M. agreed in that, but said the difficulty would be great, the empire being so large, and so spread all over the world; "The question is," Lord M. said, "whether the country is up to it; whether the feeling of the country is such." And, in which Uncle agreed, "Such an Empire as this must go on; it can't stand still, else it goes back," he added. Lord Melbourne said the British Army at any time *never* amounted to *50,000* men. Then they spoke of Russia, and the difficulty to act against it. "She retires into inaccessibility," said Lord M., "into her snows and frosts."

Sunday, 16th September.—He then read over that

[1] For fifty years there had been difficulties between Great Britain and the State of Maine with respect to the frontier line of New Brunswick, and President Van Buren, in his message to Congress in December 1837, said that a settlement seemed as remote as at the time of signing the treaty of peace in 1783. This dispute led to serious consequences in January 1839, when some lawless citizens of the State of Maine invaded the debatable territory and made extensive fellings of timber.

part of Mr. Bulwer's[1] despatch which I couldn't quite understand, and explained it to me. He told me yesterday that the only thing against Bulwer was, his being considered such a Radical abroad; "Metternich would view any thing coming from him with suspicion," said Lord Melbourne, and he added laughing, "He (Metternich) would hardly think it safe to be in the same room with him."

Monday, 17th September.—He then told me that Uncle had spoken to him on a very delicate matter, namely, about maintaining our Alliance with France. Uncle, he said, told him that if Russia were to change her tone and to say to France, "Why, let us look to our own interests, let me go on with my conquests in my part of the Globe, and you may take Savoy and the Rhine and Belgium"—Louis Philippe would be rather impressed with it; and Uncle told Lord M. that "we ought to *ménager* Louis Philippe"; for, Lord M. agrees, that an Alliance with Russia would be most pernicious to us; and it seems by what Lord M. told me, that the King (L.P.) is somewhat hurt and annoyed at Lord Palmerston, and much hurt at not having been mentioned in the Speech, Uncle told Lord M.; that is, it's not having been stated that we were on good terms with France. Lord M. said, "I must say I think that's as well got rid of;

[1] Henry Bulwer (afterwards Lord Dalling), an elder brother of the author of *Pelham*. He was Secretary of Embassy at Constantinople, and had just achieved a diplomatic success in negotiating a commercial treaty with the Porte. After a short time spent as *chargé d'affaires* at Paris, he was appointed British Ambassador at Madrid, where he was at the time of the "Spanish Marriages." Many of his various diplomatic activities are recorded in his *Life of Palmerston*. He was a man of keen discernment but of variable temper. He was one of the first public men to note the rare tact and diplomatic skill of the Prince of Wales, afterwards King Edward VII.

it's invidious to the others, and is always repeating the same Cuckoo song."

Tuesday, 18th September.—Lord Melbourne said, "I asked Palmerston if the King had spoken to him about his own affairs," and Lord P. said he had not, but that Van de Weyer had told him (Ld. P.) that he meant to do so, as he (the K.) thought it would appear odd if he didn't do so. Lord M. said he fancied Uncle was a little angry with Lord Palmerston; and "The King of the French is a good deal nettled at Palmerston"; Lord M. said Uncle told him that the Alliance with England wasn't very much liked in France, as they got nothing by it, and as we wouldn't let them take anything. "They say," continued Lord M., "'Austria has got a good deal, Prussia has got all along the Rhine, and Russia has got Poland, but we've got nothing.'" That consequently an Alliance with Russia would be very much liked. Lord M. thinks that even when France and England were so much opposed to each other, the French and English *never* hated each other.

Dressed in my Windsor uniform, and cap, like last year, and at a ¼ to 2 I mounted Leopold, and rode to the ground with Uncle *en grande tenue*, Lord Hill, the Duke of Wellington, Lord Portman, Lady Portman, Col. Fremantle, Capt. Hill (Aide-de-Camp to Lord Hill), Sir William Lumley,[1] Sir G. Quentin, all in uniform, Col. Cavendish and his son, the Page of Honour preceding us, and Lord Palmerston and Lord Cowper not in uniform, and Lord Falkland and Lord Torrington in the Windsor uniform, with an Escort. The others went in

[1] Gen. Sir William Lumley, G.C.B., son of the 4th Earl of Scarborough. He had been A.D.C. to the Duke of Wellington during the Peninsular War.

carriages, as follows :—First carriage: Aunt Louise, Mamma, Mme. d'Hogvorst, Lady Mary; 2nd, Lady Cowper, Lady Forbes, Miss Paget, and Lady Gardiner; 3rd, Lehzen, Miss Anson, and Lord Melbourne; 4th, Van de Weyer, Aerschot. We received the Salute, and then cantered up to the Lines, when Leopold (I can't think why) went such a pace that I thought he was running away, but he went beautifully down the Lines and between the ranks, the drums beating and bands playing in his face; but when I cantered back to the Standard he played me the same trick, and I could hardly stop him; but he amply made up afterwards by standing like a lamb, throughout the Review, in which there was a good deal of firing. It was a very pretty Review, and the Troops did admirably; the Duke of Wellington said that it was as pretty a one as he had ever seen; I was stationed between Uncle and Lord Hill, the Duke being next Lord Hill. I expressed my satisfaction with the Troops to Sir James Hope[1] after the Review; and I rode up to the carriage in which Aunt Louise, &c., were, and the one in which Lady Cowper, &c., were, and to the one in which Daisy and my good Lord Melbourne were. We rode back to the Castle at a ¼ p. 4; put on my usual habit, and all the other gentlemen took off their uniforms, and at a ¼ to 5 I rode out with Uncle, Aunt, Mamma (who didn't ride the whole way), Lord Melbourne, the Duke of Wellington, Lord Cowper, Lord Palmerston, Lord and Lady Portman, Lord Torrington, Lady Forbes, Col. Cavendish, and the Page of Honour, and came home at ½ p. 6. I

[1] Sir James Archibald Hope (1785–1871), had been Assistant Adjutant-General in the Peninsula. From 1814 to 1839 he was Lieut.-Colonel in the 3rd Foot Guards (now Scots Guards).

rode Tartar, who went delightfully; it was a very pleasant though short ride. I rode the whole time between Uncle and Lord Melbourne. Spoke to Lord Melbourne of Leopold's running away a little bit, which he said he thought he observed; of Mamma's horse going so slowly, and Lord M. said, "We came a pretty good pace"; of my wishing to have a monkey, which Lord M. has a great horror of. I forgot to say that Lord M. showed me in the morning a letter from Lady Holland from Paris, who complains of his being "stubbornly silent." I told Lord Melbourne that Uncle had been somewhat surprised at the Duke of Wellington's having spoken, after dinner, against the French having Algiers[1]; Lord M. said, "The King is favourable to that; we dislike it very much here; and the Duke does particularly." I said Uncle said that the French *must* have a place to fight in, and go to. Lord M. said, "There is something in that." Spoke of Uncle's having said that the Life Guards and Household Troops ought to be stronger; Lord M. replied, "It would be as well," but that the expense would be so great; the King wants them to be 600 strong, whereas they are only 300. The Empire is so great, Lord M. said, that the Army must be spread all over the World; the whole Army altogether don't exceed 90,000 men, he told me. There are 15,000 men in Canada, and 15 or 16,000 in Ireland, which, as Lord M. says, isn't too much.

Wednesday, 19th September.—Lord M. spoke of the

[1] The African expedition of the French had been successful, and Constantine was captured, the Duc de Nemours being present. In the French Chamber, however, there was much difference of opinion upon the policy pursued by the French Ministers. The occupation of Algiers was not popular in France.

people's great civility to me now, whereas they were rude to the King and put on their hats when they saw him, particularly in Buckinghamshire, "which used to annoy the King very much"; "but there was nothing to be done for it."

Thursday, 20th September.—Lord M. said that Uncle was so much surprised to hear of Lord Portman's great riches, but Lord M. thinks they must have exaggerated it in saying he had £100,000 a year; Lord M. said all his riches consist in property in London; Portman and Bryanston Squares belong to him; his grandfather, Lord M. told me, was very asthmatic and bought a Farm in Portman Square, *then* considered the Country, in order to live out of London, and thus originated his great wealth.

Friday, 21st September.—Spoke of eating and drinking, and dessert being unwholesome; as one eats it without *real* appetite; "and I am of that opinion," said Lord Melbourne; that he believed what one ate after dinner, and the few glasses of wine one drank, hurt one, and that if one was to get up before that it would be much better. "That's why I should like to get up with the ladies," said Lord Melbourne; "but it never has been the practice here." I said it was a very bad habit that of the gentlemen sitting in that way after dinner. He remembers, in the country, in the houses of fox-hunters, sitting till 11 or 12, and "coming in and finding all the women yawning." "I can't bear it," said Lord M., "though I *did* like it too, formerly. I believe the ladies like it; they like to have a little time to arrange their hair, and to talk." I said *I* didn't. He continued, "Of course the men were very much elevated by wine; but it tended to increase the gaiety of society, it produced diversity." "In every party," said Lord M., "there were generally 10 or 12 in that state." Lord M. said he never saw any body eat and drink so much as George IV.; in 1798 it was beyond everything; and his spirits and love of fun beyond everything, too. Of doing business. "All depends on the urgency of a thing," said Lord M. "If a thing is very urgent, you can always find time for it; but if a thing can be put off, why then you put it off."

Saturday, 22nd September.—Spoke for some time of church-going; and Lord Melbourne said he never used to go, after he left Eton; "My Father and Mother never went," he said. "People didn't use to go so much formerly; it wasn't the fashion; but it is a right thing to do." He said Uncle, *last* year, wanted me to go twice, but Lord M. assured him (as it is) that that was unnecessary. George III., Lord M. believes, never went twice, though a strict man; and wasn't at all for all those Puritanical notions; and he's the person, Lord M. said, to look to in all these matters. Lord M. said it wasn't well to puzzle myself with controversies, but read the simple truths; the Psalms he thinks very difficult to understand, and he thinks very probably *not* rightly translated.

Sunday, 23rd September.—We spoke of the Duke of York, and when he died. "We didn't think he was dying," said Lord M., "he always thought he would outlive the King; for I know he told to people whom I know, what he intended to do." Lord M. said if he had become King, he *never* would have consented to the Catholic Emancipation, he would have sacrificed anything sooner than have done it. I observed George IV. disliked it, which Lord M. said he certainly did, but he did it. "He was a much cleverer man," said Lord M., "and saw the necessity of giving way."

Monday, 24th September.—Spoke of the Spaniards still carrying on the Slave Traffic under their own Flag; though we have a Treaty with them; Lord M. said, "We can prevent *that*, for we have the mutual right of search"; and he added also, "by the article of equipment," which means, he said, if a Vessel is found which can instantly be recognised as a Slaver by its peculiar equipments, bolts to fasten the Chains to, we can seize it. Lord M. said, Buxton's[1] notion of our taking country along the coast, and establishing Ports in order to prevent the Traffic, would never do, for, he said, if we told the French they mightn't conquer about Algiers, we couldn't say that, "if we are taking the Coast ourselves." Speaking of Mr. Buxton, Lord Melbourne said, "He certainly is a clever man and a rational man"; and a great follower and friend of Wilberforce's; Lord M. said he heard Wilberforce's *Life* was very entertaining; spoke of their (his two sons) having published things about people which they oughtn't to have done; Lord M. told me the letter of his they had published was in answer to one Wilberforce had written to him about Queen Caroline; "They shouldn't have published that letter," said Lord M., "for it was quite confidential." He was a very little man, Lord M. said, "with a pretty expression, benevolent." "He had a beautiful voice," said Lord M., "very melodious; he sang very well; but he gave that up; he didn't think

[1] Thomas Fowell Buxton (1786–1845), co-operated with Wilberforce in his exertions to abolish slavery. He was created a baronet in 1840. He married Hannah, daughter of John Gurney of Earlham.

that right; he sang Psalms, but he used to sing after supper." Lord M. told me (what he had already done when we looked at some pictures in the morning) that he wore his hair long, as all boys then did, till he was *17*; (*how* handsome he must have looked); but that "it was always dirty"; a boy, he said, can't comb his long hair as a girl can, and that it got matted, so that no comb would go through; he only cut it just before he left Eton. I asked him if his hair was always so dark. He said, "It was about the colour of Your Majesty's hair, I should say, when I was a child." He thinks mine so much darker than it was, which it certainly is. Spoke of Uncle Leopold, whom he still thinks handsome; "he has a fine expression," he said; and Uncle Ernest he also admires; he likes Uncle Leo's low voice, and thinks it very agreeable.

Lord M. never saw Knighton. Spoke of George IV. with Lord M. for a long time; it is so interesting to talk with Lord M. on *all* subjects, and he knew George IV. *so* well, that it's peculiarly curious. He said George IV. seemed to be a Whig before he came to the Throne, but that "he did it from opposition and not from principle." "His principles all along were the contrary," Lord M. added some time afterwards. Lord M. did not see much of him latterly; Lord M. came into office for the first time in 1827, and entered Parliament in 1806. The Duchess of Devonshire and all those Whigs "were the leading people of fashion," said Lord M., "and he (Prince of Wales) naturally fell into all that." George IV.'s income as Prince of Wales, Lord M. said, was settled in 1783 at £50,000 a year, and he got into debt, and came to have his debts paid in '87. He had to pay his Establishment out of it; but, Lord M. said, an

Establishment *then* didn't cost near so much as it does *now*. Lord M. said, "The Prince of Wales is born Duke of Cornwall; he isn't made, but is born so," and the revenue is his. "It vests in the Sovereign now," he continued, "as there is no Prince of Wales." George III. educated George IV. out of this. Lord M. continued, that he thinks George III. might have managed George IV. better, for that the latter was very much afraid of his Father, and yet very fond of him.

Tuesday, 25th September.—Lord M. then gave me a most amusing letter from Lady Holland to read, which made us both laugh very much. She is ill, and unable to go out, and in a great state. She writes to Lord Melbourne: "Please write a line to say you pity me." The 4 last words are repeated twice. Her account of Molé, too, is amusing; he *was* handsome, she said, and now he is "underjawed and ugly." She likewise says Lord Coke[1] (Lord Leicester's son) is at Paris, with a French Tutor, to learn French, recommended by Guizot, but who is so taciturn that he never speaks at all, and so she says the boy has little chance of learning French. I told Lord M. that in returning from the Review, I said jokingly to Uncle, "It's a pity I cannot wear a Uniform," and he replied that I must be a *Prince* to do that, and added quite seriously, "It's a great pity you are not a Prince." This made Lord Melbourne laugh much, and he said, "You didn't like that?" I replied, "I said I thought so too." Spoke to Lord Melbourne of his being at Eton, which he liked pretty well, but home much better; of his being fagged, but never a *regular fag*. I asked him if the boys ill-treated him much. "Not much,"

[1] Thomas William, afterwards second Earl of Leicester (1822–1909).

he replied; "they beat me sometimes, but that was to be expected." He didn't like fighting much, particularly with big boys. "I never stood to be licked." "I remember going out to fight with a boy once," he continued, "and after the first round I gave it up; he was a tall boy and had much longer arms and pounded me amazingly; and I saw I never could beat him; I stood and reflected a little, and *thought* to myself, and then gave it up; I thought that one of the most prudent acts, but I was reckoned very dastardly for it." This showed already his good sense, and gentle temper. Spoke of there never being quite 500 boys at Eton; of Harrow, where Lord Palmerston was. Stayed up till 20 m. p. 11.

Wednesday, 26th September.—Of Spain, affairs looking so very ill there. Lord M. said Lord Palmerston is still sanguine, and attributes most of the bad success of the Spanish Government to France; for that the Queen Regent does not wish to have an Exaltado Government for fear of displeasing Louis Philippe. "But I'm afraid," said Lord Palmerston, "that neither *Exaltado* or *Moderado* have any talent"; and he added what a bad thing it was for the country to have a succession of Governments, one weaker than the other. Spoke of the length of time that this unhappy state of affairs has been going on; Ferdinand died in '33, and the Quadruple Treaty[1] was concluded in '34; spoke of the misfortune of Don Carlos's having escaped from here,

[1] The Quadruple Alliance of 1834 was signed by England, France, Spain, and Portugal. It confirmed Dona Maria on the throne of Portugal, which she had gained by the aid of English troops in opposition to her usurping Uncle Miguel. This treaty was Palmerston's answer to that of Münchengratz, by which Russia, Prussia, and Austria had agreed to support one another against the liberalizing tendencies resulting from the revolutions of 1830.

which nobody thought he would have had the courage and determination to do. "Nothing so bad," said Lord M., "as overrating the weakness of an enemy." Spoke of Louis Philippe's *fear* of Spain. Lord M. said he couldn't bear to take an active part in the affairs there, "as he considers it always to have been the grave of French Armies,—as it *has been*"; and then he fears any revolution taking place there, as that would affect him. . . . Spoke of the impious and dreadful things the French now introduced upon the stage, whereas formerly, Lord M. said, they never killed any body on the stage, and accused us of doing so; and Lord M. said, he believed that in none of Racine's or Corneille's Tragedies, anybody was ever killed on the stage. Spoke of these French Tragedies which Lord Melbourne admires very much; and though he says that Corneille had the most power, I'm glad he agrees with me in admiring Racine the most, and he said "that for beauty of feeling and taste" he thought there was nothing like Racine; he mentioned *Phèdre* and *Athalie* as his finest; spoke of Voltaire's *Zaïre* and *Semiramis*; he said that Voltaire copied a good deal from the English, "like a great Master he infused the same spirit," without taking the same words. *Zaïre* was very like *Othello*, and *Semiramis* very like *Hamlet*, he said; he admired the acting of these Tragedies, and Mme. Duchénois'[1] acting as very fine, though herself *so* ugly.

Thursday, 27th September.—He told me he had got a letter from the Duke of Wellington (Lord Melbourne had written to the Duke to ask him for the Will of George IV.); who said he had got the Will in London, and that if it was immediately

[1] Catherine Josephine Duchénois (1777–1835), a French actress.

wanted he would go up to Town for it, if not, he would send it when he next went to Town, to the Lord Chancellor. He also said in the letter that the King of Hanover had written to the Duke of Cambridge asking him several questions about these Jewels,[1] and that the Duke of Cambridge asked his (the Duke of Wellington's) advice as to what he was to do; the Duke of Wellington said he should not answer or meddle with it, as this was an affair which ought only to go through Ministers. Then Lord Melbourne gave me a Medal (of myself) which the City Remembrancer sent to me (and of which we looked at a silver one last night), and I observed it was very like; "It's a fine head," said Lord M., "the nose cut up, which gives a good deal of *finesse* to the look," which made me laugh. Spoke of the Duchesse de Broglie, who, Lord M. said, spoke English like any English person, and was very pretty. He knew her Mother, Mme. de Staël, very well, when she was here in '14; she was very ugly, he said; though she had fine eyes; she had a great deal of folly and showing off, but still, Lord M. said, "She was a very superior woman." Napoleon couldn't bear her, nor she him, he said; and Lord M. told me the famous anecdote; when she was making a long discourse to Napoleon, he abruptly said, "Est-ce que vous nourrissez vos enfants?"

[1] The King of Hanover claimed the Crown Jewels which had been left under the will of Queen Charlotte to the eldest living representative of the House of Hanover. The matter was inquired into by a Commission presided over by Lord Lyndhurst, the other members being Lord Langdale and Chief Justice Tindal. Lords Lyndhurst and Langdale differed in opinion, and the Chief Justice died before the award was made. It was not until 1857—nearly twenty years later—that a decision was given, under which the greater part of the jewels claimed were handed over to the King of Hanover.

Then, Lord Melbourne said, she had been great friends with Talleyrand, and then broke with him, and he told me the following funny anecdote, which is said to have given rise to the Quarrel. Mme. de Staël and Talleyrand and Mme. de Souza (Flahaut's Mother) were all in a boat together, and Mme. de Staël said it would be the proof of love to save a person in danger; and she asked which of the two he (T.) would save; he said to her, "Madame, vous, qui savez tout, savez nager."

Friday, 28th September.—Spoke of Pozzo's speaking such odd, and not always quite intelligible, French; of Lord Melbourne's disliking to speak it, which he told me last night, and again this morning, he did; he said last night, when one spoke in language one wasn't master of, "one feels quite in prison and in chains." I asked Lord Melbourne if he admired Mme. de Staël's works; he said he did, and that her conversation was very agreeable and clever; Schlegel he saw here with her, but he won't allow that Schlegel gave her the most of the fine notions in her books, with the exception of a book upon Germany, which he says Schlegel did help her in. *Corinne* he admires. Talleyrand said of Mme. de Staël, Lord M. told me, "Elle est insupportable; elle n'a que ce défaut-là." She was not tall, he said, had fine, full arms which she was fond of showing, fine eyes, a large and ugly mouth and nose, a square face, and not an agreeable expression.

Spoke of Pozzo; "He can't bear to be contradicted," said Lord Melbourne; and that "you must listen to him, and then just put in what you have to say," saying, There's a good deal in that, *but*—you must admit so and so. Spoke of Lady Holland; "She has no religion, but she has every sort of superstition," said Lord M. I asked if she disbelieved in religion; he said she did. How unhappy must this be in the end, for a person, "in the hour of death and in the day of judgment," when reliance on an all-powerful God and an all-merciful Redeemer is such a balm, and such a consolation! Lord M. spoke of the gallant behaviour of a girl called Grace Darling, the daughter of a man who takes care of a light-house on the Northumberland coast; a steamer was lately blown up there, and a number of people perished and this girl went out in a boat by herself and saved nine people.[1] Spoke of the book Lady Holland had sent him, which led us to speak of her fear of dying, which Lord Melbourne said was so very great, and haunted her night and day, though she had *no* apprehension as to what was to become of her hereafter. I said I thought people who didn't believe in religion had always more fear of death. "They generally have," Lord M. replied. Lord M. don't think there is such a total disregard of religion in France as there is said to be; though he thinks France is the country in which there is the *greatest* disregard for religion; I said I thought England was the one in which there was the most feeling *for* it,—in which Lord M. agreed; he don't like, he said, those wild notions which have sprung up lately in some parts of Germany; "I like what is tranquil and stable," he added.

[1] Grace Darling was twenty-three years old, the daughter of the lighthouse keeper on the Farne Islands. In point of fact the girl was not alone in the boat, but helped her father to row it. She was granted a gold medal and £50 by the Treasury; but a sum of £750 was raised for her. In return she was obliged to cut off nearly all her hair, as tokens of remembrance, for her admirers. She died of consumption in 1842.

Saturday, 29th September.—Lord M. told me he had seen Esterhazy, who was rather anxious about this Belgian business, and Lord M. said it was rather awkward to have to return and to be unable to state any progress to his Court. Said Lord Palmerston had complained of receiving no answer from the Belgians; and that Van de Weyer had told him Uncle rather wished the Confederation to take possession by force of Luxembourg (which they would be obliged to do) and which Lord P. said he doubted Uncle could *wish*; Lord M. doubted it also, but said Uncle might possibly wish to prove to the Belgians how impossible it was for him to prevent it, and thus get out of it. Lord M. told me Lord Clifford[1] had been with him a long time, so long that he thought he never would go. He wants us, Lord M. said, to establish a communication with the Pope, and to settle with him about sending Priests to India, for that all the Catholics there were in the hands of the Portuguese Priests,[2] who were very depraved and taught everything that was bad; he wants us to repeal the Law, which renders it criminal to have any thing to do with the Pope, and have an Ambassador at Rome, which Lord M. thinks he would like to be himself; Lord M. said it certainly was a great inconvenience to be unable to have any communication with the Pope, who was still a great man in Europe; (there has been no communication since James II.'s time).[3] "And it would be a very good

[1] Hugh Charles, seventh Lord Clifford of Chudleigh (1790–1858), a supporter of Lord Melbourne's Government. A Roman Catholic, he ultimately resided almost entirely in Italy.

[2] From Goa.

[3] In James II.'s time Roger Palmer, Earl of Castlemaine, husband of Barbara Palmer, was sent on a mission to reconcile England to the Vatican. On this he was subsequently indicted, and was one of the

thing to repeal that law, but it wouldn't do to try in this country" ; that the feeling was still so great.

I then, with Lord Melbourne, looked over a book of very fine old original Drawings (of which I told him before we began to look, some weren't quite eligible and were tacked together) ; he admired them much ; one, he said, represented Æneas with the Sibyl ; which I remembered reading in *Virgil* ; and I asked Lord M. if he didn't think *Virgil* very hard ; he said the hardest author there was, which is a consolation. We then looked at some very fine old prints, portraits, heads,—amongst which was Cardinal Borromeo's ; he is *preserved* at Milan and seen through a Crystal Tomb ; and Lord M. said Lord Dudley wrote once from Milan : "I've this morning seen Cardinal Borromeo, and Rogers, both in an equal state of Preservation." Lord M. said George III. bought all these Drawings for 25,000 Crowns ; they belonged to Cardinal Albani's Collection ; and George IV. spent £40,000 in prints.

Sunday, 30th September.—Lord M. spoke of some of the Eton boys ; of Mr. Anson,[1] whom he likes very much ; of the late Duke of Norfolk's having taken into his head once, the strange fancy of giving a dinner to all the descendants of the Jockey (I think) Duke of Norfolk,[2] in Richard's time ; and he

victims of Titus Oates. He defended himself with spirit, and was acquitted. Towards the end of the nineteenth century, the Government of Mr. Gladstone sent Sir George Errington, M.P., on a mission to Pope Leo XIII.

[1] George Anson, son of the Very Rev. Frederick Anson, sometime Dean of Chester. At this time he was Private Secretary to Lord Melbourne, and afterwards to Prince Albert.

[2] Sir John Howard (1430-85), a close adherent of the house of York, who was killed at the Battle of Bosworth with his master Richard III., who had created him Duke of Norfolk in 1483. He was famous for

went on till he found 6,000 ! ! and then he thought it was time to stop !

Sunday, 2nd October.—Spoke of Lady Lyttelton, who Lord M. said wasn't very young when she married, about 23. I said I thought 23 quite young enough to marry ; "So do I," said Lord M., "but girls begin to be nervous when they are past 19," and think they'll never marry if "they are turned 20." We spoke of Eton, the different forms. Lord M. said, "I was a deuced good scholar when I entered the 5th form ; but I went a very bad one into the sixth." Spoke of the Masters, and its being such dreadful work to have to look over 60 or 70 exercises ; said nothing the Masters used to dislike so much as when the boys used to come with an exercise of perhaps 50 or 60 Iambics, to look over ; "My tutor used to complain of that," said Lord M. "He said, 'Why do you bring me this so late at night ?'" He spoke of a very odd boy of the name of Harry Drury, who was at school with him, and who, in order to plague his Master, used to pick out all the oddest and most "cramped words" from Cicero, and put them into his exercises, and then puzzle his Master, who asked, 'What authority have you for this ?' 'Cicero,' he answered then." Lord M. said, "I never felt so lowered as when I came back (home) and had no power" ; for, Lord M. said, that a head boy has immense power ; a look of his is like the law to another boy, who would never think of disobeying ; and many tyrannize amazingly, he said. Spoke of the different ways of fagging, though he never was, or had, any particular regular fag. There were 24 boys generally

the large number of high offices which he held, and was known as the Jockey of Norfolk.

in the Upper School, he said. His brother Frederick went to Eton when he was about eight, and so did his brother George. . . .

Wednesday, 3rd October.—Lord M. said that if the Head of all didn't like or care for a thing, it couldn't thrive; George IV. and King William neither cared for flowers; Lord M. said if the Queen Dowager didn't care for flowers, it was useless expense keeping them up. "That's why I think," he added, "people should never have what they don't like." Spoke of the Farms; George III.'s liking them; old George Villiers [1] having managed them for him; of George IV. having let them, which was very inconvenient; of its being impossible to keep up Game without corn fields, or without feeding them, of pigs, which I thought ugly, which he didn't, and he said they were not so dirty as they were supposed to be.

Thursday, 4th October.—Spoke of the Queen Dowager's having embarked; of my having got a letter from Feodore in the morning, who complained of headaches, and Lord M. said funnily, "When those people get back and among their children, they don't dress, and nothing's so bad for a woman." He said Esterhazy told him that the late King of Naples [2] was a coward, and he told him, to prove it, that he went out shooting one day, and a wild boar came out after him, and he climbed up a tree and said, "Non è paura ma antipatia naturale." Now Lord M. don't think—which is true—that this is a proof of cowardice. . . .

[1] George Bussy Villiers, fourth Earl of Jersey and seventh Viscount Grandison (1735–1805), known as "The Prince of Macaronies." He held various court appointments, culminating in those of Lord of the Bedchamber and Master of the Horse to George IV., when Prince of Wales.

[2] Francis I., "King of the Two Sicilies," 1825–30.

Friday, 5th October.—Lord M. said Brougham had written an answer in *The Edinburgh Review* to Taylor's pamphlet (as we both predicted) maintaining his ground and attacking George IV. very violently. Lord M. has only seen the extract of it in the papers. George IV. hated Brougham, he said, and *he* hated George IV. The latter disliked very much his (B.'s) having the Silk Gown, Lord M. said, which however he did get, in Canning's administration; Taylor said that Queen Charlotte never intrigued, upon which Brougham answered, "George III. wouldn't have allowed it and would have treated her as George I. did his wife"; of which, Lord M. said, there is an account in Walpole; but Brougham is wrong, Lord M. said, in saying George I. murdered her. We both agreed, however, that George I. and George III. were *very* different characters. Said I thought George I. was rather a weak man. "Clever-ish man," replied Lord Melbourne. "George I. was brought to this country by one party, and he had difficult cards to play." Spoke of Prince Doria's marrying Lady Mary Talbot[1]; of his having been advised to come over and marry her, and that I thought such marriages seldom succeeded. Lord M. said, "It's not what happens before the marriage; but what happens after it, that is of consequence. They say," he continued, "that the happiest marriages are those where the woman's taken by force."

Spoke of my having read in Walpole about George II.'s death; of his fondness for Sir Robert, of his hunting in Richmond Park, and then dining

[1] Lady Mary Alathea Beatrix Talbot, daughter of the seventeenth Earl of Shrewsbury, married Philip Andrew, Prince Doria Pamphilj Landi, and was raised to the rank of a Princess by the King of Bavaria.

with Sir Robert at the Lodge; of his always talking in Latin with Sir Robert. Lord Melbourne said when he (Ld. M.) was at Glasgow, they always were examined, questioned, and lectured, in Latin; and "we answered in Latin." He went to Glasgow immediately after he left Cambridge. Asked him if it was his own wish or if he was sent there. Lord M. replied, "It was a good deal my own wish, but it was very much promoted by the Duke of Bedford and Lord Lauderdale, who were great friends of ours; Francis, Duke of Bedford." Lord Melbourne said there is "more study" there; "less mathematics and more politics." Lord M. said there were "very few gentlemen" there, *then*, but much fewer still *now*, as the Universities were very much gone off now, and were then famous for the people at the head of them, who were of the greatest eminence. Lord Palmerston, Lord Lansdowne, Lord John Russell, and Dugald Stuart, were all at Edinburgh, he said. Lord Kinnaird was at Glasgow.

Lord Melbourne looked at a picture of Queen Charlotte which was put up in the drawing-room on trial, and said she was very plain and small, "Well made and a good figure, though she had had many children; and very civil; a good manner." Lady Lyttelton asked leave to put on spectacles for working; and Lord M. said, her asking leave showed she understood *etiquette*, for he said formerly nobody was allowed to come to Court in spectacles, or use glasses; that Mr. Burke, when he was first presented at Court, was told he must take off his spectacles; and that Lord M. said he remembered as long as anything, that no one (man) was allowed to wear gloves at Court.[1] I praised Lady

[1] These customs have never been abandoned, and still obtain.

Lyttelton and said she was such a nice person; in which Lord M. quite agreed; Lord M. said he knew her before her marriage, which took place in 1810, he thinks; (she came out he thinks in 1804, the same year as his sister did, and they are just the same age), but he didn't know her, he said, "before I married." Spoke of her feeling Lord Lyttelton's death much, of Lord Lyttelton's being younger than Lord Melbourne, which I should never have believed; "he was a good man, but an odd man"; Lord M. said it was an old and distinguished name; that there had been one distinguished for his great piety and another for great profligacy, who was called "the wicked Lord Lyttelton,"[1] and who, Lord M. thinks, was great-uncle to the late Lord. The pious one "wrote the *Life of Henry II.*, a very good book, and he also wrote some tracts; his son was very different and went quite the other way, and made the country stand on ends by what he did." Spoke of the present Lord being a nice young man."[2]

Saturday, 6th October.—Told Lord M. that Lehzen

[1] Thomas, 2nd Baron Lyttelton (1744–79), known as "the wicked Lord Lyttelton," succeeded his father George, who, after holding the office of Chancellor of the Exchequer, was made a peer in 1737. The first Lord was the author of several books, including *A Monody to the Memory of a Lady lately Deceased*, *Dialogues of the Dead*, and a *Life of Henry II.*, which was reviewed by Gibbon. His wicked son was the author of two novels, and is one of the persons to whom the *Letters of Junius* are attributed.

[2] George William, fourth Lord Lyttelton, a brilliant scholar. He married a daughter of Sir Stephen Glynne, a sister of Mrs. Gladstone. His mother (see *ante*, Vol. I., p. 208) was Lady Superintendent to the Queen's children, and a writer of delightful letters which were privately printed by her grand-daughter Lady Frederick Cavendish. The fourth Lord Lyttelton was chiefly known to fame as the father of a family of sons remarkably distinguished in the domain of cricket, and subsequently in the graver service of the nation.

and I had been disputing about the right the Sovereign had here, of preventing any of the Royal Family marrying *after* they were of age, and that they must all ask his or her leave; Lehzen maintained that she had seen in Blackstone that after they were of age they might marry any Prince or Princess—*not* a *subject*—without the Sovereign's leave.[1] Lord M. said he was almost certain they could not, "but one can never be quite sure," and that we had best ask the Chancellor about it; and he believes the Princess Charlotte could *not* have married Uncle if she was of age, without her Father's permission. The Prince or Princess wishing to marry give notice to the Privy Council of their intention, and if it isn't objected to for a year, it may take place. Spoke of Charles I.'s intended marriage to the Infanta of Spain, which Lord M. said "was extremely distasteful to the nation," as they wished a Protestant Princess, and this marriage was broken off by the Duke of Buckingham, who quarrelled with Cardinal Olivarez, and they offended the Spanish Court amazingly; Buckingham then took Charles I. back by Paris, where he formed the match with Henrietta Maria, "which was not half so much" disliked as the other, though, Lord Melbourne said, the Country always

[1] By the Royal Marriage Act, 1772, no descendant of George II. (other than the issue of Princesses married into foreign families) can marry without the Sovereign's consent, signified under the Great Seal and declared in Council. A marriage without that consent is void, and certain penalties attach to persons present or assisting at it. But any such descendant, if over *twenty-five*, may, after *one year's* notice to the Privy Council, marry without the Sovereign's consent, unless *both Houses* of Parliament shall, before the year is out, express disapproval of the proposed marriage. Two points are noticeable here: 1st, no distinction is drawn between a marriage with a subject and one with a person of royal blood; 2ndly, a marriage in defiance of the Act is void, not merely "morganatic." See Vol. I., p. 390.

suspected Charles when he asked for money to defend the Elector Palatine, that he would use it in France against the Protestants; they urged him, Lord M. said, to assist the Elector Palatine, and then would give him no money; "they always suspected him of having a leaning for the Roman Catholic Religion, and I suppose he had," continued Lord M. James I., Lord M. said, was far too proud to think of "marrying his son to a little German Princess," and there were hardly any Protestant Kings then; and *he* wished a great match. Spoke of Catherine of Braganza, "who was a quiet inoffensive woman"; Anne Hyde, he said, became Roman Catholic when she married James II.

Lord M. said, "Have you read much in Guizot?" Replied I had not, and wanted first to finish Walpole. "I'm afraid that Walpole's a dull book."[1] I agreed it was very ill written; said the account of Queen Caroline (George II.'s wife) was very curious. "And I believe that's very true," he said. Spoke of her great cleverness, rigidness, learnedness; of no person succeeding who tried to gain favour with the King by paying court to *other people* than the Queen.

Saw Lord Lansdowne. At ½ p. 2 I held a Council at which were present the Lord Chancellor, Lord Melbourne, Lord Lansdowne, Lord Palmerston, Lord John Russell, Lord Glenelg, and Sir John Hobhouse. Lord Melbourne told me after the Council that Mr. Rice was not coming. Lord Melbourne talked a good deal with me about many things. He said Lord Lansdowne had come 70 miles, Lord John 40, and Sir J. Hobhouse 80, this morning.

Lord Melbourne sent me a very nice, prettily

[1] *Memoirs of the Last Ten Years of the Reign of George II.*, by Horace Walpole.

and cleverly written little letter from Wilhelmine Stanhope[1] to read; written from Cadenabbia, Lago di Como, and giving an excellent account of Sir Frederic[2] who was staying with them. They never went into Milan!! At 8 we dined. I sat between the Lord Chancellor and Lord Melbourne. I asked the Chancellor if *any one* of the Royal Family, when of age, could marry any body without my leave? He replied, "*Certainly not.*" I turned to Lord Melbourne and told him he was quite right. Spoke of its being rather severe. I said fortunately there was no law which gave the Sovereign the power to *make* any of them *marry by force*; Lord M. said there was no such power; though people often forced their daughters to marry, by their influence; and he knew many girls would obey, if their Parents told them it was for their best, and for their happiness. Said I liked best to judge for oneself in such matters. Spoke of something I had been reading in Walpole; spoke of *sleep*, and the Chancellor said he *scarcely ever* got *5 hours'* sleep, and yet was quite well; 3 o'clock was a very early hour to go to bed for him! After dinner I sat on the sofa part of the evening with Lady Lyttelton; and with Princess Augusta for the last 20 minutes; Lord Melbourne sitting near me the whole evening, and the Lord Chancellor, Lord Lansdowne, Lord Palmerston, some of the ladies, being seated round the table.

[1] See Vol. I., p. 188.

[2] Lamb. Afterwards Lord Beauvale.

INTRODUCTORY NOTE TO CHAPTER XII

In the month of October Lord Melbourne's prescience divined the early fall of his Administration. The portents were fairly obvious. A weakening Parliamentary majority and internal dissensions, coupled with the obvious murmurs of Chartist disquiet at home and the failure of the Government to give consistent support to a great public servant in Canada, pointed unerringly to political change. Lord Melbourne warned the Queen to hold herself prepared. She was naturally alarmed. To this young girl of nineteen, charged with such high and onerous concerns, it seemed a terrible thing that the statesman to whom she looked up "as a father" should be torn from her side, and that she should find herself surrounded by new faces and listening to strange voices. The clouds, however, blew over for a while.

During the closing months of the year, after the gaieties of the Coronation had become a memory, the Queen was engrossed with the troubles of her Uncle Leopold in Belgium and of her cousins in Portugal. The tiresome controversy as to the possession of Luxembourg was revived, and the civil war in Spain spread unrest throughout the whole of the southern Peninsula. The education, however, of the Queen, at the hands of Lord Melbourne, progressed rapidly. In spite of the fact that, as these Journals reveal, her Minister saw the Queen daily, his letters on public business became fuller and more careful in detail. Her replies acquired more strength and clearness. She began to realise more and more the duties of her position, and its seriousness.

Meanwhile the death of Lady John Russell had touched the Queen with pity for a Minister whom she had hitherto regarded with admiration, but with no special degree of affection. This was now changed. Not only was the Queen suddenly made aware of the political danger likely to accrue, should Lord John Russell's sensibility and grief lead him to retire from active politics, but she was moved by his human sorrow, by its simple expression in letters to herself, and by the emotion stirred in the susceptible heart of Lord Melbourne, who seemed to share to the full the grief of his colleague. For a while it was thought that Lord John's resignation was inevitable. Though "dreadfully shaken," he faced the future, and continued unshrinkingly to fulfil his duties. Thus another peril to Lord Melbourne's Administration, and to the Queen's peace of mind, was temporarily averted.

CHAPTER XII

1838

Sunday, 7th October.—" We've had a long sit of it," Lord Melbourne said to me. And he said they had agreed that Sir J. Hobhouse should write to Lord Auckland, that *no* expedition should be sent into Persia (which they hope and are almost certain Lord Auckland has *not* done), but to strengthen and protect our Indian Possession on the side of Afghanistan and Cabul; and that Lord Palmerston should write a Despatch to Pozzo strongly remonstrating with Russia; Lord M. said these were the principal points of the conversation; and that they were " all for strong measures." Asked him if Lord John or *he* (Ld. M.) should sit next to me at dinner; and he said, " Oh! Lord John! " which I was very sorry for, though Lord John is an agreeable man. Said it surprised people (foreigners) that the *Prime Minister* should not take precedence; Lord M. said that many Prime Ministers had had no rank at all; Pitt, he said, was only the Hon. William Pitt.[1]

Monday, 8th October.—Spoke of the Duchess of Sutherland, who he thought looking well. Went to look at the Duchess of Sutherland's two children asleep, who looked like two cherubs. We were seated much like the night before; the Duchess of

[1] The office of Prime Minister was given high precedence by King Edward VII. The holder takes rank after the Archbishop of York and before Dukes (other than Royal). See *ante*, Vol. I., p. 299.

Sutherland on the sofa, and Lord Melbourne near me the whole evening; and some of the other Ministers, round the table. Spoke to Lord Melbourne about the Duchess's dear children; of children's sleep being so deep that you might hold a candle to their face and it wouldn't wake them, which I said no grown-up person could bear; Lord Melbourne said a tired labourer would, and that formerly they might have done almost anything of the kind to him. Said I thought he didn't like children, which he wouldn't allow, and he said, "I like to speak to them in my own way; not if children are brought in to be paid attention to; that's a great bore."

Tuesday, 9th October.—Lord P. told Lord Melbourne that these Belgians had come with a Proposition to settle the Syndicate first, and to leave the other negotiation to a future time; "which is a proposition for delay"; and Lord M. continued that Uncle had written to Van de Weyer stating how much they had suffered since the separation, upon which Lord M. observed with great truth, that if they had suffered so much since then, why then they had better *never* have *separated.*[1]

Spoke to him of Villiers' making excuses in his letter to Lord Palmerston for staying so long at Paris; of Louis Philippe having told Villiers, Upon no account would he ever marry any of his sons to the little Queen of Spain, not that he despised the Crown of Spain, far from it, but that he knew the jealousy it would excite; at the same time he said he never would permit an Austrian Prince to marry her, but wished that Don Francisco's eldest son

[1] This alludes to the separation of Belgium and Holland. See Vol. I., p. 387.

should, to which Villiers said there were great difficulties. Lord M. thought they couldn't marry her till 16. He continued, "I think that was a very nice letter of the Princess's this morning"; and he observed he hoped she would write more, and that it would be a very good thing if she would give me some account of the feeling in Germany. Prussia was very inimical, he said, and Austria was the only *really* friendly one. Bavaria and Wurtemberg were quite on the French side during Napoleon's time. Spoke of Lady Ashley; its being so difficult to get a match just as one likes; of Frederick Robinson's love of Lady Ashley; "It's the violent feeling of a boy, which often wears off; but which kills others," he said. He then told me a story of C. Fox's [1] to prove the violence of feeling. Charles Fox, he said, "was engaged to marry Lady Erroll and was excessively in love with her"; well, he went abroad (to Malta, I think), and one day somebody said, "Oh! I see" (by the papers) "one of the Fitzclarences is married." He felt his heart coming to his mouth, and he said, "Which is it?" "Oh! I'm sure I don't remember," said the man. "Is it Sophy?" [2] "No." "Is it Mary?" "No." So at last he gulped out, "Is it Eliza?" "Yes, it's Eliza, she is married to Lord Erroll." And he fell down to the ground as if he had been shot. They had told him nothing of it. He afterwards came home and married Mary.

Wednesday, 10th October.—Shewed Lord M. a very pretty letter which I had got from Ferdinand in the morning, giving an account of George Cambridge's

[1] General Charles Richard Fox, Receiver-General of the Duchy of Lancaster. Married Lady Mary Fitzclarence.

[2] Sophia Lady De L'Isle. See *ante*, Vol. I., p. 99.

visit to Lisbon, but his incognito was so strict (quite absurdly so) that it was with great difficulty they persuaded him to dine with them. "It's a lively letter," Lord Melbourne said. Spoke of George travelling under the name of Earl of Culloden (*Baron, not Earl,* I see by the Peerage); which led us to speak for some time of all the Titles borne by Members of the Royal Family; York, Clarence, and the *Earl* of Cambridge, are old royal titles; but the Earldoms of Sussex and Cumberland were never borne by any of the *Royal* Family; the last Earl of Sussex, Lord M. thinks, was a great favourite of Queen Elizabeth's; spoke of Henry VII.'s descendants, &c.; and of how confused all those descendants of my Ancestors are; Lord M. said it was all very well explained by Hallam; spoke of Walpole, his quarrels with Pulteney, who Lord Melbourne said was afterwards Lord Bath, and a very rich man; Sir Richard Sutton, he said, *now* possesses his estate. Lord M. said it was a most extraordinary thing, that after driving Walpole from the Ministry, Pulteney would accept no office. "He was a worthless man," Lord M. said. Said I thought Walpole occasionally gave way to low feelings of revenge and party; Lord M. said, "He was a good man and a kind-hearted man, but his fault was that of lowering the country, and pursuing rather a *low* policy, of every man having his price." Speaking of learning, and Latin, Lord M. asked me if the Dean ever made me do Latin Exercises, which I said he did, but *no* Latin Verses, which I protested against. Made Lord M. laugh by an account of the Dean's horror at my false quantities; and spoke of the anecdote of Lord North's awaking on hearing Burke say *Vĕctĭgal*, and solemnly saying *Vectīgal* and going to sleep again; said I

H.R.H. Prince George of Cambridge
from a portrait at Windsor Castle

began with Eutropius, then with Cæsar's Commentaries, which Lord M. said are very hard, and too hard for a beginner; then read part of *Virgil*, also hard, part of *Ovid*, which he says is very fine but very hard, and part of *Horace*. Said I thought I had benefited but little by what I had learnt, for that I could not construe any quotation; but Lord M. said, "Oh! yes you have" (benefited). "You know that there are such books and such authors, and what they are about," which is very true. Before this we spoke of pronunciation; Lord M. says Room and Goold, for Rome and Gold; I pronounce it in the latter way; asked him if it was right to spell Despatches with an *i* or an *e*; he said he spelt it Despatches, though that was quite modern and came from *Dépêches*; asked him about how to place *who* and *whom*, which I said puzzled me.

Thursday, 11th October.—The revenue of this year exceeds that of last year. Mr. Baring writes that Mr. Rice formed two calculations; the least sanguine is considerably exceeded, and he thinks that by next April it will probably come up to his most sanguine expectations; the Excise seems to have greatly increased, but Mr. Baring says, that comes from its being collected from several quarters; "That often happens," said Lord M., "that that swells one quarter when it has been collected later." The great deficiency is in corn; Lord M. said it is an ascending and descending scale, in proportion as the price rises the duty falls, until the price rises to 70*s*. and it is brought in for 1*s*., and it has been that; Lord M. said it is now about 10*s*. 6*d*. He then explained to me that the corn is brought in without duty, but then bonded, and the duty paid when taken out. Spoke of Pitt's dislike for music being mentioned in Wilberforce's *Life*; Lord M. said he believed that much dislike for music arose from want of attention to it; "I'm sure that's the case with me"; said I thought music was a talent and a gift; he said, "It is often in a person, and can be awakened." Asked if he ever *drew*; he replied, never, though always fond of pictures and understands them; "That again can be taught," he said. He agrees with me that there is too much of Wilberforce's *own* meditations in his life; spoke of W.'s dislike or rather, as Lord M. said, *pity*, for Fox, whom he considered a fallen person; speaking of W., Lord M. said, "There evidently was a great struggle in him; the Devil had a good tussle with him." Spoke of one of Lady Ashley's dear boys (the 2 eldest are here) having fallen on the Slopes and cut his nose; "blundering fellow," said Lord M.; "I think a boy should always be licked when he falls, or puts himself in danger," which made us laugh. Spoke of Lady Ashley's knowing Windsor well; and Lord M. said he thought it was in the winter of '28 that they were here, and not in '29, when George IV. was already very ill; "It was the year of the Catholic Emancipation, and he was very sulky and saw nobody; when he was annoyed about anything, he used to go to bed. Lord M. didn't see him after the year '28.

Friday, 12th October.—Spoke of this book about the South Seas, by Williams,[1] which Lord Ashley said was very curious and which Lord M. means to run through. Lord Ashley then spoke of a book by

[1] John Williams (1796–1839), known as "the Martyr of Erromanga," at which place he was killed by the natives among whom he had worked for over twenty years as a missionary. In 1838 he published *A Narrative of Missionary Enterprise in the South Sea Islands.*

a Captain or Mr. Yates,[1] about the New Zealanders; said they were such a fine people, with one single exception—they *eat men*; Lord Ashley says, "When they have a certain number of daughters, as many as they want, they *eat* the rest."

Saturday, 13th October.—Spoke of the bad weather the Duchess of Sutherland would have for her journey; of its being so expensive to get good fires in France; they only burn wood; Lord M. said he heard that people who had a small fire in a small grate, could do with 2 chaldrons of coals a whole year; at Paris it would cost you, with wood, £2 a week. Told him Murray was stingy and wouldn't have fires in the Corridor in the morning, which Lord M. thought wrong, and said all Scotchmen were rather economical; but "it's a good thing to have economy in the Department." Lord M. said the expense of fires in this Castle must be very great, for that there must be "several 100 fires"; lighting and warming are the great expenses. Said it oughtn't to be more than in the late King's time; for he lived almost always at Windsor, and that when I lived in London, nothing need be kept up here; but Lord M. said that when the King did come to Town, he had very little lighting.

Spoke of the dulness of the great dinners at St. James's and their awkwardness before dinner; told him Aunt Louise told me how dull they were at Brussels; after dinner *she* and all the women sitting, and the King and all the men standing; which Lord M. said was a great convenience to Uncle, but must tire some of the old men a good deal. "The Queen of the Belgians," Lord M. said,

[1] *Account of New Zealand and of the Church Missionary Society's Mission to the Northern Island* by Rev. William Yates, 1835.

"doesn't seem to me to be like a French person, shy, and rather more of an English character." Showed Lord M. two small miniatures I have of George III. and Queen Charlotte, in bracelets; spoke of their children being handsome; said the Princess of Wales (George III.'s Mother) I believed had been good-looking; he said James I. and his Wife, from whom we all come, had been very ugly; Charles I., a fine head; Charles II., very ugly; James II. not so, when young; "Queen Mary" (his daughter) "was the most beautiful woman in Europe," Lord M. said. Queen Anne, plain and large, but he observed having "repeated children." Her Mother, Anne Hyde, of whom he has a picture at Melbourne, was ill-looking; he has also a picture of the Duke of Gloucester, Charles I.'s son. Lord Ashley said he had been to see Sir J. Wyattville, who showed him a remonstrance from Queen Elizabeth's Maids of Honour, which had been found amongst some old papers; which showed the uncouthness of those times; they lived all in one room, which was separated from the gentlemen by a partition which didn't reach to the Ceiling, and they begged it might be made to reach the Ceiling, as the gentlemen climbed up and looked over the other side. This made us all laugh very much, particularly Lord M., who said, "It was very right feeling of the Maids of Honour."

Sunday, 14th October.—Spoke of Lord Ashley's strictness; Lord M. said, he told him the other day that nothing would ever make him fight a Duel; he (Ld. A.) was very much bullied by a man who said he would post him for refusing to fight; upon which Lord Ashley said, "You need not give yourself the trouble, I will do so myself, I've no objection to let the world know I'll never fight a Duel." At the same time Lord Ashley says, "I must take great care not to give offence, as I refuse to give satisfaction." Lord M. said to him, "But what would you do *now*, if you were betrayed into a passion?" "Why, make an apology"; and Lord M. said, "That's the best way and the right way." Spoke of Wilberforce's piety being quite sincere; and Lord M. said, "It was of a very mild character"; that his greatest friend, William Smith, was a Unitarian whom he pitied but loved; Lord M. said, "It is very difficult to be a Unitarian according to the Scriptures"; for, Lord M. said, they deny "the atonement of Christ"; with respect "to the nature of Christ," Lord M. said, "there may be a question, but how they do without the atonement I don't know." He said, they say the New Testament was added and didn't belong to the Bible; this, Lord M. said, is a very dangerous doctrine. Spoke of Evans' book on the Sects,[1] which Lord M. said "is a very clever little book." Lord M. said the Wesleyan Methodists were the most numerous Sect now; that they differed but little from the Established Church, but were followers of Arminius and believed more *in works*, whereas the Calvinists do *in faith alone*; the latter, I said, was highly dangerous, for then some might say that, as they had faith, it did not signify how wicked they were; Lord M. said "that's *antinomianism*"; that the Calvinists didn't go so far, but said if there was true faith there could be no wicked works; I said one could get oneself quite puzzled by thinking too much about these matters,

[1] *A Sketch of the Denominations of the Christian World*, by Dr. John Evans, a Baptist minister. The book had reached its fifteenth edition by the time of the author's death in 1827.

and that I thought it wrong to do so; Lord M. quite agreed with me, and said, "It is best to believe what is in the Scriptures without considering *what* Christ's nature was, for that isn't comprehensible; the Trinity isn't comprehensible." This is all just as *I* feel; I know I have written at great length, more perhaps than I ought, but the conversation was such an interesting one, and Lord M.'s feeling so *right*, *just*, and *enlightened*, that I felt I couldn't do otherwise.

Of Uncle's letter; Edward II. was the first Prince of Wales, Lord M. said; born at Carnarvon; Henry 5th was born at Monmouth, he said. "A very clever man," he said Edward was, "but very ruthless." The Black Prince he thinks the mildest of these; Edward III. very cruel and ruthless; Henry IV. and Henry V., he said, were very religious, "but Henry V. became very much elevated with success." Spoke of when Henry VI. was born. Lord Conyngham spoke of his boy being too much worked at Eton. Lord M. said if there was too much work, the only way was not to do it; but he owned they were flogged for it; he was sometimes flogged at Eton, he told me, and that it had always an amazing effect on him; his Private Tutor used to flog him, and he said, "I don't think he flogged me enough, it would have been better if he had flogged me more." He said he was a very assiduous master, and that he (Ld. M.) should have learnt more if he hadn't always been trying to get away; he said, "I liked it" (being there) "very much when my Father and Mother were in London," which he said they often were; but when they were only 3 miles off, he was always wishing to be at home; he was there 3 years; his eldest brother had also been there. Said, flogging was so degrading; he said that never was thought so by the boys; I observed they didn't like it. "Didn't like the *pain* of it," he replied. Sir J. Herschel[1] sat near Lord Melbourne who talked to him a good deal, which *I* did not profit by, as much as I ought, for I was *stupid*. Lord M. said to me, "He's monstrously frightened," which he seemed to be; for Lord M. had great difficulty in persuading him to sit still; he guessed his age—40. Lord M. spoke to Sir J. Herschel about new discoveries, and he (Ld. M.) said, "I don't mind your discovering stars, if you don't discover men." Asked Lord M. if he admired Paley's works, "Not very much," he said; said, I had read his *Natural Theology* and his *Moral Philosophy*, which Lord M. said are considered rather loose in point of religion. Lord M. continued that when Dr. Barrington, Bishop of Durham, gave him a Living, he said to him, "I don't give you this for your *Natural Theology* and your *Moral Philosophy*, but for your *Christian Evidences* and for your *Horæ Paulinæ*." Lord M. agreed with me that his Anatomical descriptions in the *Natural Theology* were very disagreeable. His *Moral Philosophy* I liked better, but, as Lord M. truly observes, he puts every thing in such a Philosophical light as to create doubts; "You ought to do what's right, because it's right," said Lord M., and Paley puts the reasons against, and the reasons why, you should do it, and Lord M. says, if people see a doubt raised, they become disinclined to do what is right. Lord M. said, "The Rooks are my delight," watching them out of his window, and hearing their cawing; there are numbers of them here, and he was quite surprised

[1] He had discovered η Argus in the previous year.

at my disliking them. *He* also likes the large Clock in the court here, to *me* so melancholy,—which puts him in mind of the Eton clock.

Tuesday, 16th October.—Lord Melbourne told me he had been reading a long article by Mr. Macaulay about Sir William Temple; "a very good article," he said, in *The Edinburgh Review*. Spoke of the article in it Brougham has written in answer to Sir H. Taylor's remark, and of which Lord M. has only read the extracts. George IV., Lord M. said, "was very fond of his father, and monstrously afraid of him." Spoke of a letter which Lord M. said George IV. wrote to Queen Caroline, when he separated from her, in which he said, "Love and affection weren't in their power," but that he hoped civility would remain between them; and that there was no tie left between them. This he sent her by Lord Cholmondeley. Spoke of George III.'s blindness; my fear for my eyes[1]; George III. had no private Secretary till he grew blind, and Lord M. mentioned an instance of how much he used to write.

Wednesday, 17th October.—Spoke of Mr. Pitt's sister, Lady Eliot,[2] who died and who Wilberforce mentions; one of his (Pitt's) sisters[3] was Lord Stanhope's Mother, Lord M. said, and he says Lord Stanhope certainly speaks very like Pitt. "His manner, his voice, and the form of his sentences are the same, but with this difference between them:—

[1] The Queen had no cause to fear. She retained her powers of vision far beyond the normal period.

[2] Lady Harriet Pitt married Edward James Eliot, M.P., son of the first Lord Eliot.

[3] Lady Hester Pitt married Charles, third Earl Stanhope, and died before his succession to the peerage, but there was no son by this marriage. The fourth Earl Stanhope's mother was the only daughter of the Hon. Henry Grenville, Governor of Barbadoes.

when Mr. Pitt spoke, no one breathed, or thought when it would end, whereas you can't listen to Lord Stanhope for two sentences without being tired to death; that's the difference between them," said Lord M.

Friday, 19th October.—Said, I feared I teased him often so much by asking him so many questions, and often I feared very indiscreet ones. "Oh! never," he replied most kindly, and continued in such a warm affectionate manner, "You *must* ask questions, it's your right, and it's my duty to answer you; pray don't ever think that; any thing but that." I said he was too kind, for that I feared I was so young and often inconsiderate. I said I was very sorry he went; "I'm very sorry, too," he replied, and that I should miss him very much in my rides. Spoke of my dislike to go to Brighton; and he said, "I wouldn't go if I didn't like it." Said, as I had a Palace there I thought it was necessary I should go; he said not at all, for that it was only a fancy of George IV.'s to go there, nobody ever went there before. Said I thought it would vex the people if I didn't.[1]

Monday, 22nd October.—Asked Lord M. if anything had been done about changes in Government, or if it had been talked about. "Talked a good deal about it," Lord M. said, "and a good many for it." Sir John Newport[2] is better, but wishes to resign. "If Lord Glenelg could be made to accept that place, he would be safe," Lord M. said; but of course that would lead to other changes; he says

[1] The Pavilion was sold to the town of Brighton in 1849.

[2] Sir John Newport (1756–1843). An Irish banker. Chancellor of the Irish Exchequer, 1806, and Comptroller of the Exchequer in 1834. He was a man of considerable ability, and a typical Whig placeman.

Lord G. is not active enough; and that his present affliction makes him still more dilatory. But how to replace him; make Rice[1] a Peer and put him there, Lord M. replied; but then there's a difficulty to replace Rice; Mr. Baring is certainly fit for it, Lord M. said. Asked if Lord Glenelg would accept the place; Lord M. don't know, but rather doubts it; it's sure for life, he said, and G. is very poor; his father, C. Grant,[2] Lord M. said, might have made at the utmost £50,000 or £60,000, and that, if divided, would soon vanish with an election or two. "Then there's another project," said Lord Melbourne, "which some people are for, and which is very much instigated by Normanby, which is to send the Duke of Sussex to Ireland, but it would be extremely dangerous."[3]

Thursday, 25th October.—Received a letter from Lord Melbourne, which is too long to copy here, therefore I shall only transcribe the beginning and end: "Lord Melbourne presents his humble duty to Your Majesty and begs to acquaint Your Majesty that Lord John Russell did not come to Town yesterday, but that he will come up to-day and remain until to-morrow. This will prevent Lord Melbourne from returning to the Castle till to-

[1] See *ante*, Vol. I., p. 199.

[2] Charles Grant (1746–1823), father of Lord Melbourne's much-abused Colonial Secretary. A clansman of Speyside, born on the day Culloden was fought, he spent the best years of his life, after the fashion of his family, in the Indian Civil Service. Later, as M.P. for the County of Inverness, he took a leading part in Indian debates, and was ultimately elected Chairman of the East India Company. He never acquired wealth, but he was rich in evangelical faith, and with Zachary Macaulay was a member of the Clapham sect.

[3] The project of sending a Royal Prince as Viceroy to Ireland has frequently been discussed, but Prime Ministers have hitherto taken Lord Melbourne's view.

morrow. Lord Melbourne has received another letter from Lord John strongly pressing as early a Meeting of Parliament as possible, but Lord Melbourne upon consultation with Lord Glenelg, Lord Palmerston, Mr. Rice, and Lord Duncannon, finds them all much opposed to the measure. If Lord John perseveres in his opinion it will be necessary to assemble the Cabinet without delay, but in that case Lord Melbourne does not think that the Majority or any considerable portion of the Members will be induced to concur with Lord John Russell." . . . "I am afraid that times of some trouble are approaching[1] for which Your Majesty must hold yourself prepared; but Your Majesty is too well acquainted with the nature of human affairs, not to be well aware that they cannot very long go on even as quietly as they have done for the last sixteen months."

Friday, 26th October.—After dinner we were seated as usual, Lord Melbourne sitting near me the whole evening. Showed him some lithographs, Aunt Louise sent me, of Soult,[2] Talleyrand,[3] Fitzjames,[4] Benjamin Constant.[5] Talked of

[1] One of the causes of disquiet was the Chartist Agitation, now beginning, which only finally came to a head and collapsed on April 10, 1848.

[2] Marshal Soult, Duke of Dalmatia, had been the most popular figure at the Queen's Coronation a few months before. He was now 69, but hale and vigorous. He lived another thirteen years. See Vol. I., p. 309.

[3] Talleyrand had died in the preceding month of May, reconciled to the Church of which he had been a prelate, after a kaleidoscopic interlude of forty-seven years. At the age of eighty, only four years before his death, he had been the most conspicuous ornament of King William's Court, to which he was accredited Ambassador by the son of Egalité.

[4] The Duc de Fitzjames married the sister of Mademoiselle Montijo, afterwards Empress of the French.

[5] Benjamin Constant had died in 1830, aged sixty-three. His

Marie's[1] illness; of the Orleans being strong till this generation; Louis Philippe's Mother[2] was heiress to the Duc de Penthièvre, Lord M. said, and very rich; talked of Louis XIV. being very strong, and so was his brother. The Regent Orleans was also very strong, but died from indulgence; he married one of Louis XIV.'s natural daughters; Lord M. thought Mdlle. de Blois,[3] but was not quite sure. The Prince of Orange, father of our William III., wished to marry her, Lord M. said, but Louis XIV. wouldn't allow it, and William said, "Well, I've tried to have him as a friend, but as I can't do that, I must try what I can do with him as an enemy." The Duchess of Orleans was very proud, Lord M. said, and St. Simon used to call her "Madame Lucifer."

Sunday, 28th October.—Talked of poor Lady Uxbridge[4]; of perfumes; Lady Holland desires her Maître d'Hôtel to take away people's pocket-hand-

psychological novel *Adolphe*, a new departure in introspective literature, had earned for him some fame. His inexplicable attachment to Madame de Staël, and his more easily comprehended infatuation for Madame Récamier, obtained for him a greater notoriety. He, in company with many other distinguished Frenchmen of that era, oscillated in his allegiance to political principle, and while his pamphleteering led him into many duels, he fought his last one, as a cripple, seated in a chair.

[1] Wife of Duke Alexander of Würtemberg. See *ante*, Vol. I., p. 78.

[2] Louise Marie Adelaide de Bourbon, daughter of the Duc de Penthièvre. He was descended from the Comte de Toulouse, natural son of Louis XIV. and Madame de Montespan.

[3] Mademoiselle de Blois was a sister of the Comte de Toulouse. Louis Philippe was thus doubly descended from Louis XIV. and Madame de Montespan.

[4] The second Lady Uxbridge was daughter of the Rt. Hon. Sir Charles Bagot, at one time Minister to the United States, afterwards Ambassador at St. Petersburg and eventually Governor-General of Canada. Lord Uxbridge's first wife (Eleanora, daughter of John Campbell of Shawfield) had died in July, 1838.

kerchiefs when they have any scent upon them, and Lord M. said she had quite a quarrel with Lord Alvanley [1] about it, once, who wouldn't give up his.

"Don't you feel uneasy at the movement of these two great armies?" he said; I replied it was very serious, and asked him if he was; he said not, but "It is a great crisis; it is a stroke for the Mastery of Central Asia." [2] These armies, he said, are gone to Candahar and Cabool; the danger, Lord M. said, is that it may convulse the Mahrattas behind. Talked of the siege of Herat being raised; "If the Shah has raised the siege, then it'll all subside," he said; that if this was the case, it was all owing to the brave and heroic defence of the Afghans; and he quite agrees with McNeill that we ought to assist them and to stand by our friends; Lord M. says Lord Auckland has done quite right in moving this army; "It's in fact," he said, "revolutionising Cabool and Candahar"; upsetting the present Chiefs, and putting on the Throne whoever we choose and whoever may be friendly to us. It may perhaps, if the siege of Herat is raised, be brought to an accommodation,

[1] William Pepper Arden, second Lord Alvanley (1789–1849). Possessed, in a high degree, that least tangible of intellectual gifts, a fine wit. Sir Walter Scott found him the most entertaining of men. His powers were considerable, his achievements slight.

[2] Some years earlier Dost Mohammed, having usurped the throne of Afghanistan, drove the Ameer, Shah Sooja, into exile. Lord Auckland, the Governor-General, sent Captain Burnes (who had been presented to the Queen before her accession and had described to her many of his adventures: see Vol. I., p. 89) on a mission to Cabul. The Ameer received him civilly, but afterwards somewhat unceremoniously dismissed him. Accordingly Lord Auckland decided on the restoration of Shah Sooja, and in the autumn of this year published a proclamation dethroning Dost Mohammed. A military expedition was forthwith sent across the frontier. See *ante*, p. 47.

he says. The army Lord Auckland has put under arms consists of 25,000 men; and Runjeet Singh,[1] Lord M. said, on whom we depend, but who is old, has agreed to furnish 50,000; in all 75,000 men; but Lord M. said an Indian army of 75,000 men is in fact one of 500,000; for that each person has such numbers of servants with them. Talked of boys who go to Eton getting money. Lord M. said he generally got 9 or 10 guineas after each Holidays, to go to Eton with; "Besides that, my father told the old man at the Inn, Kendal, to give me ½ a Crown every Monday and every Thursday; that's five shillings a week," Lord M. said, which he thought a very odd way of giving it, quite independent of the Tutor or any body. He generally spent it at the Pastry Cooks, and later too to Dog-fighters, rabbit-catchers, and boatmen.

Monday, 29th October.—Lady Lyttelton, who is a most agreeable amiable woman, talked to me a good deal of Lady Caroline Lamb, who was her 1st Cousin; she had a very pretty slight figure, but very red hair, and her face a little *en beau* like Lady Mary Stopford. She was amazingly in love with Lord M., which, handsome and agreeable as he was, was no wonder, but acted the gentleman's part and told him of her passion; he could not marry her as long as his eldest brother lived, but when he died he married her.

Sunday, 4th November.—At a ¼ p. 4 I walked

[1] Ranjit Singh (1780–1839). "The Lion of the Punjab," strong-willed and energetic, uneducated but acute, he created for himself a kingdom out of incongruous elements, and maintained his authority unchallenged. He is said to have preferred the "Koh-i-noor" diamond to all his conquests. This was the penultimate year of his life. After his death in 1839, the Punjab was plunged for years into a state of anarchy, from which it was rescued by British annexation in 1849.

BARONESS LEHZEN.

From a sketch by the Queen before her accession.

out on the Terrace with Lord Melbourne and all the ladies except Lady Barham and Lehzen, and all the gentlemen, and came home at 5. It was a fine bright evening, and a good many people out. I walked between Lord Melbourne and Lord Surrey. Lord Melbourne came out in his Windsor uniform,[1] which I told him I was delighted to see (all my gentlemen wear theirs when I go to Church and walk on the Terrace).

Tuesday, 6th November.—Talked to him of a report (which I fear is quite true) of ——'s boy, who is at Eton, having stolen some money; "It is better to treat it as a childish trick," he said; "and I should speak seriously to the Boy." This is very true; when he was there a boy stole a pair of buckles, and is now grown up, a very gentlemanly man, but it disgraced him for the time. Said, I heard this boy hadn't had enough money; if a boy couldn't pay a Pastry Cook's bill any more, the boy kept away from the shop, Lord M. said, a very good thing, and was dunned whenever he came near it. Talked of boys telling lies whenever they had done wrong at school, which wasn't considered wrong, and which Lord M. said was the same thing as pleading not guilty at the Bar, which *everyone* would do. Lord M. talked to Alava[2] of a person of the name of

[1] This custom was continued for many years after the Queen married. See Vol. I., p. 351.

[2] Don Miguel de Alava (1770–1843). One of the many modern soldiers of distinction who, like Sir Evelyn Wood and Sir John French, began his career as a sea-officer. Alava was present at Trafalgar, in the Spanish flagship, but this did not hinder him from becoming A.D.C. to the Duke of Wellington in the Peninsula and serving on the Duke's staff at Waterloo. He was Spanish Ambassador in London in 1834. He was one of the few distinguished men during the tempestuous years of the Napoleonic era, who retired into exile from sheer weariness of taking new oaths of allegiance.

Montrond,[1] whom Louis Philippe gives money to, to gather news for him; he is a man of bad character, Lord M. said; was a great friend of Talleyrand's, and of Lady Holland's; he has had several fits, and Lord M. said, "When he had one of these fits one day, and was grasping the ground, Talleyrand who stood by him said, 'Il veut absolument descendre.'"

Wednesday, 7th November.—We then talked about this affair of ——'s boy during the greater part of dinner time, Conyngham telling us what he heard from Slane about it; how they bullied the little boy, knocking off his hat, kicking him, and calling him, "Thief who sharped £5," which he did from *several* boys. "They are like so many demons—boys," said Lord M. "I should have taken the boy away." —— was sent for, but left the boy; the boy stole 12*s*. at a private school, and came with this reputation to Eton; Lord M. said it certainly was doing it "in a systematic way," stealing it from various boys; two of poor ——'s boys did the same thing, and were obliged to be taken away, but weren't flogged; Lord M. thinks he would have tried the effect of giving little —— a good flogging. He knows the boy, who is very clever and studious; it's a great disgrace, he said, and would hurt his parents very much. "Bad thing to take him away too," said Lord M., "for they'd say, That boy was taken away from Eton for thieving."

Thursday, 8th November.—Talked of Alfred Paget and his sisters, who Lord M. thinks such complete Cadogans; George he thinks the best-looking. Talked of George IV.'s liking Lord Anglesey, which Lord M. said he did, only that he was jealous of

[1] Protégé of Talleyrand, and notorious roué. He married the Duchesse de Fleury. He died in the odour of sanctity.

him; of his figure, and used to say to the Tailor, "Why don't you make my coats fit like Paget's?" which made us laugh, as the King might well think his own figure wasn't quite as slim as Lord Anglesey's; Lord M. said they all tried to vex him by having their things made better and tighter than his, particularly some "leathern clothes" (breeches) which people wore then, and which annoyed the King. Lord M. turned and looked at the picture of George IV. by Gainsborough in my room, and said, "I think that's like you," which it is; told him I was reckoned very like him when I was little.

Friday, 9th November.—Asked Lord M. if he really thought Lord John meant to retire; Lord M. said, "I don't know; that wouldn't at all do what he proposes." Lord M. says that with rather a difficult task before him, meaning the Ballot, Lord John might be a little discouraged. "His wife[1] had influence with him," Lord M. continued; "she was ambitious, she would have prevented his retiring; she restrained his eagerness, being against any thing tending to radicalism in her heart; it's a great break-up for him; he was very happy and thought himself settled for life; it loosens all that again."

Thursday, 15th November.—Lord M. looked at 2 Annuals, talked of the Author of Junius never being known; and Lord Holland told us a curious story of what happened in Spain to (he thinks) Philip IV.; whenever he sat down to dinner he found a sheet of satirical verses about his Court, in his napkin, and this went on for several days; he very angry, and nobody could discover who did it; one day, a curtain fell down and another copy of

[1] The first Lady John Russell, widow of the second Lord Ribblesdale. She had died on 1st November of this year.

these verses appeared; at last they appointed a commission to try and find it out, and for six weeks it ceased; but then it began again, and it never had been discovered. Lord Holland also told some other curious mysterious anecdotes. Talked of the Duchess of Portsmouth,[1] whose pictures Lord Holland said were "very Dolly"; she lived to be ninety or a hundred; Lord Holland's grandfather *saw* her in 1729; and she believed Charles II. to have been poisoned; Lord M. said he died of apoplexy. Talked of its being seldom that people were really poisoned; Lord M. thinks that the Duchess of Orleans,[2] Mme. Henriette, was poisoned in a glass of chicory water, for that she died immediately after taking it. Talked of Prussic Acid; Lord M. said it won't kill if it's alloyed, but otherwise one drop is certain death.

Friday, 16th November.—Talked of Lord Holland; of Lady Holland's talking of going to Bowood; Lord M. said he thought she would move about "once she has got on her legs again." Formerly she wouldn't go in a carriage; when she does travel, he says, she chooses her own horses, and her own boys whom she has taught to drive as she likes. Of the Duchess-Countess[3] and her complaining of her poverty, and that she hadn't more than £12,000 a year of her own; that she had £32,000 a year in all, but was obliged to spend all but the £12,000 in

[1] Louise Renée de Quéroualle, created by Charles II. Duchess of Portsmouth in England and by Louis XIV. Duchesse d'Aubigny in France.

[2] Henrietta, Duchess of Orleans (1644–70), daughter of Charles I. She married the only brother of Louis XIV. It was an unhappy marriage, and her sudden mysterious death at the age of twenty-six led her contemporaries to think that she had been poisoned by order of her husband. Bossuet preached her funeral sermon.

[3] *I.e.* of Sutherland. See *ante*, Vol. I., p. 68.

Charities. Lord M. said he thought that was true. Talked of his elder brother's name having been Peniston, but they called him Pen; it was also his father's name, but where the name originally came from he don't know. "All I know is," he said, "that in 1670 there was born at Southwell a fellow called Peniston Lamb, in very humble circumstances; he went up to London, studied the law, and became a Conveyancer and an Agent, and made a very large fortune; he died in 1734, and bequeathed his fortune to his nephews, Matthew Lamb and his brother Robert; how they were his nephews and who their father was I haven't the least idea, nor have I ever been able to find out."[1] Lord M. told this so naïvely and simply. "Matthew Lamb also studied the law," he continued, "and then he married Miss Coke of Melbourne, who was a great heiress; he became Sir Matthew Lamb, and left a very large fortune to my father, who contrived to get rid of it very speedily; still *he* has left a good fortune; my father was somehow connected with Lord Bute, and through the interest of Lord North and the Prince of Wales, he was made, first Baron, then Viscount Melbourne; and in the year '15 he was made a Peer of England, also by the Prince of Wales; that's the History of the thing." This of course interested me exceedingly; and to hear it related by this great and excellent man, and in this unostentatious, delightful manner, rendered it still more so. He reverted again to his not knowing who his grandfather's father was. The family of the Cokes, he said, was well known; they were a very ancient and highly distinguished Family. His great-uncle, Robert Lamb, Bishop of Peterborough,

[1] See appendix to this volume.

had no children; Lord M.'s only relations on his father's side are the Binghams and Wombwells. Asked Lord M. who that old Mrs. Howe was, who I heard him mention; he said she was sister to Lord Howe; she had 3 brothers, one (whom I forget about), Lord Howe who so eminently distinguished himself on the 1st of June, and William, afterwards Sir William Howe, who, Lord M. said, was not so distinguished; "as brave as a Lion but no more of a Commander—than a Pig," he said, laughing. That had always been said of him, Lord M. said. They were descended from Sophia Walmoden, "Countess of Yarmouth," he said; "it was the last time that a title was given to such a person." Mrs. Howe married her cousin, and Lord M. said, was a very clever woman, though very rough, and more like a man than a woman always; George III. and Queen Charlotte, Lord Melbourne said, treated her always like a relation. Talked of when Lord M. first knew Lord Holland; at Eton, though Lord Holland is 6 years older than Lord M., and when Lord M. left Eton, Lord Holland asked him to Holland House. He formed this connection at Florence, Lord M. said; Lady Holland was a Miss Vassall,[1] daughter of Mr. Vassall, a great Proprietor in Jamaica, married Sir Godfrey Webster when she was only 16; "she was very handsome, hated her husband, was a very ambitious woman, and thought it would be a very good thing to marry Mr. Fox's nephew."

Talked of Mr. Harcourt[2] (Lady Elizabeth's husband), who, Lord M. said, was a very strange man, though a clever man. He was a Whig but is now an

[1] See Vol. I., p. 101.

[2] George Granville Harcourt. See *ante*, Vol. I., p. 132.

adherent of Stanley's. Lord M. said that when his brother Frederick was over here last, he went to Nuneham to see Elizabeth, and when he came back he said, "What a country this is,"—that there were only 3 people in the Family, but that there were 3 parties: Elizabeth herself, a great Wellingtonian; Lord Norreys,[1] a most violent ultra Tory; and Harcourt, a follower of Stanley's; and all so violent that they would hardly speak to each other.

Sunday, 18th November.—Talked of Clark's boy wishing to have gone into the Navy, but that the risk was so great and the promotion so slow, as there is no buying as in the Army; talked of the buying seeming to be a bad system, and Lord M. said quite unlike any other Army; that there was no discipline and system like ours in the World, that it had "every possible defect and yet it certainly has produced one of the finest armies," which it certainly has. Speaking of the Army, Lord M. said, "It's a department of the Government I don't understand very well," which I won't allow, for there is hardly *any thing* he don't understand; but he said he believed the Army to be on a much better principle than the Navy, that there was less favouritism in the Army; he is quite alarmed, he says, at the numbers of Pagets and Russells there are in the Navy; he thinks the Navy belongs more exclusively to the Aristocracy than the Army. "I always supported Lord Hill and Fitzroy Somerset[2] from the beginning of Lord

[1] See *ante*, Vol. I., p. 132.

[2] Lord Fitzroy Somerset (1788–1855), afterwards first Lord Raglan, was a son of the fifth Duke of Beaufort. An officer described by the critical historian of the Peninsular War as of gracious manners, discreet, and of sound judgment. Wounded in the arm at Waterloo. He asked the surgeon not to "carry away that arm" until he had taken off the ring given him by his wife. Courageous, high-minded,

Grey's Government," he said. Lord M. likes Lord Hill and thinks he managed well; if there had been any other great commander to put in his place perhaps he wouldn't have hesitated removing him, he said; but there is nobody, but people like Lord Anglesey, who *never* would do, and Lord William Bentinck,[1] "who is a worthy man as can be, but a wild-headed man." Talked of the fire at the Chapel, which I said gave him so much trouble; of the stove, as he said, giving no warmth; Lady Barham talked of how churches should and could be warmed, and Lord M. said, "Those very religious people always make everything very comfortable." And we talked for some time about the Sermon, church-going, our Liturgy, most cleverly and agreeably. Lord M. said he remembers churches never being warmed, or people ever thinking about their being warmed or not; Lord M. said there was formerly more *real* feeling for religion, "less show"; not "ostentatious." "You should be humble." Lord M. said, "I was thinking this morning how I should curtail it" (the Service); "I think I would have the Psalms and the concluding Prayer"; not the Lessons, as they are detached; the Commandments he would also have; but he don't think it would be *well* to change it *at all*. He admires the Psalms very much, thinks them very fine, but that

and with a noble and intrepid spirit that suffered but never quailed before hostile criticism. He bore the brunt of the Crimean struggle as Commander-in-Chief of the British Force, and died in harness before Sebastopol. "His loss," wrote the Prince Consort, "is irreparable."

[1] Lord William Bentinck (1774–1839). This judgment of Bentinck is curious, if compared with the eulogy of Macaulay engraved on the base of the Governor-General's statue at Calcutta, in which such expressions occur as "wise, upright, paternal, simple, moderate, prudent, honest, and benevolent."

there are some odd things in them, and he thinks some of the translations were imperfectly done, the language not being so well understood 200 years ago as now; but he said, it would not do to attempt to translate them again. Talked of Mant's Bible, which I used to read, with Notes; "I've got that book," he said, "it's a very good book," and done in a manner to avoid cavil; it's done by Mant,[1] Bishop of Down (I think), and Dr. D'Oyley,[2] Chaplain to the Archbishop of Canterbury, who Lord M. knows.

Begged him to be kind enough to let me hear from him what was going on; and he turned towards me and said, "I'll take care you shall be informed of all; one feels a little nervous meeting them all, what they may do"; and I begged he would also let me hear what else of importance might be going on, and he promised he would, as I said I was always very curious, and heard very little when he was not here. "Oh! it's right you should know," he said. Talked about what they would discuss in the Cabinet; about the measures for next Session and the general aspect of Affairs, he said, not about changes in Government; "You can't discuss those in the Cabinet," he said, as they concern the Cabinet itself too much. "I must talk to them separately about that." In reply to a question of mine about Lord John's absence, he said, Lord John's being away was an inconvenience, for that he had great influence, on

[1] Richard Mant, Bishop first of Killaloe, afterwards of Down, Connor, and Dromore, a voluminous writer of verse and theological essays.

[2] George D'Oyly, for many years Rector of Sundridge, Kent, and of Lambeth. He was treasurer of the S.P.C.K., for which the annotated Bible here referred to was prepared.

account of his situation people looked to him; there was a great deal in *Situation*, Lord M. said.

Monday, 19th November.—Talked of Lady Mary Fox,[1] who dislikes Lady Holland very much, Lord M. says, and vice versa. Lady Holland likes C. Fox,[1] he says, but has quarrelled with him very much; he has very much her temper and "spars in a moment." That she was particularly anxious to prevent Henry Fox's going to Florence, and begged Lord M. to oppose it, he believes merely because H. Fox wishes it. Talked of the late King's having known Lord Holland, but Lord M. thinks he never liked his Politics; Lord Holland was too fond of the French; George IV., Lord M. said, feared the French Politics, but liked French Society; made much more of Louis XVIII. than George III. ever did; Lord M. had only seen Louis XVIII. at Carlton House, but didn't know him; the Comte d'Artois (Charles X.) he knew; had been in the same house with him, had been out shooting with him at Lord Talbot's.[2] Lord M. said he was a very lively, agreeable, pleasant man, and very easy; used to keep *Maigre* very strictly and used to reprimand the Duc de Berry for not doing so; *he*, Lord M. said, was proud and harsh; talked of the Duchesse de Berry[3] being very strange, of there having been an intention at one time of Uncle's marrying her, but that he couldn't make up his mind to it.

Begged Lord M. not to forget about his sister's

[1] General Charles and Lady Mary Fox. See *ante*, p. 49.

[2] Charles, second Earl Talbot, K.G. He was appointed by Peel in 1817 Lord Lieutenant of Ireland, but had to give way to Lord Wellesley in 1822. He opposed Catholic emancipation, but supported the repeal of the Corn Laws.

[3] Caroline Louisa, daughter of King Ferdinand I. of the Two Sicilies.

coming down here on Saturday, which he said he would not, as also his writing to me. I pressed him to take care of himself. I then took leave of him, gave him my hand, which he pressed so warmly, saying so kindly and affectionately, " God bless you, M'am," and then kissed my hand. This was done in such a hearty, warm, affectionate yet respectful manner, as quite touched me.

Wednesday, 21st November. I forgot to say that Lord Conyngham's 2 youngest children, Cecilia,[1] 7, and Francis,[2] who they generally call Peacock and sometimes Franky, 5, arrived here yesterday, and I saw them when I came home from riding. Peacock is a beautiful boy, with long black hair ; Cecilia has fine eyes but is not otherwise pretty and is very like poor Lady Agnes Byng.[3] Went into the Gallery and played with the children for an hour while Lord Conyngham and Lehzen stood talking. They are charming, delightful children, quite at home with me and treated me quite like a playfellow, which pleased me much ; played at ball with them, and then I sat in the window-seat and looked at picture-books of animals with them, and told them the names of the animals. They would hardly let me go.

Saturday, 24th November.—Talked of a letter of Clanricarde's[4] which we think curious ; he (C.) owns the Emperor's power of fascination, and that he took him twice by both his hands, which Lord Pal-

[1] Afterwards wife of Sir Theodore Henry Brinckman.

[2] Afterwards Lieutenant R.N., and M.P. for Co. Clare.

[3] Daughter of first Marquess of Anglesey and wife of Hon. G. Byng (see Vol. I., p. 205), afterwards second Earl of Strafford.

[4] Ulick John, first Marquess of Clanricarde, Ambassador to St. Petersburg. In 1858 he served as Privy Seal in Lord Palmerston's Administration. See Vol. I., p. 318.

merston told Lord M. he hears he always does in his eagerness in conversation; that when Lord Clanricarde broached the subject of Persia, the Emperor said, "I'm so glad you've touched on that subject, it's just what I wished." The Empress[1] he mentions as plain; she denied to him ever having any things made at Paris, which I know she *has*; the Grand Duchesses, beautiful. The Cabinet had not been very long, he said, it was about these Belgian affairs, and Lord Palmerston explained how it stood; it was a little difficult, he said, to restrain Bülow and Senfft[2]; Uncle complains in his letter, Lord M. said, of the tone taken in the Conference, which he considers as ill-tempered; and he speaks of his great difficulties, and says he went to Belgium by the wish and desire of England and not of his own accord. Then Lord M. said, Bülow and Senfft wouldn't believe what the King of the French said about the difficulty he had to restrain the feelings of the French Nation, for they would say the King of the French can always carry everything he wishes. Lord M. thinks Senfft very agreeable; he met him at Lord Holland's, as he did also Alava who dined there yesterday.

Sunday, 25th November.—Talked of various things and of Lord Holland's grandfather having seen the Duchess of Portsmouth,[3] which I thought most extraordinary. Lord M. said, both his grandfather

[1] The Empress of Russia, Charlotte Louise (Alexandra Feodorovna), daughter of Frederick William III., King of Prussia. The Grand Duchesses her daughters were Marie (who married in July 1839, Duke Maximilian of Leuchtenberg) and Olga (who married King Charles of Würtemberg).

[2] See *ante*, Vol. I., p. 388.

[3] Henry Fox, first Baron Holland, was born in 1705, and the Duchess of Portsmouth died in 1734.

and grandmother, Lady C. Fox, saw her; she used to go with her father and mother, the Duke and Duchess of Richmond,[1] to see the Duchess of Portsmouth at Aubigny; the Duke was her grandson. Talked of there being some difficulty about the Duke of Richmond's properties in France; by the French law they ought to be divided amongst every branch of the Family, by which Lord Holland would have some, and the Beauclerks (who are descended from the Duchess of Leinster, who was the handsomest sister of Lady Caroline Fox and Lady Sarah Lennox) some. Nell Gwynn was Mother to the Duke of St. Albans, and Lord M. said she used to ridicule Mdlle. de Quéroualle, Duchess of Portsmouth, and used to say, "Whenever anybody belonging to a great family in France dies, she puts on mourning, whereas if she thought of it, she ought to die of shame at what she is."

Wednesday, 28th November.—Got a letter from Lord Melbourne in which besides other things he says he sends me a note from Lord Minto, stating that Durham had arrived at Plymouth on Monday night, but had not yet landed. Lord Melbourne says he had "received an answer from Lord Spencer[2]

[1] This was the second Duke, who inherited the dukedom of Aubigny direct from his grandmother, Louise de Quéroualle, at her death in November 1734 (Charles II.'s son, the first Duke, had died in 1723). Lady Caroline was his eldest daughter; she married Henry Fox (afterwards Lord Holland).

[2] John Charles, third Earl Spencer (1782–1845), better known as Lord Althorp, in which capacity he led the House of Commons with singular force and captivating modesty, was at this time employed in the, to him, congenial occupation of losing £3,000 a year by farming at Wiseton. No one in public life ever declined high office with greater persistency. Like Lord Hartington (eighth Duke of Devonshire), whom he somewhat resembled in character and disposition, Lord Spencer inspired confidence in men of both political parties, and was universally respected by his fellow-countrymen.

decidedly declining both Ireland and Canada." Lord M. says also that he had likewise received a letter from Uncle Leopold by Van Praet,[1] which he would send me, and which was "very kind"; "but I am afraid points at an impracticable arrangement respecting the Territory, namely that Belgium should retain it upon payment of a sum of money to Holland."

Thursday, 29th November.—He said he had seen Van Praet, and that he feared there would be great difficulty in this new Proposition of Uncle's, namely, to buy part of Luxembourg and Limbourg from the King of Holland, the part along the Meuse, and Lord M. thinks the others will *never* consent to this. Talked of this for some time, of the danger of force being employed; said I would show him Uncle's letter after the Council; he told me that he had sent me this, and that he thought I ought to ask Van Praet, but would speak to Palmerston first about it. . . .

Sunday, 2nd December.—Asked him who Lord Ligonier[2] (whose bust is in the Corridor) was; he was a French Protestant who entered our Service, he said; was made first Sir John and then Lord Ligonier; "he was quite the right hand of William Duke of Cumberland." At the Battle of Fontenoy, Lord M. said, he got mixed with the French, and thought he could save himself by his being a Frenchman, and leading on the French "en avant," and

[1] Jules van Praet, as Secretary in 1831 of the Belgian Legation in London, had been concerned in the negotiations for the offer of the Belgian Crown to King Leopold.

[2] John (or Jean) Louis, first Earl Ligonier, a skilful and intrepid soldier. He fought in Marlborough's four great battles, and commanded a division at Dettingen. Ligonier died in 1770, and was buried in Westminster Abbey.

thus get back; but they discovered his red ribbon of the Bath, and they took him prisoner. . . .

Wednesday, 5th December.—Lady Holland is going to Bowood on Saturday, and Lord M. said he found her sketching out the road and settling where she would sleep. He said to her, "I suppose you will sleep at Hounslow the first night and the next at Maidenhead?" She didn't like that at all and said "Nonsense." She makes 3 days of it; Lord M. and Lady Cowper made us laugh by talking of all she takes with her when she travels,—bed, arm-chairs; she puts her coachman, a very clever Italian, Lord M. says, called Gigi, who she has had many years, on the box, who keeps telling the Postboys not to go so fast; Lord M. said she had excellent servants, who were like those in former times and put in a word in the conversation occasionally. . . .

Friday, 7th December.—Lord M. says Lord P. [Palmerston] has only one Private Secretary, which is little considering what an immense private correspondence he has; but the Précis Writer, James Howard,[1] Lord Suffolk's son, Lord M. says, helps Spencer[2]; the Précis Writer, he told me, has to make the Abstracts of all the Despatches and write it on the backs; said I believed Spencer was very clever; which Lord M. says he is; told Lord M. I heard he took to playing lately; "So I am afraid, from what I hear," replied Lord M., "that he plays at Crockford's; *bad* thing."

Friday, 14th December.—Lord M. said he had seen a boy killed by a waggon which passed over his neck and chest and left him quite dead on the road,

[1] James Kenneth Howard, afterwards Commissioner of Woods and Forests.

[2] Spencer Cowper, Lord Melbourne's nephew.

without any laceration, and "the face as placid as if he was asleep." Said I dreaded anything of the kind, and had never *seen* death. "I can't bear to see it," Lord M. said. I observed I thought it was right to do so; he replied not, but it was well to accustom yourself to blood; that Goethe wouldn't go and see his greatest friends when they were dead, as they say the expression changes so; said, I thought if you were with a person you loved, to the last, you wouldn't mind it.

Saturday, 15th December.—Lord M. also told me an anecdote of General Keppel [1] (Uncle to Albemarle); George III. rode very hard, and when he was a young man he rode from Windsor to London one day, very hard, General Keppel was with him, who was very old and fat, and he couldn't keep up with the King, and got so knocked up that he was obliged to stop at Turnham Green and go to bed. Talked of Brougham's letter,[2] which I had read on coming home, and which I told him made me angry; not the offensiveness towards me, but the villainy against himself; he said it was in fact an attack on Hereditary Monarchy. Lord M. then repeated with tears in his eyes, and most emphatically, what Lord Eldon once said: "The *King* of *England* is *always King; King* in the helplessness of infancy, *King* in the de-

[1] General William Keppel (1727–82), Commander-in-Chief in Ireland and Gentleman of the Horse to the King.

[2] This letter accused the Ministers of deserting their offices in Downing Street and Whitehall, and spending their time in the royal palace; of being indifferent to the public service so long as they retained the Sovereign's favour. Consequently, Brougham argued, the due preparation of despatches and State papers is neglected. The effect of the letter, apart from its bad taste, was neutralised by the well-known malice of the writer and his notorious grievance against Lord Melbourne. See Vol. I., p. 244.

crepitude of age." Talked of the Provost of Eton,[1] and Lord Melbourne said, "I always liked this man"; he said he had always very great spirits which Lord M. says is absolutely necessary for a School Master; and that he always made the lessons so very agreeable to the boys. He was one of the under Masters when Lord M. was at school; the Head Master, Dr. Heath, and the Provost, Dr. Davis; Lord M.'s Tutor, Dr. Langford. Told Lord M. that the Provost told Lady Mary he overheard the late King saying to somebody, *whom* he would make Provost when he died; and Lord M. and I observed how singular it was he should have outlived the King; Lord M. thinks Dr. Keate *ought* to be his successor[2]; but he thinks the Provost don't look like dying yet awhile.

Sunday, 16th December.—The King wasn't at all open with Lord M., he said, though very civil; "he liked me," said Lord M., "he liked me as much as any body could, under the circumstances; that was a very disagreeable affair in '34." "I don't believe he possibly could have carried it on without Taylor[3]; Taylor was a very fair man; *upon my honour* I don't see how it could have gone on; the

[1] Joseph Goodall, Provost. See *ante*, Vol. I., p. 119.

[2] Dr. Keate did not succeed Goodall when the vacancy occurred in 1840, and never was Provost of Eton. Kinglake's fine tribute to him in *Eothen* describes Keate as he was a few years before this period. He had retired from the headmastership in 1834. He was a Canon of Windsor and Rector of Hartley Westpall, where he died 1852.

[3] Sir Herbert Taylor (see Vol. I., p. 394), Private Secretary to William IV., died in March of the following year, 1839. He was at this time First and Principal A.D.C. to the Queen, and living on a pension of £1,000 per annum from the Civil List granted to him by George III. for his services as Private Secretary to Queen Charlotte. What happened to the correspondence of William IV., which was presumably in charge of Sir Herbert Taylor, has never been discovered.

King used to go and talk to Taylor, and Taylor softened matters."

Monday, 17th December.—Lord M. said Hoppner[1] had made 2 pictures of him when he left Eton, and was about 17; one is at Brocket, and the other, which was painted for Dr. Langford and sold after his death, was bought by his brother George and is at Melbourne; the Provost was asking after it, and Lord M. said, "I know where it was. I could get it." Lord M. said it was very like, and "I think a very handsome boy,"—which I'm sure it *is*, and he *was*; I regretted much there was no print of it. Lord Melbourne has a very pretty head of his sister by Lawrence, at Brocket. Talked of the picture of her and his other sister, by Hoppner, which is in George Street; of the one of him when a little boy of a year old, by Cosway, playing or rolling with 2 dogs; and talked of the one by Reynolds, of him (when 4 years old), his eldest brother, and his brother Frederick, which is also in George Street and a beautiful picture, he says; I've got a print of it. "Leslie was talking of it the other day," said Lord M., "he says it's like me now," which I think it is; Lord M. said, that Leslie told him, and it certainly is so, that all the pictures Reynolds painted of people when they were children, are like them now. Talked of Reynolds being the greatest painter England ever produced; of his great talent for painting children; of the fine picture he painted of George IV. and which George IV. gave to Lord M.'s father in '84; it is at Brocket. Talked of George III.'s dis-

[1] Hoppner, whom Lawrence in 1810 called "my most dangerous rival," died in that year. The portrait of Lord Melbourne painted for Dr. Langford is believed to be one which is now the property of the King and is in the Corridor at Windsor Castle.

like of Reynolds, and of his predilection for West.[1] Lord M. told me that he heard it had been remarked that I didn't bow to the Officer when the Escort changed; I thanked Lord Melbourne for telling me so, and I said I would take care and do so. One of the first things Lord Wellesley told him, he said, was that "Lord Plunket[2] had made a most excellent joke." Lord W. asked Lord Plunket what Personal Narrative meant, and Lord P. answered, that *Personal* was in general in opposition to *real*; Lord M. told this so funnily, imitating Lord Wellesley's way of speaking. . . .

Sunday, 23rd December.—Read in *Eugene Aram*[3] for some time while my hair was doing, and finished it; beautifully written and fearfully interesting as it is, I am glad I have finished it, for I never feel quite at ease or at home when I am reading a Novel,[4] and therefore was really glad to go on to Guizot's *Révolution de l'Angleterre.*

[1] Benjamin West (1738–1820) was Reynolds's successor as President of the Royal Academy. There are some charming portraits of George III.'s family by West, now hung in Kensington Palace, to which they were brought from Hampton Court in 1901. Gainsborough was a greater favourite with the King than even West. He, too, painted a series of portraits of the King's children. They are in Queen Mary's audience-room at Windsor, a room beautifully decorated in the Victorian manner by Crace for the Prince Consort. This series of portraits, very little known, is among the best work of Gainsborough.

[2] William Conyngham, first Lord Plunket, was Attorney-General for Ireland during Lord Wellesley's Lord-Lieutenancy. He was Irish Lord Chancellor under Lords Grey and Melbourne, but was induced to resign the post in favour of Campbell.

[3] Bulwer Lytton's well-known melodramatic novel.

[4] This feeling of doubt as to the propriety of reading novels lingered in the minds of young people for another twenty years. It was not until Dickens had become a household word, in the 'sixties, that the tone of fathers and mothers in regard to novel-reading changed, and their rigorous prohibition was relaxed.

Wednesday, 26th December. Lord M. asked if Seymour[1] was gone; I replied he was to be at Brussels last Sunday. . . .

Friday, 28th December.—The first actresses, he continued, began in Charles II.'s reign, and were Mrs. Ness, Mrs. Marshall, and Nell Gwynn, all women of bad character; there is an account of them in Pepys' Memoirs, he says. They were succeeded by others in William III.'s and Queen Anne's reigns, whose names he mentioned but which I've forgotten; and they again by Mrs. Yates, "who were beautiful actresses, and very clever women, some bad, some good." Mrs. Jordan died in '16, he said, at Paris, but acted till '13 or '14; Mrs. Jordan[2] was very good-natured, Lord M. said, and George IV. liked her. Asked Lord M. if he ever knew her to speak to; he said no, never; that one day when he went behind the scenes with Mr. Lewis,[3] the author, they met her just coming off the stage in man's clothes; she had been acting Hippolyta.

Sunday, 30th December.—Lord M. said he felt much better. Talked of Anderson's preaching;

[1] Sir Hamilton Seymour (1797–1880), who held various diplomatic posts, including that of British Ambassador at St. Petersburg when the Crimean War broke out, was at this time Envoy Extraordinary at the Belgian Court.

[2] Dorothy Jordan (1762–1816). Her "good nature" plunged this clever and attractive actress into many difficult situations. She was equally lavish of her affections and her resources. She bore the Duke of Clarence ten children. There are two portraits of her in the Garrick Club.

[3] Matthew Gregory Lewis was one of Byron's intimate associates in the days of his youthful dissipation. He wrote many plays and some poems, and a novel against which legal proceedings were taken on the score of immorality. This novel, *Ambrosio, or The Monk*, gave rise to the nickname of "Monk Lewis," by which he is generally known. He died of yellow fever on his way home from the West Indies in 1818.

and Lord M. said, "I'm afraid to go to church for fear of hearing something very extraordinary." I laughed and said he never went, and that he always managed to be very conveniently either unable to come down for a Sunday, or to be ill, which made him laugh very much. Talked of when my boxes arrived in London, and Lord M. said he always tried to prevent their bringing boxes to him when he was at dinner at Lady Holland's, for that she was always wanting to know what was in it, and would say, "What's that? Let me see what that is." That he always made as good a fight as he could, but that it was often very difficult to prevent her. Lord M. then said, "No woman ever wrote a really good book; no sterling book." Hannah More and Mme. de Sévigné were mentioned, and he admitted that those were both exceptions; H. More he thinks a very clever writer, and said she drew the distinction between the intellects of *man* and *woman* uncommonly well; "a woman has a much quicker intellect, much acuter, seizes a point much quicker, but somehow or other they don't keep it," he said, which made us laugh; Mme. de Staël he thinks the best female writer, and that she was very clever, "but she was a great humbug." Mrs. Somerville,[1] he agreed, was very clever, and said that Lord Harewood said of her, "She is good from the attic to the kitchen." When La Grange saw her at Paris, Lord M. continued, he said that he only knew one as clever as her, and that

[1] Mary Somerville (1780–1872), daughter of Vice-Admiral Sir William George Fairfax. A lady of masculine intellect and rare scientific attainments, but of so fair and fragile appearance that in girlhood she was called "The Rose of Yedburgh," her birthplace. She was the most remarkable woman of her generation, if judged by the standards usually applied to scientific thinkers of the sterner sex.

was a Miss Fairfax. "That's me!" she replied. Talked of Miss Edgeworth's writings; also *Oliver Twist*,[1] which I must say is excessively interesting; of Mr. Pitt's way of dressing, which Lord M. described as being a blue coat, a pair of nankin breeches very tight over the knees, blue silk stockings, and shoes with buckles; "that was the dress of a beau in those days." Lord M. said he had never had his hair dressed, or worn powder, but that he had great difficulty to persuade his father to let him crop his hair. Lord Normanby reminded Lord M. how very black his hair was when he first knew him; Lord M. said it was beginning to turn then; "I began to be seriously alarmed about it," said Lord M., "when I was at Paris; I had all the grey hairs pulled out; I had three women at it, and in a week's time there were just as many; and you have no idea how painful it is, when you go on doing it for an hour together." He said this so funnily. Before Lord M. told us this, he said that when Lord Morley cut off his tail, Canning said, "that he had heard so much of it, that he wanted to look at it."

Monday, 31st December.—Lord Melbourne and I looked at a Vol. of small Prints after Reynolds's pictures. He observed upon each, in his amusing manner, knowing who most of them were. Mrs. Abington,[2] who was a famous Comic Actress, and

[1] *Oliver Twist* began to appear in January 1837, and was not completed until March 1839, so that the Queen was now more than halfway through the novel.

[2] Frances Barton, afterwards Mrs. Abington, was of obscure origin, and her early life was full of hard and painful experience. She gradually acquired fame in all branches of comedy. Her costume and elocution were much admired. At forty, she originated the part of Lady Teazle, and to Walpole she appeared the "very person" for the part. When past sixty, she acted Beatrice, a feat only equalled

who he knew afterwards in society as an agreeable woman; there were several other very handsome women; Lady Charles Spencer,[1] who he said had been a most beautiful woman. The Duke of Rutland's mother,[2] a very great beauty, and who Lord M. knew very well, and he said, "She used to be very fond of me." Talked of Mrs. Fitzherbert,[3] her beauty; of Lady Holland, her not allowing any print to be taken after her pictures; her having had 3 children by her 1st husband, and 4 by her 2nd; there not being much love between her and Henry Fox; and Lord M. said it was hardly possible for people who knew her intimately *not* to quarrel with her. . . .

by Helen Faucit in after-years, who appeared at much the same age in the trying part of Rosalind.

[1] Mary, daughter of Vere, Lord Vere, and sister of Aubrey, Duke of St. Albans, married Lord Charles Spencer, second son of the third Duke of Marlborough.

[2] Mary Isabella, daughter of Charles, fourth Duke of Beaufort.

[3] Maria Fitzherbert (1756–1837), youngest daughter of Walter Smythe, a Roman Catholic country squire. She was twice married, and when for the second time a widow met George IV., then Prince of Wales. It is a curious coincidence that as a child she had been presented to Louis XV. She was married to the Prince of Wales on 21st December, 1785, but under the Royal Marriages Act the ceremony was illegal and the alliance invalid. By George III. and Queen Charlotte and by all the members of the Royal Family she was treated with high consideration and much kindness. It was not undeserved.

INTRODUCTORY NOTE TO CHAPTER XIII

DURING the first three months of 1839 the Queen's days were passed in the normal atmosphere of Lord Melbourne's congenial society. Trouble, however, there was, and owing to the incaution and want of prudent reserve shown by some of those about the Court, a false accusation made against one of the Duchess of Kent's Ladies caused strong private and public resentment, which very unfairly reacted against the young Queen. For a time her popularity suffered. There were deeper reasons for anxiety, due to the Government's lost hold upon Parliament. Lord Roden carried in the House of Lords a motion for a Select Committee to inquire into the state of Ireland. Lord Melbourne, inclined as he was to resign his office, felt that he could not do so in the face of the declaration made by him in 1836, that he would maintain his post so long as he possessed the confidence of the Crown and of the House of Commons. Of the former he was assured, but he resolved to test the latter, and the result was a resolution of confidence from the Commons by a majority of twenty-two votes. That his Ministry, however, was likely to be short-lived was now clear to every one, including the Queen.

Louis Philippe was at this time in considerable difficulty to find a serviceable Minister. It was thought in this country that Thiers was inevitable, although the King, unwilling to accept him, had appointed Soult to the post. It is curious to find the Queen, in view of her strong reluctance to face the probable advent of Sir Robert Peel into her Councils, writing to her Uncle Leopold that "it is a pity that Louis Philippe should show so much dislike to a man he *must* take." As a tribute to the teaching of Lord Melbourne, and to his unwearied efforts to convince the Queen that she should look kindly on the Tories, this phrase from one of her letters is illuminating.

It was at this time, when the young Queen's horizon was darkened by the Lady Flora Hastings "incident" and the prospect of losing the guidance of Lord Melbourne, that the King of the Belgians was eagerly pursuing his scheme for marrying her to her cousin Prince Albert of Saxe-Coburg. The youthful Prince was travelling in Italy under the wing of Baron Stockmar, who had been withdrawn from the English Court by Leopold for the express purpose of acting as Prince Albert's mentor and travelling companion. Although there were rival candidates, and although Lord Melbourne looked coldly upon Leopold's choice, the King was obdurate and firm. It was arranged that Prince Albert should visit the Queen in the month of October.

CHAPTER XIII

1839

Thursday, 1st January.—Got up at 9. Most fervently do I beseech Almighty God to preserve me and all those most dear to me safely through this year, and to grant that all may go on as it has hitherto done, and to make me daily more fit for my station. Sir George Grey [1] must, Lord Melbourne thinks, be eventually Judge Advocate-General [2]; "but John Russell wishes to have him in the House on the Address; and Lord Glenelg is very unwilling to part with him." It will be difficult to replace him, Lord M. says, but he is very desirous of being Judge Advocate. Talked of my getting on in *Oliver Twist*; of the descriptions of "squalid vice" in it; of the accounts of starvation in the Workhouses and Schools, Mr. Dickens gives in his books. Lord M. says, in many schools they give children the worst things to eat, and bad beer, to save expense; told him Mamma admonished me for reading light books.[3] Lord M. took 2 apples (Newtown pippins), put one on his plate, and wrapped up the 2nd in his napkin, and hid it in his lap; he did this in such a playful manner as made me and himself laugh very much. When the one was eaten, the 2nd was produced from its hiding place. He

[1] See *ante*, Vol. I., p. 300.

[2] He was appointed during this year, 1839.

[3] This view of novels was widely held at this time. See *ante*, p. 83.

then mentioned Mrs. Jordan as such a charming actress, though a little vulgar; "there was nothing like her," he said, her spirits and all. Talked of Mme. Vestris, her being half Italian; Garrick's mother being Italian,[1] which Lord M. told us and which I never knew. "It's very rare to see a good actress," said Lord M., "it's very rare to see a good anything, that's the fact." Lady Ashley said, she should like so much to act, and Lady Fanny too, though neither has ever acted. "Would like to smell the lamps," Lord M. said to Lady Fanny; talked of its being easier to sing and act; Lord M. said, it took away from the sameness; "Music takes away the sameness of a tragedy,—that is to those who *like* it"; these last words Lord M. pronounced in a very marked and sly manner, and made us all laugh. Talked of the Italians' good acting; Grisi's; of Private Theatricals; Lord M. was a great actor himself, but hasn't acted for *many* years.

Wednesday, 2nd January.—Lord M. then spoke to me about some new Puisne Judge who would be appointed, but which I must ask him once more about; I then showed him a letter I had got the day before from Sir J. Hobhouse about another Judgeship. Lord Melbourne was very cheerful and seemed in good spirits when out riding; I observed that he had a green coat on, since he was here, which I hadn't observed him wear before; he smiled and said, "Is it a bad colour?" I assured him quite the contrary, but that it was new for him to wear it, as also an olive-green velvet waistcoat.

[1] Lord Melbourne probably meant Garrick's grandmother, and not his mother. David de la Garrique, the actor's Huguenot grandfather, may have married an Italian. Garrick's mother was Arabella Clough, the daughter of a vicar-choral of Lichfield Cathedral.

Thursday, 3rd January.—He had seen his sister. "She says," he continued, "that that picture[1] which the Maids of Honour wear, is wrong." That it was throwing it away upon them and ought to have been given only to the Ladies in Waiting; I said it was a very small picture, and that the Ladies had a picture in a bracelet; he continued that it's considered the very highest distinction the Emperor and Empress of Russia can give, to wear their Portrait on the shoulder with a red ribbon; "She says Mme. de Lieven would die of it if she saw it." Talked of George IV.'s giving his picture to so few; Lady Conyngham, Lady Cowper, and Lady Aboyne[2] being the only 3 English Ladies who had it. Talked of my feeling low and ill, which as I had felt it both times I was here, at different seasons, was a proof, I thought, that the place [Windsor] disagreed, which he wouldn't allow. He said very funnily, "You have got some fixed fancies; Your Majesty has settled in your mind certain things." Lord M. asked if I had got on far with *Oliver Twist*; I said into the 2nd volume, and liked it so much and wished he would read it, which he said he would one day; talked of it, and of the story; of the *Beggars' Opera* by Gay,[3] which Lord M. has seen very often,

[1] The "picture" was a miniature portrait of the Queen. The Queen *always* wore up to the time of her death a *small miniature* of herself surrounded by diamonds on a bow of crimson ribbon. The Ladies in Waiting wore a bracelet with the Queen's miniature up to the time the 2nd Class of the "Victoria and Albert" Order was instituted, when the Queen gave the 2nd Class to the Ladies in Waiting. The Women of the Bedchamber wore the Queen's monogram in pearls and diamonds on a white watered silk bow.

[2] Lord Aboyne, afterwards tenth Marquess of Huntly. Lady Aboyne had been Lady Elizabeth Conyngham, sister of the Lord Chamberlain.

[3] See Vol. I., p. 330.

and which is coarse; but he says they have refined it down so much and scratched out so much as the times got more polished, that there was hardly anything good left. Gay had some talent, Lord M. said; he was at Court about the Duke of Cumberland, and was offered, Lord M. said, the situation of gentleman Usher, which however he didn't think good enough, and left the court; upon which he was taken up by the Duchess of Queensberry,[1] a great beauty and leading person of the day, but who was always in opposition to the Court; she was a Hyde, Lord M. said, daughter to Lord Rochester and grand-daughter to Clarendon; talked of Gay's fables which Lord M. knew by heart when he was 4 years old; of children learning fables; their not understanding them "as they are generally deep." He thinks the French fables the best. He mentioned Lafontaine's, "though he's a writer not to be mentioned generally; he's not a correct writer"; his *tales* are not to be mentioned, but his fables are excellent; Lord M. thinks him, Molière, and another, the best French writers; I observed Molière was not very proper; Lord M. said pretty well, that there was a great difference in what was so "from the coarseness of the times, and what is avowedly so," which is very true. Talked of Barante's[2] *History of the House of Bur-*

[1] This lady died of a surfeit of cherries in 1777. Her correspondence with Swift and Gay, her influence over the elder Pitt, her intimacy with Pope and Prior, her eccentricity in dress, and her youthful appearance in old age made her famous. Walpole at Twickenham used to thank God that "the Thames is between me and the Duchess of Queensberry."

[2] Amable Guillaume Prosper de Barante, Baron de Bongière, born in 1782, held important civil posts in France under the Empire and after the Restoration. He was also Ambassador at St. Peters-

gundy, which Lord M. says is so excessively interesting, though rather a long book; "more like a novel"; that there were many things in History which he thinks very extraordinary—hardly credible; all that about the murder of the Duke of Orleans by the Duke of Burgundy (in the book) and of the Duke of Burgundy by the Dauphin was very curious; it all arose from an offence given; the Duke of Orleans was a violent man, Lord M. continued, and he showed the Duke of Burgundy into a room full of pictures, "and he said to the Duke, 'All these ladies have been my mistresses,'—and the first was the Duchess of Burgundy." That offence was the cause of the Duke's murder; there's the whole account of Joan of Arc in it, "and beautifully told," Lord M. said; "I suppose it was enthusiasm at first, but she certainly *became* an excellent commander." Talked of the English behaving so cruelly to her; Lord M. said he really wasn't quite surprised, considering the times, and how extraordinary it was.—Lord Alfred brought in his dog; she is a fine large black dog, half Newfoundland, half retriever, called *Diver*, but also sometimes *Mrs. Bumps*; she's a dear affectionate gentle creature and took a great liking to me and lay near me; Lord M. said, "Dogs get so familiar that they behave as well as any man,—*better* than some."

Friday, 4th January.—He then gave me a Warrant to sign, saying, "I thought it best to bring this Warrant myself to you; somebody ought to bring it to you; the Lord Steward ought by rights." It is a Warrant for a sum of money given to a

burg. His *Histoire des Ducs de Bourgogne de la Maison de Valois*, published in 1824, led to his admission to the French Academy.

number of servants' Widows, from (I think) the Lord Steward's Department, and which Murray[1] wanted to bring to me himself, and about which I had talked to Lord M. when he came out from dinner the day before; Lord M. said it was a large sum, and that it rather encouraged servants to marry and not to provide for their wives. Lord M. gave me a copy of it to keep. He then gave me a note from William C. to read; it was to say that he had set Stanley at the newspapers, to prevent their making so much noise about the Corn Laws; it's *The Times*, I think, Lord M. mentioned. He then said, "Here's a very long and a very good letter from Lord Howick about Canada; and what is to be done; I'll leave it with you, and perhaps you'll send it me." No one ever dined with George III. except perhaps on very great occasions the Archbishop of Canterbury and the Lord Chamberlain; George I. used to dine at Richmond with Sir Robert Walpole, Lord M. said, and was very fond of joviality; George III. introduced that very strict etiquette; "It suited him," said Lord M.; "he dined with great rapidity, was very temperate and hardly ate anything—it would not have suited him" (to have had company) "and he would not very probably have made it very agreeable to others." . . .

Tuesday, 8th January.—Lord M. again took two apples, but only ate one, and put the other before him; I asked him if he meant to eat it; he thought not, and said, "But I like to have the *power* of doing so." I observed hadn't he just as well the power

[1] Charles Augustus Murray (1806–95), diplomatist and author. Son of the second Earl of Dunmore. At this time he was Extra Groom-in-Waiting and Master of the Household (1838–44). He was afterwards a K.C.B., and Minister successively to Persia, Denmark, and Spain.

of doing so, when the apples were in the dish on the table? He laughed and said, "Not the *full* power."

Wednesday, 9th January.—Talked of Lady Stanhope not having written very often. "Why, pretty well," said Lord M., "considering that I've not written to her once; not once." He said he didn't answer all the letters he got, which I didn't wonder at; "But the Duke of Wellington would," he replied; "he would answer all and if he didn't answer them all he would at least acknowledge them and that's the right way." Talked of Sedan Chairs and being carried in one, which Lord M. said "is a very pleasant sensation." "My mother used always to have her chair, and it was the usual mode of conveyance; the Town is grown too large for it now." Talked of it for some time, and Lord M. said there used to be 300 Chairmen in London, all Irishmen, very strong and very skilful. "That man opposite," said Lord M. looking at Pocock, "has very often walked before my mother's chair; he knows it all perfectly." He don't like Masquerades much, he said, "It's a mixture of profligacy and malignity." I had the beautiful picture of the dogs brought in; and then I sent for Dashy who Lord M. accused of having crooked legs, which I wouldn't allow; we put him on the table, and he was very much petted and patted and admired by Lord M., who was so funny about him; we gave him tea, and Lord M. said, "I wonder if lapping is a pleasant sensation," for that it was a thing we never had felt.

Talked of the picture of him and his brothers (now Lady Cowper's) not having been his father's; and I said Lady Cowper told me his father was displeased with part of his (Lord M.'s) dress; Lord M. said, "I believe my father didn't like to pay for the picture." It cost Lord Cowper, Lady C. told me, £600, and Lord M. said, the original price was £300; talked of the print of it, and Lord M. said the picture was very bright and light. That Leslie said when Queen Elizabeth said she wished to be painted without any shade in her face, that she meant "in an open garden-light," which was too much for the artists of that time, and that it was no ignorance whatever. Talked of the fine picture Reynolds did of his (Ld. M.'s) mother, with his eldest brother, of which I said no print was now to be had. He said the picture was a very fine one, done soon after she was married; like a Titian. Lady Cowper finds her house (which Lord Cowper left her) an expense, and £3,000 a year, though considered a good deal, Lord M. said is hardly enough. It's a rather large house; larger than his; his is not a large house[1]; "It wouldn't hold any one else besides me," he said; "No one else?" I said; and he replied laughing, "No one else; not by any means"; which made us both laugh very much. He pays £1,000 a year for it; "It's all my idleness not to look out for another"; he has had it since '30; "Mrs. Lamb took it for me." He had lived in Dover House,[2] where his father died, ever since

[1] Lord Melbourne's house during his Premiership was 39, South Street, Mayfair.

[2] Lord Melbourne's father purchased from the Fox family in 1770 the fine house in Piccadilly which stood on the site of what is now the Albany. Here the future Prime Minister was born in 1779. About the year 1790 the Duke of York, who occupied the house situated between the Horse Guards and the Treasury, expressed a strong wish to exchange houses with Lord Melbourne, and the transfer was carried out, including the names, York House in Whitehall becoming Melbourne house. It has been known since 1830 as Dover House, from George Agar Ellis Lord Dover, who purchased it in 1830, and died there in 1833. It is now the office of the Secretary for Scotland.

'92; having more servants then; coals cost him £400 a year then, and £70 now. His father built a magnificent house called Albany (which is now Chambers) and exchanged it for Dover then Melbourne House, with the Duke of York, on the Duke's marriage. Lord M. said, he can see traces of Albany in all George IV.'s Palaces; talked of George IV.'s excessive high spirits and good humour when he was young,—which last he lost latterly. Lord M. remembers meeting him on the stairs in that house, and "We had just done our dinner, and the Prince said, 'Have you done your dinner?' 'Yes, we have'; 'Why, you ought to have only been eating your soup in that time.'" His spirits were beyond everything, "fit to leap out of his skin a'most."

Sunday, 13th January.—I looked with Lord Melbourne at 2 vols. of Engravings (small) after Reynolds' pictures; and he knew who almost *all* of them were. I shall only name a very few of those he observed upon. *Mrs. Masters,*—"She was supposed to be the handsomest woman that ever lived," he said, "I knew her particularly well; she died about 20 year ago," was 65 years old. Sir Joshua died in '93, Lord M. thinks.[1] Reynolds was perpetually painting those women; Kitty Fisher, Nelly O'Brien. There was a pretty picture of a Miss Collier; a *Mrs. Mary Robinson,*[2]—"She was the

[1] In 1792.

[2] The famous "Perdita," whose intimacy with George, Prince of Wales, afterwards George IV., was notorious. She is never likely to be forgotten so long as Gainsborough's lovely portrait of her hangs in Hertford House. She was not only a beautiful and talented actress, but a writer of passable prose and verse. Charles Fox found her society as well as her person to his taste, and Garrick liked her as an actress and as a woman. After many vicissitudes she died, aged 40, at Englefield Green, and was buried in the churchyard at Old Windsor. Gains-

1st about whom there was any noise." A *Miss Emily*, a famous picture, as Thais, and a great beauty. Lady C. Spencer,[1] whom Lord M. only saw (did not know) when she was old, and *then* a great *dévote*, walking with her spaniels. There was the print after his mother's picture; and of him and his 2 brothers; and he said, looking at it, "That's me." Then there was one of a Mrs. Stewart,[2] who he said was very much engaged in the Douglas Quarrel Trial, which I never heard of before, but which he told me all about. The last Duke of Douglas had no children but an only sister; and if she had children the property was all entailed on them; if not, it went to the Duke of Hamilton. She married a Mr. Stewart; the Court decided in favour of her children; but Lord M. said people are almost certain and it is generally believed, that she never had any children. "It is supposed," he said, "that she purchased two children in Paris and had a feigned accouchement." The Courts of Scotland decided against her, and against the legitimacy; but it was brought up to the House of Lords, where it was decided in favour of her; and Lord M. said, Lord Mansfield is supposed to have behaved rather unfairly about it. Talked of Sir H. Taylor's being very ill; and Lord M. said kindly, "Poor fellow! I had always a feeling that it never would do for Taylor to have no-

borough's sketch for her famous portrait, a work even more beautiful than the finished picture, hangs in the Queen's private sitting-room at Windsor Castle.

[1] See *ante*, p. 87.

[2] Lady Jane Douglas, sister of the last Duke of Douglas, was born on 17th March, 1698. On 4th August, 1746, she married, as his second wife, Colonel John Stewart. When fifty years and four months old she gave birth to twin sons. The younger lived to be M.P. for Forfar, and was created Lord Douglas of Douglas.

thing to do." Talked of his having a number of the papers, which Lord M. hopes he'll be careful about.[1]

Monday, 14th January.—Lord Melbourne told me in going in, that Lord Holland had sent him a note from Lord Granville, in which he said that the French Ministry could not stand, he thought; that they had lost many of their supporters; Lord Holland is very sorry for it. "I'm sorry," said Lord M., "for I'm afraid we shall have Thiers." Lord Palmerston and Lord Granville both dislike Molé[2]; Lord M. says Thiers did everything we wanted, but then he did it all without telling the King; and Lord M. said, "One never knows what he will do next."

Asked Lord M. if he thought Lady Holland felt her being unable to come to court[3]; he shook his head and said, "Perpetually; oh! she feels it very much." George IV. knew her, he said, but disliked her very much latterly; and she one day was very rude to him (George IV.) when he came into her box at the Play; and he was perpetually recurring to that; "He said to my brother, 'Don't you remember, Frederick, when we went into the box that night, how she treated me?'" George IV. was excessively fond of Lord Holland,

[1] This allusion is to King William's correspondence. He was so "careful" of the papers that they have disappeared.

[2] Count Molé, who had been President of the Council since 1836, dissolved the Chamber of Deputies in 1838, and as the ensuing general election gave him an indecisive majority, M. Thiers dexterously seized the opportunity of forming a junction with Guizot and opening the way to power for himself. His characteristic obstinacy and arrogance, however, led to a dispute about appointments to offices, and, a popular disturbance ensuing, Marshal Soult was appointed President of the Council and Minister of Foreign Affairs in May 1839.

[3] She was the divorced wife of Sir Godfrey Webster. See *ante*, p. 70, and Vol. I., p. 101.

Lord M. said; and Lady Holland rather expected he would have received her, as he used when Prince Regent to go there so often; said, I thought perhaps she mightn't feel the exclusion; Lord M. said, "Oh! she feels it deeply; there's nobody who doesn't feel it; I have never known anybody who didn't feel it bitterly; many don't wish to go, but they don't like the exclusion." Lord Melbourne told me after dinner before we sat down that he had seen Duncannon, who had seen Durham; Durham sent for Duncannon, Lord M. said, and Duncannon found him very mild, and saying it was a mistaken idea that he meant to take a line in opposition to the Government, that he never meant to do so, and only meant to defend himself; he is very much annoyed, Lord M. says, Duncannon told him, at my not having answered the letter Lady Durham wrote from Portsmouth. He promised Duncannon to see Howick.

Talked of the French Ministry, and *who* it was likely might replace them, which Lord M. can't at all tell; he don't think the King will name Broglie; probably Guizot.

Talked of Clocks, Lord Melbourne's never having one in his room; "I always ask the servant what o'clock it is; and then he tells me what he likes," said Lord M. Talked of large clocks which strike the quarters, which Lord M. likes; he thinks the Eton clock the best in the World. Asked Lord M. *when* George IV. gave his father that fine picture[1]; in the year '84 or 5, he said; talked of Lord M.'s father having been one of the first of George IV.'s Lords, when his Household was first formed in '83. Of his having been in waiting when the Prince of

[1] Portrait of George IV. by Sir J. Reynolds.

H. M. Louis Philippe.
King of the French.
from a portrait by F. Winterhalter.

Wales married,—which he said George IV. did in desperation; Lord M. does not think George IV. could have kept Queen Caroline in bounds, even if he had treated her well; they were not calculated to go on together for a moment, he said. . . .

Wednesday, 16th January.—Lord M. had seen all Chantrey's works in his studio; and he said, "I saw Mrs. Jordan's statue"; the late King, Lord M. told me (Chantrey told him) sent for Chantrey about 4 or 5 days after he came to the Throne, and desired him to make this statue, which he had *always* intended to have done when he had the means for it; the King's Executors tell Chantrey it belongs to Munster, but Lord M. said Munster doesn't know what to do with it; it's too large for a house; it's with 2 of the children, and done after the picture Beechey did of her when she was quite young and thin, and not like what Lord M. remembers her. Then Lord M. said, they didn't know what to write under it, so they called it, "Sacred to the memory of an affectionate Mother, Dorah Bland." But I asked Lord M., why shouldn't it be Dorah Jordan? Bland was her maiden name; Lord M. said he had no idea who Mr. Jordan was,[1] or if she was married to him. Asked Lord M. if he liked pictures or busts best; pictures, he said. That Chantrey said their difficulty was the absence of colour, and that they were obliged to produce by shadow what painters do by colours. Lord M. asked him how it was that Sculptors generally took fewer sittings than Painters; "They *ought* to have more," he said; "but Sculptors are generally cleverer fellows than Painters." Talked again of Mrs. Jordan. She died at St. Cloud in '16.

[1] Mr. Jordan was a myth. She was never married.

Her brother, called Bland, was not a good actor, but was very like her, and used to act with her in the *Twelfth Night.* "She was beautifully formed," Lord M. said, "her legs and feet were beautifully formed, as this statue is"; and she used to be fond of acting in men's clothes; she used to act Hippolyta in *She Would and She Would Not*, and Rosalind in *As You Like It*; "a lovely play," said Lord M., "the prettiest play in the world; and her acting in that was quite beautiful." "She had a beautiful enunciation," he added. She was an Irish girl.

Sunday, 20th January.—After dinner Lord Melbourne came up to me and said, "I've seen Sir James Clark this morning; he's very anxious about this vaccination." Lord M. then talked for some time to me about this, urging me to have it done; I resisted. "You'll have it done," he said; "if it doesn't take, why then you're safe; and if it does, it can do no harm." I said I did not mind the thing,—but thought it quite useless [1]; he owned there was a degree of fuss; "You think it's childish," he continued; "now that's nonsense; I shall see Halford [2] to-morrow morning; shall I ask *him*?" I said he might. Lord M. then looked at a new Translation of *The Arabian Nights*, illustrated; he said it was quite another book to the one he was accustomed to read; "This is an amusing book too," he said; and he read out some accounts of the Mahommedan religion given in the Notes, which

[1] Although Jenner's discovery was about sixty years old, vaccination was by no means universal in 1839, and revaccination rare. It was not made compulsory in Great Britain until 1853.

[2] Sir Henry Halford (originally Vaughan), Bart., Physician to George III. and IV., William IV., and Queen Victoria.

put him into fits of laughter. He said *The Arabian Nights* were a very extraordinary production, and were first known in England a hundred years ago; Lord M. talked of Wilkinson's[1] book about the Egyptians, which he says is so very curious, and he said, how very curious it was that the Egyptians drew everything. Talked of my disliking Ancient History and Rollin,[2] which Lord M. said he never did, but most people did; of reading without attention; and Lord M. said one never learned well unless one was interested; "You can't get on," he said, "if you can't enlist the pupil on your side"; and he said that was why some boys got on very well at school and others not at all. Said to Lord M. I should resist about this Vaccination; "Oh! no, you'll do it," he said kindly; I said No, and that no one could force me to it; he agreed in that, but strongly urged it and said earnestly, "*Do.*" "Think if you were to have it; think of the responsibility, of the scrape you'd get them into; of the scrape you'd get us all into."

Monday, 21st January.—Talked of poor Princess Charlotte's fondness for Uncle, and his for her; of his constantly recurring to those times. "He had acquired great influence with her," said Lord M., "was very quiet and patient, and that's the only way in which a man can have any power with a woman."

Tuesday, 22nd January.—Talked to Lord M. again about what he had told me the other day, viz. that people said I showed no particular liking to any

[1] John Gardner Wilkinson, an explorer and Egyptologist. He was knighted in 1839.

[2] It is not surprising that the Queen disliked Rollin, if only because her copy of the book was in folio!

of the Ladies, and I asked if it included *all* my Ladies and all the Men (of the Court) also; he said it did, and that it "is strange for so young a person not to show any preference"; I said I dared not, though I was very fond of some, but that I never saw a great deal of them, and never talked of anything that interested me much, to them. Lady Portman, Lady Barham,[1] and Lady Normanby[1] I was very fond of, I said; Lady Tavistock[2] I also liked, I said, as she was very discreet.

Talked of my going to the Play in State next week, and of my having no lady hardly to go with me, and that I must write and ask Lady Tavistock to come up for it, which he said would be the best thing to do. Talked of Sheridan Knowles saying I had promised through Lord John that I would have one of his Plays acted when I went in State; talked of that, and Lord M. said, "All Sheridan Knowles's Plays are very proper." Said I thought *The Love Chase* wasn't quite the thing for me to see; "Perhaps that's the most questionable." I asked if he had seen it; he said, "No, but I think I read it"; but *The Hunchback* and *The Wife* he mentioned as the prettiest modern Plays that could be; said, they would never let me see *The Hunchback*, though I begged so to see it; which he was quite surprised at; for he said it's a most moral Play. Talked of my seeing *The Tempest*, which I asked his advice about; he advised me to do so. . . .

Thursday, 24th January.—Lord M. said there had been rather an important Cabinet yesterday, about the Corn Laws, which lasted from 3 till 6.

[1] See *ante*, Vol. I., p. 175.

[2] Anne Maria, daughter of third Earl of Harrington. See Vol. I., p. 202.

"There was a good deal of difference of opinion," he said, "I hope it'll go no farther." Thomson and Howick, he said, were very anxious, and urged it very strongly, that the Government should take advantage of the present clamour about the Corn Laws "and change the present fluctuating duty upon corn to a fixed duty of 10*s*." Lord M. said that the greater part of the Cabinet were for the change, but think it would be extremely unsafe for the Government to change at this moment, the course the Government has hitherto pursued; it was an Open Question, and everybody voted as they liked, he said; "But they" (Thomson and Howick) "urged it very strongly; it was a very eager debate, and they may urge it farther." Interests and opinions in the country, he says, are very much divided upon it; some think the present system, which almost entirely excludes the Importation of Foreign Corn, is very injurious to the Country; others just the contrary. At 8 we dined. Besides we 13, Lord Conyngham dined here. We came in about 20 minutes before the Lions came on. Van Amburgh[1] surpassed even himself, and was miraculous; he stayed a much longer time than usual in the 1st cage, and all the animals were much more lively than usual; in the 2nd cage, as usual, the little lamb was brought in, while he was reclining on the Lion's body and head, and put before the Lion's nose, which he as usual bore with indifference; when one of the Leopards, the smallest of all the animals and a sneaking little thing, came, seized the lamb and ran off with it; all the others, except the lion, and all those in the other cage making a rush to help in the slaughter; it was an awful moment,

[1] A celebrated lion-tamer of the day.

and we thought all was over, when Van Amburgh rushed to the Leopard, tore the lamb unhurt from the Leopard, which he beat severely,—took the lamb in his arms,—only looked at all the others, and not one moved, though in the act of devouring the lamb. It was beautiful and wonderful; and he was immensely applauded; he held the lamb for a few minutes in his arms, and then sent it out of the cage, but remained himself some little time in the cage, making these animals obey as usual. After the Pantomime was over, we waited in a little ante-room till everybody was gone, and the house quite cleared, and then we all went down on the stage, which was walled in by Scenery, and the cages with the animals again brought on; there they were, and most beautiful beasts they are, so sleek, so well-conditioned—and so *wild*—that really Van Amburgh's power seems little short of a miracle. They had *not* been fed *since* early the *preceding day*, and consequently were wilder than usual; Van Amburgh, who was in plain clothes, is a tall but not very powerful-looking man; young, very modest, quiet and unassuming; with a mild expression, a receding forehead and very peculiar eyes, which don't exactly squint but have a cast in them. I asked him if that had ever happened before with the lamb; he replied, "Sometimes it does; it did the first time I took one in," but the lamb was unhurt; they then fed them, and they roared and fought with one another terrifically; but it was very fine. I didn't allow Van Amburgh to go into the cages, but he went up to them and stroked them and they obeyed him wonderfully; he told Lord Conyngham that they were all full grown but two, when he first had them; the large lion in the furthest cage is the fiercest, he says; and the weight of the leopard which he carries on his head and shoulders and makes it perform every sort of beautiful trick, is 14 stone. He scarcely ever uses an iron bar to them, but only a stick made of Rhinoceros hide, which he showed us. . . .

Sunday, 27th January.—Talked of Lady Barham's boy [1] disliking learning, which led us to talk of children learning; *his* (Ld. M.'s) having feigned to be ill so often when a child; a Mr. Cuppage taught him to write before he went to his Private Tutor's; his having hated learning Latin so, and wishing, he said, at the time, he could work in the fields instead. "I remember thinking it most fervently," he said, "and I used to think how I wish I was one of those happy fellows in the fields, instead of learning this consumed Latin!" . . .

Tuesday, 29th January.— . . . Asked Lord M. if they had had no Cabinet about the Ballot; he replied that they had not. "This (the Corn Laws) has rather superseded the Ballot." Asked him if this Question was one of more difficulty than the Ballot; "No, but people are apt to forget it" when taken up with a new subject. He thinks there will be a good deal at first when Parliament meets; I observed they had got through several long questions last year, and Lord M. said, "Oh! yes; I think the danger doesn't come so much from our adversaries as from ourselves."

Wednesday, 30th January.—Lord M. said he was well, but I thought him looking pale and black under the eyes. He had not seen Lord John this morning. Asked why should Lord John resign (as

[1] Roden Berkeley Wriothesley Noel, afterwards Groom of the Privy Chamber, 1867–71.

Lord M. wrote me last night he meant to do) if Lord Howick did ? Lord M. said, he supposed Lord John thought it would affect him, and that probably since his recent loss he hadn't the same spirits. Talked of Lord Howick's saying he was always in a minority, which he has often been, Lord M. says ; Lord M. said in this West Indian business,[1] which is one of difficulty, he started a new Proposition ; the Legislative Assembly of Jamaica are pursuing the same course as the Legislative Assembly in Canada did, and refusing to obey and to carry into execution what they are ordered to do. " The question is, what is to be done ? " said Lord M. ; it is therefore intended, he continued, to empower the Government and Council to do it ; well, Lord Howick wishes, Lord M. said, that this should be done for *all* the islands, and a Commission sent out, of 5 Commissioners, to legislate for all the Islands ; now Jamaica is the only island that has positively acted contumaciously, though the others have done their duty inadequately. Asked Lord M. if Lord John agreed with Lord Howick upon this ; Lord M. said, he did not ; why therefore should he resign, I observed. Lord M. said because Lord John thought that Lord Howick's resignation would be said to be on account of his having more popular feelings than Lord John, which would weaken Lord John's influence ; I asked Lord M. if *he* thought so ; " No,

[1] Reference has already been made to the apprenticeship question in Jamaica, *ante*, Vol. I., p. 294. The planters' severity in punishment had also placed a strain on the accommodation in the prisons, and an Imperial Act for their regulation was passed. The Jamaica Assembly was opposed to this, and a second house, elected after a dissolution by the Governor, Sir Lionel Smith, took the same view. This state of things induced the Melbourne Government to introduce a Bill to suspend for a time the constitution of Jamaica.

I don't see the least reason why he should do so," said Lord M.; at the same time, it would be inconvenient and embarrassing if Lord Howick was to resign, as it would be difficult to fill up his place; asked Lord M. if he always gave trouble; Lord M. said he always did, even when out of the Cabinet, during Lord Grey's administration, under Lord Ripon. Lord M. said, "He is a very clever man, but a very obstinate man, and excessively eager about what he takes up, and very angry when every body don't immediately adopt his views." Lord M.'s eyes filled with tears in speaking of England's glories; he *loves* his country *truly*. "George III. said," Lord M. continued, "'I've been both the most unpopular and the most popular of monarchs; the first I owe to my Ministers; the last I owe to my son'; rather a bitter *mot*, if he said it." Talked of Lord M.'s house in Downing Street, which is a "large rambling house, badly furnished."[1] He made a contract with a man in '34, just before Lord M. was out, for furnishing it for 6 and 20,000£, and paid £300 to be off. They have the Cabinets at his house in Downing Street instead of at the Foreign Office, now.[2]

Thursday, 31*st January*.—Talked of my going to the Play in State again, and Lord M. said, "If you

[1] The official house of the Prime Minister. It was left by Sir Robert Walpole to his successors. It has not, however, always been used by the Prime Minister. Lord Salisbury, for instance, did not occupy it, but gave it to Mr. Balfour, who at that time was First Lord of the Treasury and Leader of the House of Commons.

[2] The practice has varied under different Prime Ministers. At the present time (1912) the Cabinet Councils are again held in the old Cabinet room in Downing Street, in spite of the size of the Cabinet. The room has double doors, for the purpose of greater secrecy, and a "messenger," by immemorial custom, is stationed at the door.

like it, it's a popular thing." Talked of the standing for the Attendants being rather a hard thing; and Lord M. said, he believed George III. and Queen Charlotte introduced that,—and particularly George III. Talked of George III. using to go once a week to the Play in State; George IV. used to go often before he became King, and understood acting well, Lord M. said. Lord M. said there had been hardly any Court till George III.'s time, since Queen Caroline (George II.'s wife),[1] and she was only Queen for 10 years; "She had a literary society," Lord M. continued; "Dr. Clark, and Leibnitz." Lord M. admires her; talked of Frederick Prince of Wales. Said I thought he was stupid, which Lord M. doesn't think, but said, "He wrote ridiculous verses; he was always writing love verses." I forgot to say that before dinner I received a letter from Lord Melbourne, sending 3 letters from Lord Howick; the 1st to Lord John saying he could not alter his mind, and enclosing a letter to Lord Melbourne tendering his resignation; and the last (to Lord John), having heard Lord John would resign if he did, which shook him a good deal in his decision. He had not been at the Cabinet, Lord M. said, and Lord M. was going to see him at 12 next morning.

Friday, 1st February.—He had seen Lord Howick, whom he found calm and reasonable enough; he had written Lord Melbourne a letter before he came to see him, which Lord M. had sent to Lord John. Lord M. said Lord Howick said, that he did not like to take the entire responsibility upon himself of breaking up the Government, and that he would remain if he was sure that the Government of the

[1] That is, between 1737 (when Queen Caroline died) and 1760, when George III. succeeded to the throne.

Colonies would be put on a sure footing, in fact, Lord M. said, meaning the removal of Lord Glenelg. Lord M. said, "Lord Glenelg certainly does it very indolently and loosely, and is so slow about bringing anything forward." I observed how inconvenient it was, this happening just now, in which Lord M. agreed, and Lord M. said, "I said to him (Howick), You should have told me this a month or two ago." But he replied, he was obliged to wait for a fit moment for doing so, which hadn't before appeared. I asked again why should Lord John resign; Lord M. said, what he had said before, that Lord John fears that if Howick resigns, it would be said it was because he had more popular notions than Lord John, which Lord J. thinks would lessen his influence, and he cannot stand unpopularity,—still less now that his spirits are a good deal broken.[1] Talked of Glenelg's resignation, and his (G.'s) disliking to resign. Lord M. said, the only way seemed to be, to *make* Lord Glenelg resign, which I said was a disagreeable thing to do, in which he agreed, but which he said had been done in the case of Lord Ripon; when Mr. Stanley wouldn't remain in Ireland and would only be a Secretary of State, Lord M. said, Lord Ripon was made to resign.[2] Lord M. said, it was a disagreeable thing to do, "but it's the only alternative of their resigning." Said I thought it not right in Lord Howick bringing this

[1] By the death of his first wife. See *ante*, p. 67.

[2] This was the more remarkable because Lord Ripon (1782–1859) had formerly (under the name of Lord Goderich) been Prime Minister. He became a member of the Whig Cabinet in 1830 as Colonial Secretary, and under pressure in 1833 gave up that office and became Privy Seal. At this time Lord Ripon was out of office, but he became President of the Board of Trade in Sir Robert Peel's second Administration formed two years later.

on, just now, and Lord M. said, "No, it's not right, it's very awkward"; and I observed it wasn't right in Lord John minding unpopularity. "He shouldn't mind it," said Lord M. "*I* think he's quite mistaken." Lord M. would see Lord John almost directly; there was to be a Cabinet about the Speech, and Lord M. had got Lord Howick to come, as his absence was observed; asked if Lord Howick did his business well. "Very well," replied Lord M.; "but too actively, quite the opposite extreme to Glenelg." Said I regretted so *very* much Lord M.'s having all this trouble; "Yes, it's a great difficulty," he replied, "and what's worse I don't see my way through it."

Got at dinner a letter from Lord Melbourne, in which he gives me an account of an arrangement to get over our present serious difficulties. This is Lord Melbourne's communication: "Lord Melbourne presents his humble duty to Your Majesty, and begs to acquaint Your Majesty that he has seen Lord John Russell. Lord John is of opinion that the only mode of keeping the Government together is to take immediate measures for replacing Lord Glenelg at the Colonial Office. He proposes that Lord Normanby should be sent for from Ireland and receive the Colonial Seals, and that Lord Glenelg should have the Privy Seal with a retiring pension. Lord Melbourne must speak to Lord Lansdowne, Lord Palmerston, and others, before he can decidedly submit such an arrangement to Your Majesty, but Lord Melbourne fears that there is no other mode of preventing the dissolution of the Administration."

Saturday, 2nd February.—Lord M. then said, "Now, Ma'am, I wrote to John Russell this morning, very strongly, representing the great difficulty of a change at this moment, and how strange it would appear, and here is his answer." In this he says he thought he had been *punished by the dreadful calamity he had endured for meddling in other people's business*, and that he did not mean to bring it forward again; but that Lord Howick's opposition had roused all his feelings again, and that he would resign next week. Lord Melbourne then read over the part in which he says he thought himself punished by the calamity he had undergone,[1] and Lord M. said, proved how full he was of his misfortune, and that he was always harping upon it; and Lord M. observed that people are always thinking why they in particular should be afflicted. "Now this looks very unfavourable," said Lord M., but he continued that he had met Palmerston (on Constitution Hill, which had made him late, he said) whom he had desired to speak to Howick; Palmerston said he had conversed fully with Howick; Howick said, though he quite agreed with Lord John upon the bad state the Government of the Colonies was in, still he knew and saw the impossibility of a change now, and therefore he would be content to remain, if he could be sure that the Colonial Department would be better conducted; Lord M. said, "So I hope to be able to prevent their having a blow up, before the Address is over; and then try and settle it with them; but I don't know." I repeated to Lord M. that I thought it not at all *right* of either of them, that they should bring this on just now. "No, it isn't right," said Lord M., "and that's what Thomson says; he says, 'You won't have a leg

[1] Lord John's usually well-balanced mind was temporarily unhinged by his domestic loss. He was a man exceptionally sensitive and tender in the more intimate relations of life.

to stand upon, for if you put it upon the total incapacity of Glenelg, why that's been known for a year or two,—and if it's only upon this last decision of the Cabinet, why that's not ground enough,'" which is exceedingly true. I asked Lord M. if he thought Lord John would have resigned if his Wife were alive; Lord M. thinks certainly not, for that she wouldn't have let him do so.

Talked of the Princess Sophia Matilda; of the Duke of Gloucester being so exceedingly obstinate; of the obstinacy in the family; George IV. was not obstinate, Lord M. said, and could easily be managed by his own fancies. Talked of the Duke of York, and he said that people relied on his word and his steadiness, which he carried to a most unfortunate extent, declaring several times "he would have gone to the Scaffold" sooner than give way about the Roman Catholics; over-good-natured, and allowing people to take liberties with him, of which Lord M. gave me several instances.

Monday, 4th February.—Lord M. then told me he had asked Lord Palmerston about the Pronunciation of the word *Guaranteed*; that if I wished to be very English I ought to say *guar*antee, for that the English word was *warranty* and *warrantee*; and the French way of pronouncing it was *garantée*, as Lord M. pronounces it; the g was introduced in Charles II.'s time. Talked of Glenelg; the letter was to go in the evening. Asked Lord M. if Glenelg was at all aware of what was brewing; Lord M. said not, and I asked him what would they give him: "We must give him the Privy Seal"; I said, then Lord Duncannon[1] must give it up. Lord M. said, "He only holds it,

[1] John William, afterwards fourth Earl of Bessborough. See Vol. I., p. 73.

H.R.H. Princess Sophia Matilda of Gloucester
from a portrait by Dalton after Sir G. Hayter

without having any salary; he takes the salary from the Woods and Forests." . . .

Wednesday, 6th February.—Said, I felt happier to read the Speech at the Proroguing than at the Opening of Parliament; which he quite understood. But, he said, "You seemed more at your ease yesterday, seemed less nervous; you were very steady." Said I was less so, but that I *always* felt nervous; and Lord M. said that no one ever got over that, and that there were very few who didn't feel the same nervousness before making a Speech even if you had done it a 100 times; he feels that, he says; and Pitt, he said, never came to the House that he didn't feel certain he should break down; but Lord M. said, it is said, nobody speaks well who hasn't that feeling.

Thursday, 7th February.—Said to Lord M. I was never satisfied with my own reading, and thought I put the wrong emphasis upon words; he said, "No, you read very well; I thought you read it very well this morning"; and I said I often felt so conscious of saying stupid things in conversation, and that I thought I was often very childish.[1] "You've no reason to think that," said Lord M., and that I feared I often asked him tiresome and indiscreet questions and bored him. "Never the least," he replied; "you *ought* to ask."

Friday, 8th February.—At 20 m. to 2 came Lord Melbourne and stayed with me till 5 m. p. 2. He had ridden here; and said he was "well in health"; he showed me a letter from Glenelg persisting in his resignation; Lord M. said, when I had read it,

[1] The Queen was still in her teens. These Journals show how modestly she underestimated her intelligence, her perspicacity, and her fine memory.

"The only way is to say that his resignation has been accepted, and to send for Normanby." Said, I thought it very hard upon Lord M. all this happening at this moment. "It puts us into immense difficulties and dangers," he replied, "when once such a shake has begun, you never know where it may end." Talked of Glenelg's being very much hurt at all this; and Lord M. said, "I never should have done it if I hadn't known that nothing but that could prevent the dissolution of the Government." I said certainly John Russell and Howick had brought all this difficulty upon them, in which Lord M. agreed; and I said it was very wrong of them. Talked of people's being like their Parents; and Lord M. said Pitt was the son of Lord Chatham by Lord Grenville's sister; and Lord M. said that when he made a speech people could tell exactly from which it came; "That's from *Pitt*—that's from *Grenville*." Talked of what the other Ministers would say about Glenelg's resignation; "I daresay it may be better as it is" (these are not *exactly* his words, I *think*), "but still I should have liked to have gone on," he said; in which I quite agree. Glenelg feels it much, we fear; we agreed Normanby was a man who would require more notice to be taken of him by me, than Glenelg did. Talked of Glenelg having no *decision* and never being able to decide promptly, which in Politics, Lord M. said, is absolutely necessary; of his being too late, and never ready; of his being a mild, agreeable man.

I asked him if Normanby would be sent for soon. "I've written to him," replied Lord M. He wrote to him yesterday; he said Normanby was quite ready to come, and read me a letter from him; Normanby says O'Connell and Brougham are well matched; he is desired to come over as quickly as he possibly can. The Cabinet he told me was to be about the general state of affairs, and the Estimates. Talked of the answer from the Russian Government to the Despatch from Lord Palmerston about their reducing their Navy, not being very favourable. "Not so unfavourable," said Lord M., "it's a clever paper." Lord Palmerston, he said, put it (in the Despatch) upon what we should say in the House of Commons; and the Emperor replies to that, that they need only say the Emperor's great moderation was well known, and could well be stated by the known cleverness of the English Debaters. . . .

Sunday, 10th February.—Lord M. made us laugh very much with his opinions about Schools and Public Education; the latter he don't like, and when I asked him if he did, he said, "I daren't say in these times that I'm against it,—but I *am* against it." He says it may do pretty well in Germany, but that the English would not submit to that thraldom; he thinks it much better be left to Voluntary Education, and that people of any great genius were educated by circumstances, and that "the education of circumstances" was the best; what *is* taught in Schools might be improved, he thinks. "All this was beginning when I was a boy," he said, "when I was with a Clergyman at Hatfield, all those Sunday Schools were beginning." I asked him if he didn't think that Asylum[1] of Miss Murray's for poor criminal children very good; he shook his head and said, "I doubt it." I said they would else commit every sort of atrocity and wickedness; "And so they will now, you'll see," he replied. Then he talked of those Normal Schools where they are going to

[1] See Vol. I., p. 162.

educate Schoolmasters, and he said, "You'll see they'll breed the most conceited set of blockheads ever known, and that'll be of no use whatever; now mind me if they don't," he added, turning to me.

He examined my bouquet and talked of forcing flowers, and said in his funny way, "Forcing flowers is questionable." I then talked about all these unfortunate difficulties, and Lord M. said this was the last of many other difficult things they had to discuss; asked if they agreed well about those. "Middling," he replied. Asked Lord M. if Howick's resignation were *not* to be followed by John Russell's, would it be a bad thing? "Why," Lord M. said, "it's not good *any* resigning, as it gives a shake, but it would not be a bad thing; it would not be a bad thing." Talked of Lord John's resigning and *his* (Ld. J.'s) reasons for so doing, and Lord M. said, "*I* think it's all nonsense," but that if Lord John had once taken a thing into his head it was almost impossible to make him change; and Lord M. thinks he is obstinate when he gets such notions; Howick, excessively obstinate and eager." Said to Lord M. I regretted so much that I was of no use, for that I *felt* I was of no use. "Oh! no," he said, "quite the contrary"; and I said I hoped, if he thought it would be of any use, he would use my name whenever he thought proper. "Thank you, Ma'am, I'll do so," he replied; "I'll do what I think right and best about that." Lord M. says he believes there will be little difficulty from the Opposition; "the real danger always comes from ourselves," and he said *he* didn't mind being helped by the Tories, for that he knew their faults and merits as well as he did those of our friends, but Lord John dislikes it exceedingly, and can't bear unpopularity in his own party. Talked of Palmerston's thinking it very wrong of Austria and Prussia to have withdrawn their Ministers from Brussels, in which Lord M. agreed, and said, "It's very rough," and he says Palmerston has written a very good draft about it.[1] Lord M. talked of the Chancellor[2] who was called to the Bar the same day as he (Ld. M.) was; he is just Lord M.'s age.

Monday, 11th February.—He had seen Lord Lansdowne last night, and they agreed that either Lord Tavistock or Lord Clarendon[3] would be the best for a Lord Lieutenant. I am quite of this opinion; Lord M. doesn't know if Tavistock would take it; Lord Clarendon we both think would be very fit for it. Lord M. said, "All the Irish Members are in despair at Normanby's leaving Ireland," which I can quite understand. Talked of Charles II. going to the House of Lords during Debates; "he used to stand by the fire and talk with the Peers like anybody else,"[4] said Lord M.; but it has never been done since. Talked of its being very hard I could never go, for that I would give anything to go.

Wednesday, 13th February.—Talked of Lady Portman's little girl, who had been very naughty in the morning and had quite resisted and refused to read when I asked her to do so, before I went to sit to Chantrey; and Lord M. said, "I never heard of such a thing, I never heard of a child who refused to

[1] A dispute as to carrying out what were known as the twenty-four articles was in progress between Belgium and Holland, and hostilities seemed probable. By the intervention of the Powers, war was averted. See *ante*, p. 48, and Vol. I., p. 387.

[2] Lord Cottenham. See Vol. I., p. 282.

[3] Sir George Villiers (see Vol. I., p. 229) had succeeded to the Clarendon earldom in 1838.

[4] While listening to the discussion in Parliament of Lord Ross's Divorce Bill, Charles exclaimed that it was "as good as a play."

do what he was asked," which made us laugh very much. "That must be a very refractory child." "You never hear," he continued, "a boy who has been brought up at a public school, say *I won't* or *I wouldn't*"; that those who were brought up at Private Schools did so; I said *I* always did, and most children did, and we asked him if he hadn't done so when a child. "Not much, very little, I knew I couldn't." "We shall see what this Board of Education will do," he added funnily.

Thursday, 14*th February*.—He had had a letter from Normanby which he read to me, in which N. wishes to have the new Bishop of Cashel,[1] one of the Lords Justices; talked of his (N.'s) successor, and Lord M. said (what he had already told me the day before), "Upon the whole we think Lord Clarendon will be the best, but it's not yet finally settled upon." Normanby will be here by Monday. Then Lord M. said that Sir George Grey was very anxious to be Judge Advocate, "and I think we can't well refuse him," though it is rather awkward vacating his place. "Perhaps you'll leave it to my discretion," said Lord M., "whether it ought to be done or not; if so, it may be done to-day."

At 20 m. to 3 I rode out with Lord Uxbridge, Lord Fingall,[2] Lord Alfred, Daisy, Miss Murray, Col. Wemyss, Major Keppel, and came home at ½ p. 5. I rode Comus who went delightfully; and rode between Lord Uxbridge and Col. Wemyss; it was a long and pleasant ride, and a most lovely day, warm like Summer. We rode 1st through Kensington by Addison Road, into the Acton Road, and

[1] Dr. Stephen C. Sandes.

[2] Arthur James, ninth Earl, for some time Lord-in-Waiting to Queen Victoria.

across into the Harrow Road, and so home by the Park. We saw no less than *4 trains* pass close to us, and had to wait for one where we have to cross the rail-road; once we were lost, or rather mistook our way, and had to retrace our steps.

Friday, 15th February.—Lord M. said, "There's a great difficulty about this Lord Lieutenancy for Ireland; we rather wish to keep Lord Clarendon for Canada." I asked who would they send; some have mentioned Charlemont,[1] Lord M. said, and "I think Charlemont would do very well," he added.

Monday, 18th February.—It was Shakespear's tragedy of *King Lear*, acting according to the text of Shakespear; we came in soon after the beginning; Macready acted the part of Lear; in parts he was very fine, particularly in the last Scene where he brings in Cordelia's body; but at times he was much too violent and passionate. Miss P. Horton acted *the fool* delightfully. Mrs. Warner[2] was Regan, and old Mrs. Clifford a shocking Goneril; Miss H. Faucit, Cordelia; Mr. Anderson, Edmond; Mr. Elton, Edgar, and of course Madrone; Mr. Bartley, Kent; and Bennett, Gloster.

Tuesday, 19th February.—Saw Lord Glenelg at 2, to whom (according to what Lord Melbourne had written to me to say) I expressed my thanks for his services and my regrets to be unable to keep him in my Councils, and the high esteem I should always entertain for him. Talked to Lord Melbourne of my having seen *King Lear* and its being a fine play; talked of it for some time; of the way in which it was acted now at Covent Garden. "I always thought him (Lear) a foolish old fellow,"

[1] Francis William, second Earl of Charlemont, K.P.

[2] Mary Amelia Warner, at one time manageress of Sadler's Wells.

said Lord M. "It's a rough coarse play," said Lord M., written for those times, with exaggerated characters. "I'm glad you've seen it," he added.

Wednesday, 20th February.—After dinner before we sat down, I talked with Lord Melbourne and Miss Murray about Schools, about which he was very funny; talked of these Normal Schools; "Normal Schools,—conceited name," said Lord M. "Normal means a rule, so a normal school is a school for teaching schoolmasters to teach." Talked of teaching the poor people to cook, and all those sorts of things, and Lord M. said Plato never could bear that sort of useful knowledge, which he called lowering Science. "You'll never teach English people to cook," said Lord M., and he added, "Walter Scott said, 'Why do you bother the poor? leave them alone'; don't you think there's a great deal of truth in that? Nothing's learnt that way."

Talked of Plays, and Shakespear's; Lord M. said there is a great dispute as to which are the first plays that Shakespear wrote, and that it is not easy to ascertain; there are 36 plays acknowledged to be written by him, and some more, Lord M. said, which are not quite decided to be his. Talked of Fletcher who wrote plays at the same time; of Ben Jonson's plays; "The only one that keeps the stage," said Lord M., "is called *Every Man in his Humour.*" Talked of a play called *The Honeymoon* which Lord M. said is written by a man of the name of Tobin[1]; of Katherine and Petruchio, and Lord M. said, "It's a coarsish plot." . . .

Sunday, 24th February.—Talked of Lord Douro's marriage to Lady Elizabeth Hay,[2] one of Lord

[1] John Tobin, also author of *The Curfew* and *The School for Authors.*

[2] Daughter of eighth Marquess of Tweeddale. She became Lady

Tweeddale's daughters, being settled; both Lady Normanby and I said we should not believe it till we saw Lord Douro really married, for that he was so very changeable; they said Lord Douro had been out shopping with the young lady; and Lord M. said, "Shopping is very demonstrative," which made us laugh; and "There is a day when even the most *volage* is fixed, and has his wings clipped." Talked of the picture of Van Amburgh and the Lions Landseer is making. "Why, he" (V. Amburgh) "quite brings Daniel down," said Lord M.; and he talked of the Power the ancients had with Music over beasts, and passions; we said that would have no effect on him (Ld. M.); he said Orpheus would; which made us laugh; he said the formation of the organ of the ear was different, and also that the dislike came from want of attention. "I have music in me," he said, "if it was awoke; only I never attended to it." If he really had *liked* it, I said, he must have attended to it. "I never could dance in time," he said; "I never knew when it began. Sir Isaac Newton said," he continued, "'The only difference between me and a carter, is attention.'" "I despised music when I was young, beyond everything," said Lord M., "and everybody who liked it; I was very foolish." It was the fashion, he said, then, to dislike music and dancing, and to lounge upon the sofas. . . .

Sunday, 3rd March.—Talked of having a Council next Wednesday or not; of the coat he wears at the Council, which he says is comfortable; of his having been in full dress the day I came to the Throne, which he said was right for him, as the Duke of

Douro, and afterwards Duchess of Wellington. She outlived the Duke (see Vol. I., p. 191) many years.

Wellington had been so when he went to William IV.; but none of the others ought to be, as it is a Council, he said, which assembles of itself and is not summoned; and that, he said, was the mistake when George IV. came to the throne, they put in the Declaration that he had *assembled* them.[1] Talked of the number there were at the 1st Council, and my being less frightened in reading the Declaration, [quite the 1st thing I had ever read before many, or any, people,] than I had since, &c. He said, "You didn't *seem* much frightened at the 1st Council; it was a trying morning altogether; you had been up so long."

Tuesday, 5th March.—Lord M. said that he had received a letter from the Duke of Wellington the day before yesterday, in which the Duke says that there is a gentleman in Hampshire whose son was Aide-de-Camp to the Emperor of Russia, and that he had written over (I suppose to his Father) that he had seen a large plan on the Emperor's table of an intention to attack the East Indies with his fleet, that the Emperor had referred it to his Ministers, and that he had afterwards seen it on the Emperor's table marked "approved"; the Duke says he does not think it at all probable that such a large and difficult undertaking should really be in contemplation, but he thinks it possible that the Emperor would get his Fleet into the Mediterranean, and wishes that something should be done to prevent their coming out; the Duke thought this intelligence ought not to be totally disregarded and therefore brought it before the Government. "I don't think it very probable," said Lord M., "but it mustn't be totally disregarded."[2] Lord M. then said

[1] This mistake has occurred since.

[2] This ridiculous story was proved afterwards to be a pure fabrica-

he was afraid they were in a scrape about the Registrar's Certificate for a marriage, of which he already told me the other night; it sounds exceedingly absurd, a man has married his grandmother; Lord M. told me the case; an old man of 70 named John Payne married a girl of 17; he had a grown-up son who had an illegitimate son; and on the death of the old man, this same natural son married his grandfather's widow,—which is, of course, quite wrong; and the mistake arose, Lord M. said, from the Registrar saying that an illegitimate child was no relation, "nullius filius," Lord M. said, and that therefore he might marry his grandmother; now, Lord M. said, this is quite wrong, and only applies to inheritance of property and not to a thing of this sort; "else," he said, "a man might marry his Mother or his Sister."[1] . . .

Sunday, 10th March.—I asked Lord M. how old the Bishop of Chester[2] was; he said, older than he was, and that he had been in the form above him at Eton; "Crumpet Sumner," said Lord M. he was called, "because his face is said to be in the shape of a crumpet, like dough," which made us laugh. Talked of that, and of his singular voice. "That singing manner that all the Methodists have," he said; which Lady Barham wouldn't allow, and said

tion. It is interesting as an illustration of the type of sensational gossip that finds credence in all countries and under all forms of government.

[1] The registrar was giving effect to what is still the popular idea on the subject. The Courts, however, have decided that a widower may not marry even the niece of his dead wife, although the niece's mother was illegitimate.

[2] John Bird Sumner (1780–1862), made Bishop of Chester 1828, and Archbishop of Canterbury 1848. He was one year younger than Lord Melbourne.

that Dr. Chalmers had not; Lord M. said, "I've never heard him; I don't go to those Presbyterians; I'm an Episcopalian," which he said in such a funny way as to make us all laugh.

Monday, 11th March.—I asked Lord Melbourne how he was—in going in—and he said quite well, and I told him I thought I was going to have the Influenza, as I had pains all over; he replied most funnily, "It's the best time to have it,—no Levée; you can't go through the year without being ill." Talked of Lord Headfort's having lost 6,000 trees by the hurricane at Headfort, and large trees, which Lord M. wouldn't allow, and said, "Can't be; there are no old trees in Ireland." . . . Talked of the late King's serious and real intention to marry me to the second son of the Prince of Orange; "He was very eager about it," said Lord M., "he was very angry with me about that, for I made a great many objections to it." Lord M. said the King meant to have managed it any how, and he was always afraid of being "forestalled" about it, which I said he very likely would have been. "The Prince of Orange was very anxious about it," Lord M. continued; "he came to me about it, and said the King wished it very much, but that he knew that wasn't the only thing in this country; and he wished to know if I had any decided objection to it." I talked of my Uncle being greatly alarmed about it. Pozzo, Lord M. said, and all the Russians, were anxious and always wishing for the Dutch alliance. I asked Lord M. did he think Pozzo was still for it; Lord M. said, of course they always wished for such an alliance; I asked was there in general much said about my marrying. "I haven't heard anything," he said, "but there will be some day a great deal;

but I'll ask." The best way to prevent that, I said, was by never marrying at all; and that I used to frighten my relations by saying so. I asked him did he think the Country was anxious I should marry, for that I wished to remain as I was for some time to come; he said he didn't believe they showed any wish for it as yet." . . .

Wednesday, 13th March.—I said to Lord M. I knew I had been very disagreeable and cross in the morning, which he didn't allow. I said I had been exceedingly angry with John Russell for not letting me go to Drury Lane; Lord M. laughed and said, "But it can't be." I couldn't get my gloves on, and Lord M. said, "It's those consumed rings; I never could bear them." I said I was fond of them, and that it improved an ugly hand. "Makes it worse," he replied; I said I didn't wear them of a morning. "*Much* better," he said, "and if you didn't wear them, nobody else would." Ear-rings he thinks barbarous. I said I thought I was not getting stronger. "Why, you have every appearance of getting stronger," he said, and "You should take the greatest care of your health; there's nothing like health; particularly in your situation; it makes you so independent; bad health puts you into the power of people." Mr. Cowper came up to us, and said he had been talking to Bulwer about his Play,[1] and that he wasn't at all satisfied with the way in which it was acted. "Pooh, pooh!" said Lord M., "the man's very unreasonable, he's got his Play through, and I dare say it ought to have been damned." Talked of Richelieu, his character, and Lord M. said that if the people were alive and here they could often tell us in a moment why they did things,

[1] The play referred to was *Richelieu.*

whereas we write volumes to prove the reasons why people did so-and-so; he said people always accused Lord Burleigh of being so unkind to his nephew Bacon, and Lord M. said he was certain if Lord Burleigh were alive he would give his good reasons for it, and we knew "what an infernal scamp" Bacon was.

Friday, 15th March.—At a little after 1, Lady Cowper (the young one) came with her little Niece, Lady Mary Vyner's little girl,[1] the loveliest child I ever saw, and such a nice child, called Henrietta and 6 years old. Wrote my journal. At 10 m. p. 2 came Lord Melbourne and stayed with me till 3. He was looking particularly well and in high spirits. I asked him how he was; and then I said I must wish him joy of this day (his 60th birthday) and I shook hands with him and pressed his hand, as he did mine, most warmly; I said to him, for many years I trusted. He seemed pleased and said, "Thank you, Ma'am." God knows, I wished him joy and pressed his kind hand with all my heart, and I am quite certain few could have done it with more earnestness than I did—or be more attached and thankful to him than I am. Asked where Duncannon lived. "In Cavendish Square, where his father and grandfather lived," he replied; "something very respectable in living where your father

[1] She married, when very young, Lord Goderich, who, better known as Lord Ripon, served the State honourably and with great distinction in many high offices, including that of Viceroy of India. The Marchioness of Ripon, as she ultimately became, was, like her husband, an earnest and consistent Liberal in politics. Her health was never strong, so that she went little into society, but no woman of the late Victorian era enjoyed and shone more in intimate causerie. Her instinct and judgment about public affairs were remarkably acute and wise. Her capacity for friendship was unusual, and her society was sought by some of the most brilliant and eminent of her contemporaries. Her memory is deeply cherished by her friends.

and grandfather lived," which made us laugh, as also my not knowing where Cavendish Square and Harley Street are. "Harley Street leads out of Cavendish Square," he said, "and consequently leads into it." We were seated as usual, Lord Melbourne sitting near me; Islay[1] sat on the sofa next to me and was good, but rather bewildered and alarmed at the Band and at the number of people. Lord M. said, "He doesn't mind it; he is not disposed to take part in it," and when I desired them to take the dog away to give him a little water, Lord M. said, "You had better leave him alone, else he'll soon learn to think he's the first object." "He's a dog of retired habits," and "You should encourage those habits of abstinence." I said I hoped he would always tell me whatever he heard; he said, "I always do." Not lately, I said; "I haven't heard anything lately." "For," I added, "I was sure I made a great many mistakes"; "No, I don't know that at all." People said, he continued, that I was "lofty, high, stern, and decided, but that's much better than that you should be thought familiar." "I said to Stanley,"[2] he continued, "it's far better that the Queen should be thought high and decided, than that she should be thought weak. 'By God!' he said, 'they don't think that of her; you needn't be afraid of that.'" Lord M. seemed to say this with pleasure. "The natural thing," he continued, "would be to suppose that a girl would be weak and undecided; but they don't think that." I said that I was often very childish, he must perceive; "No, not at all, I don't see that in any respect," he said.

Sunday, 17th March.—Talked of the Archbishop

[1] A Scotch terrier, and a great pet of the Queen's.

[2] Afterwards Earl of Derby, and Prime Minister. See Vol. I., p. 73.

of York and his being so wonderful for his age; I made Lord M. laugh by saying he told me that Lord M. had said to him, "You Bishops are sad dogs." "He's a good-natured lively man," said Lord M. "He was always very kind to me when I asked his advice about people." Lord M. went to the Speaker's Levée after his dinner. "Several people came dressed to my dinner," he said, "which put me in mind I ought to go." Not a great many people there, he said; Stanley, Peel, and Graham, and the Duke of Norfolk there. I said I thought it was so odd that the Speaker should have a Levée[1]; and Lord M. not. Lord M. said Prime Ministers always used to have them, and they were given up by Mr. Pitt out of laziness; they used to be in the morning and Lord M. said there was a curious account of the Duke of Newcastle's levées in one of Smollett's novels[2]; "He used to run in to it half shaved, with the lather on one side of his face," said Lord M., "but that was the right thing; it's meant to be while you are getting up; I hold a levée; I see people while I'm dressing." I asked him if that didn't tire him. "No, not at all, and it don't keep them waiting," he replied. Talked of going to bed so much earlier formerly; of my going to sleep quickly; of Louis XIV. never being hungry till he came to dinner, and then after the 2 first spoonfuls eating quantities; I said it was quite the contrary with me, and that when I had had a little, all appetite went. "That's not so well," he said.

[1] The Speaker's Levée still remains an institution. The Commander-in-Chief's Levée died with the office in 1904.

[2] "A shaving cloth under his chin, his face frothed up to the eyes with soap-lather." See letter of J. Melford to Sir Watkin Phillips of Jesus College, Oxon, of June 5, 17— (*Humphry Clinker*).

Monday, 18th March.—We were seated much as usual, Lord Melbourne sitting near me. He said he had desired Hobhouse to send me the letters from Lord Auckland about his visit to Runjeet Sing[1]; that there were 250 women, all mounted, and all beautiful girls; and Runjeet said *that* was the Regiment that gave him the most trouble. Talked of Weddings being affecting; and he said no one who had ever gone through it and known its consequences, could look on it lightly. Talked of the Sovereign's great power over the marriages of his relations, being great tyranny in my opinion, but Lord M. said, "No, quite right, it's much better." Of its being better in my opinion that they should not be allowed to marry a subject, as they got so mixed up else. Talked of this new Assam tea, and Lord M. said they told him the other day at the Coffee Mill in St. James's Street that they sold it for 36*s*. a lb. Talked of the Opera, and Lord M. said some East India people had outbid Lady Stanhope by £20, in consequence of which she had lost her box.

Wednesday, 20th March.—He said there was to be a Cabinet this morning about this Motion of Lord Roden's to-morrow. Lord M. said, "I am rather for letting them have this Committee for inquiring into the state of Crime in Ireland," but that Normanby was very much against it, and considered it an imputation on his Government; "and he may resign, which would bring on a great crisis."[2] "His fault," continued Lord M., "is great personal touchi-

[1] See *ante*, pp. 63 and 64.

[2] Lord Roden moved for, and obtained, in the House of Lords, the appointment of a Committee to enquire into the state of Ireland. The Ministry retaliated by getting a vote in their favour in the Commons by 318 to 296.

ness,—about his dignity." I went and fetched in the Sketch I bought from that Mr. Smith, done by Sir Thomas Lawrence when 15, and for which I paid 150 guineas, an immense sum, for the Drawing is rough and small and evidently done by a child. I brought it in and put it in Lord M.'s hands, who was quite astounded at the price and said, "I should say it wasn't worth 5 guineas." He looked at it and criticised it for some time, and said, "Why, there are 100 girls in London who could draw better than this." Yet he thought parts of it clever.

Asked Lord M. why the City were so very much against the introduction of the Metropolitan Police.[1] Lord M. said because (though this would be much better) they have their own Police, which is very bad, and they consider it an infringement of their rights. "Rather dangerous to stir," said Lord M.; "it shouldn't have been done without some previous arrangement with them"; this is John Russell's doing. We talked of Lytton Bulwer, and the book *she*[2] has just published; Lord M. said she has been writing since long, in Reviews. "No woman should touch pen and ink," Lord M. said, and talked of that; he said they had too much passion and too little sense. "Women write letters better than men do," he continued, "they write with greater facility and freedom, less formal and stiff." He quoted Mme. de Sévigné's beautiful letters.

We began by talking of Chess, and of Sydney Smith's having said the 1st thing he remembered of the Archbishop of Canterbury was he (the Arch-

[1] The Metropolitan Police were instituted in 1829. Their organization, was improved and their sphere of action extended in this year 1839.

[2] Lady Bulwer had just published *Cheveley, or the Man of Honour*, an attack on her husband. See *post*, p. 145.

bishop) throwing him down at Winchester School for being beat by him at Chess. Talked of Sydney Smith's age; and I asked the Bishop of London how old the Archbishop of Canterbury was; 73, he said, just 20 years older than he was; Lord M. was quite surprised and could hardly believe it; Lord M. said he knew him 43 years ago at the Priory.[1] Talked of Lambeth, its beauty; of the Palace at Chester being so bad; and Lord M. said the Bishop of Hereford told him the Palace at Hereford was built in 1150! The Bishop of London said Fulham had been the Residence of the Bishops of London for 1,200 years; for that the land had been granted in 639!! Talked to Lord M. of the Dean of Chester's being a year younger than Lord M., by which Lord M. said the Dean must have been at Cambridge at the same time that he was; Lord M. was at Trinity, and the Dean at Christ's; the Bishop of London said he took his degree in 1808; and Lord M. in 1798; "and *then* I pottered a good deal" (meaning that as a Nobleman he might have taken it sooner). "They were very useless years to me," said Lord M., "but that was not *their* fault; the time when I was at College," he said to me, "was the time of my life when I attended least to study." Lord M. then went to Glasgow for 2 years; all his brothers were at Cambridge, but none of them with him; talked of the difference between Cambridge and Oxford,—the former being best for clever people and the other for people of no talents.

Thursday, 21st March.—At a ¼ to 11 I got the following communication from Lord Melbourne: "Lord Roden made the Motion in a very long and

[1] The Archbishop of Canterbury was seventy-three and Lord Melbourne sixty.

not a very bad speech. Lord Normanby answered and defended himself extremely well and very ably. The Duke of Wellington made a short speech, supporting the Motion but denying that he meant any imputation upon Lord Normanby. The Duke was rather eager and excited. Lord Charleville is now speaking. It will be late—the Tories are united and eager and numerous, and we shall be beat."

Friday, 22nd March.—Got up at ½ p. 9. Very anxious and nervous. Saw by the papers we were beat by 5; and they had sat till 4! I am in a sad state of suspense; it is now ¾ p. 12, and I have not yet heard from Lord Melbourne; I hear he was still asleep when my box arrived, and I desired they shouldn't wake him. Arranged things; wrote. Heard from Lord Melbourne: "It is now twelve o'clock and Lord Melbourne was so tired with the debate of last night that he has slept until now. The majority, as your Majesty sees, was very small. We must have a Cabinet this morning in order to consider what steps are to be taken. It must be at Lord Lansdowne's, as he is confined with the gout and cannot go out. Lord Melbourne will be with Your Majesty by one—if possible." At 5 m. to 2 came my excellent Lord Melbourne and stayed with me till a ¼ p. 2. I asked how he was and if he wasn't very tired. "Not very," he replied, "I was very tired last night." It was so late. "I don't know what's to be done, really," he said. "We are going to have a Meeting at Lansdowne's this morning to consider it; it's a direct censure upon the Government." I asked Lord M. who had been appointed on this Committee of Inquiry into the state of Ireland. "Oh! they have appointed it fairly enough; we can't complain of unfairness in the appointing of it;

but it is *having* the Committee that is the difficulty to get over," said Lord M. Lord Melbourne told me he was sure we would be beat last night, and expected "by a much larger majority." He also said to me, "I'm afraid you were very uneasy at not hearing, but I thought 5 o'clock was too late to send." Received at a ¼ to 5 the following communication from Lord Melbourne: "that the Cabinet have decided—1st, that it is impossible to acquiesce in the Vote of last night in the House of Lords; 2ndly, that it would not be justifiable to resign in the face of the declaration which I made in the year 1836, in the House of Lords, that I would maintain my post as long as I possessed the confidence of the Crown and of the House of Commons, particularly as there is no reason to suppose that we have lost the confidence of that House. 3rdly, that the course to be pursued is to give notice in the House of Commons to-night, that the sense of that House will be taken immediately after the Easter Holidays upon a Vote of approbation of the principles of Lord Normanby's Government of Ireland. If we lose that question or carry it by a small majority, we must resign. If we carry it, we may go on.—This is a plain statement of the case, and this course will at least give Your Majesty time to consider what is to be done."—I forbear making any observations upon this until I have talked fully to Lord Melbourne upon it, with the exception of one, which is—that as for "the confidence of the Crown," God knows! *no Minister, no friend* EVER possessed it so entirely as this truly excellent Lord Melbourne possesses mine![1]

[1] NOTE BY QUEEN VICTORIA, 1*st October*, 1842.—Reading this again, I cannot forbear remarking what an artificial sort of happiness *mine* was *then*, and what a blessing it is I have now in my beloved

Lord M. didn't hear Lord Carew,[1] as he went out of the House for a moment when he was speaking; I said I heard he didn't speak well; "He speaks with that Wexford shriek," said Lord M. He said to Lady Normanby, "Normanby is too thin-skinned, too susceptible; and that's his fault; he shouldn't mind being abused; nobody should mind that. Brougham said to Duncannon, 'Tell that foolish friend of yours, Normanby, not to mind being abused, for he is paid to bear it.'" Talked of Brougham being a bad man with no heart; Lord M. said, "No, he *has* a heart; he has feeling, I should say he was too susceptible and acted from sudden impulses." Talked of contradicting abuse in the papers, and Lord M. said, there might one day come something one couldn't well contradict, and therefore it was better not to contradict at all. We were seated much as usual, my truly valuable and excellent Lord Melbourne being seated near me. I said to Lord M. that I was sure I never could bear up against difficulties; Lord M. turned round close to me, and said very earnestly and affectionately, "Oh! you will; you must; it's in the lot of your Station, you must prepare yourself for it." I said I never could, and he continued, "Oh! you will; you always behaved very well." I said to Lord M. I was sure he hadn't a doubt we

Husband *real* and solid happiness, which no Politics, no worldly reverses *can* change; it could not have lasted long, as it was then, for after all, kind and excellent as Lord M. is, and kind as he was to [me], it was but in Society that I had amusement, and I was only living on that superficial resource, which I *then fancied* was happiness! Thank God! for *me* and others, this is changed, and I *know what* REAL happiness is.—V. R.

[1] Robert Shapland, first Lord Carew (1787–1856), sometime Lord Lieutenant of the County of Wexford.

should carry it.[1] "Upon my word I don't know," he said; "but it was absolutely necessary to bring it to this, to see if our friends would really support us, for they have been running riot so much lately." I said that the Majority being so small in the House of Lords, we were sure of being supported in the House of Commons. "I think if they are brought up to the Post they will," he replied. I felt sure, I said, the Tories couldn't stand a moment; Lord M. wasn't so sure of that, as he says, "they've been gaining ever since the Reform Bill," and that a Government always gathered some odium as it went on. He, however, said that John Russell's announcement had been very well received. I said I felt so helpless; "I don't see what any Sovereign can do, old or young, male or female," he said, "but to put themselves into the hands of the person" that they have chosen as Minister; talking of the whole thing, Lord M. said, "We'll do everything we can to avert it; I never thought we should have carried you on as far as we have done." I said, though I liked all the others,—yet *he* was the person I really cared for; he smiled and said, "But that can't be helped." Talked of other things; my regretting I should lose him on Sunday, and begged him to let me have one other day in the next week to make up for it, which he promised. He thought I looked well, though pale; he wasn't sure if he was going to Lady Stanhope's or home. I urged the latter.—Stayed up till 25 m. to 12. . . .

Monday, 25th March.—I told Lord M. Sir Herbert Taylor was dying; and Lord M. said he hoped he would take care of his Papers, which he thinks he will leave to his brother Sir Brook Taylor. . . .

[1] The vote of confidence to be moved in the House of Commons.

Wednesday, 27th March.—Lord Melbourne was rather silent during dinner; but I *never* saw him *so* much so as he was after dinner,—so completely absorbed, so totally disinclined to enter into any conversation whatever,—and merely just answering a question in as short a manner as possible, and then relapsing into the same silence; yet he did not look nor was he ill; I was quite grieved and distressed to see him so; I fear he has got something to annoy him by what I hear, and that I conclude produced this effect. . . . Lord Melbourne said he felt better when he came up to me after dinner, but sleepy. We were seated much as usual; Lord Melbourne sitting near me. He called Islay "a dull dog," which really makes me quite angry, for Islay is such a darling, and lay so affectionately near me. Lord Melbourne said, Lord Clarendon thought Spain in a better state than France; Thiers told him that he had said they meant to throw themselves entirely into the hands of England and follow England's footsteps; upon which Dupin[1] said, "I'm not prepared for that; I'm very much for a cordial alliance with England, but I'm not prepared to follow in the wake of England; France has a *politique à elle*."

Friday, 29th March.—Talked of the water in the garden here being in very good order; of the garden, in which Lord M. has never been. "I would cut down all the trees," he said, "and plant rare trees." Elms he would cut down, and "some nasty oaks, which I wish cut down every time I drive down Constitution Hill," he said. We said there would be no shade. "*Shade?* What's the use of *shade* in this country?" he said in his funniest way. I said there were some very hot days in England.

[1] The new President of the Chamber of Deputies.

"Then you stay at home," he replied. We talked of Maundy Thursday and what it could mean and be derived from.[1] Lord M. said, "Can't tell." Talked of that. At dinner I made Lord M. smile by saying I thought the poor people who got coins on that day, must feel the difference between the late Reign and this; for they always got as many coins as the Sovereign is old; in the late Reign they got *70*, and now only *19*.

Sunday, 31*st March*.—I showed Lord M. in a Peerage I've got, an account of his (Ld. M.'s) Family, which he said was "correct enough." "Oh, Ma'am," he said, after looking at it for some time, "we think it would be right to mark these Treaties by making Lord Ponsonby a Viscount and my brother a Peer." I was much pleased at this, particularly at the last, and I asked Lord M. what title his brother would take. "He thinks of calling himself Lord Beauvale," said Lord M., "which is a place I have in Nottinghamshire; I only mention it to Your Majesty, you'll not speak of it." He then put down the Peerage and said, "It's all correct but *that*" (making Lady Anne Wombwell his Aunt instead of his Cousin). Talked of Mr. Vizard, Lord Normanby's attorney. "He is my attorney," said Lord M. Lady Normanby said he was a hard man. "I quite agree with you," said Lord M., "he's a very hard man; I never saw an attorney in my life that I didn't hate." A Solicitor he thought better.[2] Talked of making people April Fools, which some

[1] Apparently from *mandatum*. The antiphon for the day before Good Friday (the day of institution of washing the feet of the poor) began "*Mandatum novum*" ("A new commandment give I," etc.).

[2] The distinction is now obsolete. An attorney practised in the Courts of Common Law, a solicitor in Equity.

people said could only be till 12 o'clock mid-day. "I didn't know that it was bounded and limited," said Lord M. "It's a practice which I very much disapprove of," he said. "I've seen it have such serious consequences and produce such dreadful enmities; people are always taken in, and it makes people make fools of themselves, which people hardly ever forgive." We talked of Nourrit,[1] the French Singer, who Lord M. had never heard of, having killed himself on account of his feeling the ingratitude of the Parisians who neglected him for Duprez.[2] "That's the lot of every one," said Lord M., no Actor should kill himself for that. Lord M. said that Carlini, a famous Clown at Paris, went to a Physician and complained of being so ill, upon which the Physician said, "Go and see Carlini." This is the original story, which I have heard told of Garrick and Liston. Lord M. said Banti[3] was the first famous Italian Singer he remembers; and he said Mrs. Billington,[4] who had been a very good English singer, went to Italy and when she came back, Lord M. said, quite crushed Banti, though she wasn't to be compared to her. Banti used to say of her, Lord M. said, "C'est très bien, mais elle n'a pas la dolcessa di Banti." Lord M. continued, "Grassini[5] is Grisi's aunt; *she* was the best Italian actress

[1] Louis Nourrit, French musician and composer.

[2] Gilbert Louis Duprez, a much younger singer than Nourrit.

[3] Georgina Brigida Banti (1757–1806).

[4] Elizabeth Billington (1768–1818) had already had a brilliant career when, at the age of twenty-six, in consequence of some scandalous rumours, she left England, visited Italy, and sang at Naples, Milan, and elsewhere. During her stay abroad her husband died, and she was accused of murdering him. On her return she had an immense success, making £10,000 to £15,000 in the year 1801. She appeared with Banti on the occasion of the latter's farewell concert.

[5] Napoleon, at Milan, had been captivated by Grassini's voice and

MADAME VESTRIS.

From a sketch by the Queen before her accession.

ever seen on the stage; her voice hadn't much compass." I asked Lord M. if she was handsome. "*I* thought the prettiest woman I had ever seen." She had long given up singing, but Lord M. said he dined with her at Paris in '25. Lady Normanby said she saw her in '15 act with Vestris.[1] We talked of Mrs. Siddons, my having seen her at Cobham Hall; of her being very pompous; of John Kemble also very pompous. Of Bulwer's new play of *Richelieu*; of the way of pronouncing Richelieu; Lord M. thinks it better to pronounce the French and other names as they ought to be pronounced; but he says some people wouldn't do so; that Mr. Fox, who could speak French very well, used always to say *Touloon* instead of Toulon; Bordeaux, pronouncing the *x* at the end; Fontblanky instead of Fontblanque. Talked of duelling for some time, and Lord M. said, "I should be very sorry to shoot at a man, for I should feel very confident I should kill him." Talked of the Duels abroad being so very fatal, and not so here; of fighting with swords, which Lord Gardner[2] thinks better. Lord M. went on talking again about what horses could do; and he said, "Brotherton used to say to me, 'They always treat the Cavalry as if it was made of china.'" . . .

beauty, and she used to be a guest at Malmaison. Reluctant to cause excessive jealousy to Josephine, the Emperor only paid the *cantatrice* surreptitious visits; this did not accord with her ambitious temperament, and, becoming enamoured of the celebrated violinist, Rode, she ultimately fled with him from Paris.

[1] As to Madame Vestris, see Vol. I., p. 148.

[2] Alan Legge, third Lord Gardner (1810–83).

INTRODUCTORY NOTE TO CHAPTER XIV

In May 1839 the Government of Lord Melbourne was practically defeated in the House of Commons upon the Jamaica Bill. The event so feared by the Queen had at last happened. The Ministry resigned, and the Queen sent for the Duke of Wellington. He at once advised her to place the duty of forming an Administration in the hands of Sir Robert Peel. Her first interview with the statesman to whom in after-years she became much attached was harassing to both. Although Peel had been warned of the importance of the "first impression on so young a girl's mind," he was unable to put aside that stiffness of manner and reserve which were habitual to him.

Lord Melbourne had, two years before, recommended to the Queen, as members of her Household, Ladies all of whom were connected with the Whig Party. It was a very natural error, but, as events proved, a grave mistake. The Queen resented Sir Robert Peel's proper and reasonable demand that some of these Ladies should be replaced by others representing the party of which he was the chief. There is no more human episode in the history of the Queen's reign than what was called, in the slang of the day, the Bedchamber Plot. An anxious, austere, and not undictatorial Minister desired to remove from intimate association with his Sovereign, Ladies hostile to him and his party. A young girl, of imperious will and passionate temperament, determined to keep about her person the friends to whom she was accustomed, and refused to adopt "a course which she conceives to be contrary to usage and which is repugnant to her feelings."

Imagine the irony of the situation. The Queen a mere child, and these grave statesmen accepting her verdict, and telling her that unless there was "some demonstration of *her* confidence, they could not undertake to govern the country." These were the very words of a man, proud and cold, to a young girl not twenty years old. The Queen remained firm. She refused to part with her Whig ladies, and she parted, for a while, with Sir Robert Peel. The Whig Government returned to office, and for two years longer remained the Counsellors of the Sovereign. In later years the Queen, reviewing the events of 1839, said to one of her private secretaries, after eulogising Sir Robert Peel, "I was very young then, and perhaps I should act differently if it was all to be done again." Thus, by an afterthought, based on mature experience, did the Queen vindicate the Whig doctrine which has become an axiom of constitutional practice, that the Sovereign should accept and act solely upon the advice of Ministers, and in accordance with the views of the people as represented in Parliament.

CHAPTER XIV

1839

Thursday, 4th April.—I asked of Sir Herbert Taylor, who Lord M. thinks was a very good-looking man; of Princess Augusta having told me that there was a coolness between George IV. and Taylor because Taylor refused to tell the Prince of Wales anything about George III.; Lord M. said he thought it very likely; that "Taylor was a very honourable man; but I don't think he was a very clever man." . . .

Saturday, 6th April.—Talked of the news from France not being very comfortable [1]; Lord M. said the opening of the Chambers didn't seem at all pleasant; "they seemed rather to dread disturbance." I asked Lord M. did he think the King might have managed it better; he replied, "Oh! yes, he might have managed it better; if he had yielded at once to the Majority of the Chambers and done that with good grace." I said Louis Philippe couldn't bear Thiers. "I believe that's at the bottom of it all," said Lord M., but that he thought he couldn't fight against him. We talked of Pozzo's being so *passé*; his saying he preserved the peace of Europe by

[1] The French elections had taken place on 4th March, and the Molé Ministry were left in a minority. The King sent successively for Soult, Thiers, and De Broglie without success, and on the eve of the meeting of the Chambers was without a ministry. Accordingly on 3rd April a provisional Cabinet was formed, and M. Passy was elected President of the Chamber of Deputies.

making the foreign Ambassadors remain at Paris when Charles X. fled; Lord M. said this was true; I said Pozzo told me this some years ago at Kensington, and Lord Holland said he would tell him I recollected it, and that it would please him very much. Talked of Sebastiani being slow and pompous, but Lord M. said clever and clear; of Senfft; of Bülow; of the Belgian business; of Alava, his open manner. "That very open honest manner is never to be trusted," said Lord M. Asked Lord M. if he liked my dress, a cherry-coloured silk with a magnificent old lace flounce. "It's very pretty," he said, "I like those bright colours; it's very handsome." The dress I had on the day before, a striped one, he didn't think ugly, but said it was like the pattern of a sofa.

Sunday, 7th April.—Lord M. was talking of some dish or other, and alluded to something in *Oliver Twist*; he read half of the 1st vol. at Panshanger. "It's all among Workhouses, and Coffin Makers, and Pickpockets," he said; "I don't like that low debasing style; it's all slang; it's just like *The Beggar's Opera*; I shouldn't think it would tend to raise morals; I don't like that low debasing view of mankind." We defended Oliver very much, but in vain. "I don't *like* those things; I wish to avoid them; I don't like them in *reality*, and therefore I don't wish to see them represented," he continued; that everything one read should be pure and elevating. Schiller and Goethe would have been shocked at such things, he said. Lehzen said they would not have disliked reading them. "She don't know her own literature," said Lord M., for that Goethe said one ought never to see anything disagreeable; he wouldn't look upon the dead; "and that's just the same thing." "It's a bad taste," he continued, "which will pass away like any other, but depend upon it, while it lasts it's a bad, depraved, vicious taste; now just read *Jonathan Wild*," he said to Lord Torrington, "and *Amelia*, and see if it isn't just the same thing." He kept us in fits of laughter by all this,—as also in talking of Lady Bulwer's book,[1] he said, "I daresay she was a scribbling woman[2] all her life."

Asked Lord M. if he approved of children calling their Parents by their names; he did not, but said all the Greys called Lord and Lady Grey, Charles and Mary[3]; "I don't like it," he said, "it's unnatural." "I like respect." He likes Sir, to a father; "I'm for forms; there's no harm in too much respect; there's no danger of there being too much of that *now*." He told an anecdote of Napoleon; when he came on board one of our ships "he saw the Lieut. take off his cap to the Captain, and he (Napoleon) said, 'That's right; I always told my people to do so, and they never would, and depend upon it that's one of the reasons why they'll

[1] In 1836 Mr. and Mrs. Bulwer were legally separated. In 1839 she published *Cheveley, or the Man of Honour*, an attack on her husband. On Bulwer seeking re-election at Hertford in June 1858, upon his appointment as Colonial Secretary, his wife appeared on the hustings and denounced him to the crowd. After her death in 1882, a book containing letters to her from her husband was published without authority and was very properly suppressed. See *ante*, p. 132.

[2] This phrase was much in vogue in the early years of the last century. Even as late as 1867, when it was thought the retirement of Lord Derby was imminent and Mr. Disraeli would succeed as leader of the Tory Party, this eminent statesman, who happened to be also the author of *Coningsby*, etc., was stigmatized as a "scribbler" by certain distinguished members of his Party who were opposed to his leadership.

[3] It was the practice at that time in certain families, and is so to this day. See *post*, p. 196.

never be a Navy.'" Lord M. told this with much emphasis and earnestness. "There must be a little of that, depend upon it, in society," continued Lord M., "it's quite a mistake to think there's anything humiliating in that." We were seated much as usual; Lord Melbourne sitting near me. He said, "You should see those Indian papers, to see what Auckland's about.[1] He then talked of the immensity of the undertaking, and I wish I could repeat all he said about it; he said it was an immense move, and there was going to be a great war; in fact, he said, it is a struggle between Russia and England, which is to have possession in the East. We depend upon Runjeet Singh, who has always been our friend, and who he says we have no reason to doubt; but he is very old; "he has an army of 70,000 disciplined troops," Lord M. said; "he is a Hindoo and not a Mahomedan, and won't allow any cows to be killed;" Lord M. said he stipulated in all the

[1] In 1837 Captain Alexander Burnes went as British agent to Kabul to arrange a commerical treaty with the Amir, Dost Mohammed. The sudden threat of a Persian attack on Herat, led by the Shah, and favoured by Russia, however, entirely altered the aspect of our relations with Afghanistan. Burnes was for confirming our friendly relations with Dost Mohammed, but the Amir's brother, Kokun Dil Khan, ruler of Kandahar, opposed this scheme and advocated friendship with Russia and Persia. See *ante*, p. 63, and Vol. I., p. 89.

Meanwhile, without consulting Burnes, Lord Auckland, instigated by Macnaghten, arranged a treaty with Ranjit Singh, who had seized Kashmir from the Afghans in 1834, whereby it was agreed that by the joint action of British and Sikh troops, Dost Mohammed, the strong usurper, should be deposed, and Shah Sooja, the legitimate but weak claimant of the throne, should be put in his place.

The failure of the Siege of Herat, owing to the skill and bravery of a young English officer, Eldred Pottinger, rendered our interference unnecessary; but Lord Auckland, none the less, carried out his unfortunate policy, which led to the first Afghan War and, in 1841, to the murder of both Burnes and Macnaghten at Kabul.

Treaties "against the killing of Kine," and that it was impossible to make him alter his mind, and no persuasions of its not being our custom could make him give way. "One can understand the origin of it," said Lord M., "the Cow being the mother of the Calf and giving milk; I have no doubt that's the origin, and with the Egyptians the same." I spoke to Lord M. of the Grand Duke's coming. "You must be very civil," said Lord M. earnestly; that the Emperor made so much of the opinion of England and of personal opinion.

Lord M. then talked again of these Indian papers, which he said I couldn't read through. "It's an immense move," said Lord M. "There'll be an immense crisis; it's coming to a crash in Central Asia; I dare say it'll be staved off for the present," but must come to something hereafter, to be decided whether England or Russia should reign there; both pushing from different sides. Lord M. talked of those pictures of Beechey. Talked of fair and dark hair; I preferred so greatly the latter. "I know it's more specious-looking to the young, but not to those who have had experience." This made me laugh. Talked of black hair becoming sooner grey; I had said fair did, to which Lord M. said, "That's a bold proposition." Talked of Queen Charlotte, whom Lord M. saw first when he was at Eton; he said she was good-natured. Lord M. said Taylor told him that in the administration of 1806, under Lord Grenville, Queen Charlotte once asked two of the Opposition in to tea; and the King was exceedingly angry, and sent Taylor to her "saying he hoped such a thing should never happen again."[1] Lord M. said the Queen (Adelaide) was

[1] It was contrary to the practice of the Sovereign at that time to

civil to him (Ld. M.). "When I was Secretary of State I used never to go near her, but used to talk to the Maids of Honour; she complained of that, but it was much better; so I used to go and talk with the girls." Lord M. said the King (William IV.) was always very civil to him. "It was a bitter dose for him to swallow in '35, to have to take us again," said Lord M. He couldn't bear Lord John. "He called him 'that young man,'" continued Lord M., "'as for that young man, I don't understand what he means.'" We then had a great deal of fun with Miss Murray, about Education, and I only wish I could repeat all Lord M. said. "You had better try to do no good," he said, "and then you'll get into no scrapes." "All that intermeddling *produces* crime," he said. But we said if people didn't know *what* was wrong, they couldn't help committing crime. "I don't believe there's anybody who doesn't know what is wrong and right," he said. He doubts education will ever do any good; says, all Government has to do "is to prevent and punish crime, and to preserve contracts." He is FOR labour and does not think the factory children are too much worked; and thinks it very wrong that parents should not be allowed to send their children who are under a certain age, to work. He said to Miss Murray, "If you'd only have the goodness to leave them alone," which made us laugh; we asked did *he* derive no benefit from education? "I derived no morality from it," he replied funnily; "that I derived at an earlier date."

Monday, 8th April.—He said there were no news

receive members of the Opposition. George III. never spoke to any leading members of the Party opposed to his Government. This practice was first departed from after the illness of the King in 1810.

from France. Lord M. said, "Palmerston lays it all to the King"; but we think this can hardly be so. Palmerston dislikes Louis Philippe, Lord M. says, on account of his conduct about Spain. Lord M. says Lord Clarendon thinks Louis Philippe wishes Spain to be divided and never to flourish. "It would be a wicked policy," continued Lord M., "and I should think a foolish one." Talked of Portugal being in an uncomfortable state. "I don't think the King thinks Louis Philippe is acting well, by his saying so little about it," said Lord M.

Tuesday, 9th April.—I observed, the Radicals couldn't gain by turning out the present Ministry, as they couldn't stand themselves. "No, they couldn't stand alone; but they like a general shuffle, as they think they may gain by it," he replied. I observed I thought the Tories couldn't stand. "I don't know," said Lord M., "they are a very powerful party." I said Palmerston told me they weren't at all prepared for Office *now*, and very much divided; "I know he thinks so," said Lord M., "but I think they are less divided." I told Lord M. I heard some people said they meant to make it[1] a general vote of Confidence, which I doubted. "It entirely depends upon what his followers may compel him to do," said Lord M. I asked what Lord John thought about it. "He thinks we shall carry it, and Stanley thinks we shall carry it," said Lord M. So, I said, everybody did but Lord M. Lord M. smiled, and said, "Oh! no, only I can't tell at all."

[1] In answer to the majority of five in the Lords against Ministers, Lord John Russell moved a vote of approval of their recent policy in Ireland. Sir R. Peel proposed an amendment deprecating any interference with the Peers' prerogatives. Amendment after four nights' debate negatived by 318 to 296.

Wednesday, 10*th April*.—Talked of the Dance at the Duchess of Gloucester's the night before; of Augusta,[1] who I said was to go out everywhere, like any other girl; Lord M. said that it was the first time a Princess of England did such a thing. "I don't think the King (George III.) would have liked that," said Lord M. "If she goes out like any other girl, she runs the risk like other girls of forming attachments," which is very true and very awkward. "She may take a liking to somebody whom she couldn't marry," he added. Talked of Stanley's having refused to take office under Peel, of their being better friends now. "I think Peel is the best of them," said Lord M., but that he didn't know him well, though he had been in office with him in '28, under the Duke of Wellington, for a short time when Lord M. was in Ireland. Talked of Peel's not being much liked[2]; Lord M. said, "A very bad manner, a very disagreeable *abord*." He don't think he means to be cross, and says, "that's all *gaucherie*." "Stanley everybody knows," said Lord M., "to be a man of great abilities, but of much indiscretion; and he is extremely unpopular"; "he says things out of place, and that you would feel he shouldn't say; he says just what he should not say." Talked of the Tories being divided between themselves; I

[1] Princess Augusta, daughter of the Duke of Cambridge. She married Frederick William, Grand Duke of Mecklenburg-Strelitz. The Grand Duchess is still in enjoyment of excellent health (1912). Her memory is a storehouse of knowledge and of intimate details of the early Victorian Court. She is an excellent correspondent, writing fluently and well, in a singularly clear and firm hand.

[2] It is well known that the Queen and the Prince became devoted to Sir R. Peel. When he died the Queen wrote: "Poor dear Peel is to be buried to-day. The sorrow and grief at his death are most touching, and the country mourns over him as over a Father. Every one seems to have lost a personal friend."

said Lord John felt almost certain of a Majority of 20, but I said to Lord M. wouldn't he be satisfied with less? "Oh! yes," he replied; "15 or 16—or 10; *I* think myself it would be very foolish resigning upon *any* majority." I said they really shouldn't make it too difficult. "I won't," said Lord M.; "if I can keep them up to it." He then said I should not forget the Seymours.[1] "She's about as handsome a woman as you can see." The beauty comes from the paternal Grandmother, a Miss Linley, who Lord M. remembers dined at Brocket in '92 when she was already dying of the consumption, which she died of in '95. Brinsley himself had "fine eyes." His 2nd wife was an Ogle, Lady Dacre's cousin, a clever, dark, and when young, he said, pretty woman; he knew her well.

Sunday, 14th April.—Told Lord M. (what I had already told him at dinner) that my Uncle had written me a cross letter.[2] I said I was very angry but didn't know if I ought to answer him sharply. Lord M. leant close towards me and said in his kindest manner, "You mustn't get into any controversy; you must waive it, and speak of something else; some allowance must be made for him; I mean you mustn't be angry with him." That he might be anxious for the fate of his family, for Belgium was a new State, her position not settled. "The King has a great many enemies in Europe; that enmity of the Emperor of Russia is no slight thing; it would

[1] See note, Vol. I., p. 192, on the Sheridan sisters.

[2] King Leopold was at this time annoyed with the British Government. "You know from experience," he wrote to the Queen, "that I never ask anything of you. I prefer remaining in the position of having rendered services without wanting any return for it but your affection."—*Letters of Queen Victoria*, vol. i., p. 170.

be a most unequal strife"; all which is most true, and was said so kindly.

Talked of different-coloured damasks, of light blue, and Lord M. said, "I don't like blue, it's an unlucky colour; I don't like a blue gown." Talked of some upholsterers; and Lord M. said, "No English tradesman has any taste"; that when he was Secretary of State (every Secretary of State,[1] he said, used to have a sum to buy plate with, which is done away with now; he was the last who had any)—he went to Garrards to choose some plate, and he said, with the exception of what he bought, everything was shocking; "I said to them, 'Good God! they are infamous!'—so clumping." I asked, had he seen any foreign things which were better?[2] He said, "No, I'm only saying what is bad,—not praising any other; I have them in my head." We asked, could he give us any designs; that, he said, he could not, "But I've the principles in me," which made us laugh. Some of my plate he admires.

Monday, 15th April.—Talked of some people, and Lord Melbourne said, "An Italian and an English makes the finest animal in the world; it's the mixture of nations that makes the finest specimens of the human race." Talked of Wilhelmine,[3] her being long-faced; he said, a Norman face; Lady Tavis-

[1] Secretaries of State and Ambassadors, as well as the Lord Lieutenants of Ireland, were allowed services of gold plate, with the Royal Arms engraved. This plate was the perquisite of the holder of the office.

[2] The plate by Rundell and Bridge made during the reign of George IV. was, some of it, of fine workmanship. At this period, however, taste deteriorated, and some of the simple plate of the Queen Anne period was "embossed" to suit the rather vulgar taste of the day.

[3] Lady Wilhelmina Stanhope. See Vol. I., p. 188.

tock, Lady Theresa, dearest Daisy, Miss Murray, were Normans.[1]

Thursday, 18th April.—Lord M. then said, "Now, Ma'am, for this other matter." I felt terrified (foolishly) when it came to the point; too silly of me to be frightened in talking to him. Well, I mustered up courage, and said that my Uncle's great wish—was—that I should marry my Cousin Albert—who was with Stockmar—and that I thought Stockmar might have told him (Ld. M.) so; Lord M. said, No—Stockmar had never mentioned a word; but, that I had said to my Uncle, I could decide nothing until I saw him again. "That's the only way," said Lord M. "How would that be with the Duchess?" he asked. I assured him he need have no fear *whatever* on that score; then he said, "Cousins are not very good things," and "Those Coburgs are not popular abroad; the Russians hate them." I then said, who was there else? We enumerated the various Princes, of whom not one, I said, would do. For myself, I said, at present *my* feeling was quite against ever marrying. "It's a great change in the situation," he said. "It's a very serious thing, both as it concerns the Political effect and your own happiness." I praised Albert very much; said he was younger than me. I said Uncle Ernest pressed me much about it; Lord M. said, if one was to *make* a man for it, one would hardly know what to make; he mustn't be stupid—nor cunning. I said, by all that I heard, Albert would just be the person; Lord M. asked if he wasn't coming; I said, he would

[1] It is also asserted that the nasal intonation, more common nowadays in America than in England, is of Saxon origin—whereas the dropping of the "aspirate" is pure Norman. A curious inversion of probabilities, if true.

come with his elder brother in the autumn. Lord M. thinks his not being the heir, a good thing; he said, he was surprised there was not more anxiety, considering the King of Hanover was the heir. "I think it would be wished for; still I don't think a foreigner would be popular," said Lord M. I observed that marrying a subject was making yourself so much their equal, and brought you so in contact with the whole family. Lord M. quite agreed in this and said, "I don't think it would be liked; there would be such jealousy." I said, why need I marry at all for 3 or 4 years? did he see the necessity? I said I dreaded the thought of marrying; that I was so accustomed to have my own way, that I thought it was 10 to 1 that I shouldn't agree with any body. Lord M. said, "Oh! but you would have it still" (my own way). : : .

Saturday, 20th April.—Received at a ¼ to 8 a box from Lord Melbourne containing a note from William Cowper, dated a ¼ p. 4 from the House of C., saying *we*[1] had a majority of 22 on Sir Robert Peel's amendment,[2] and of 218 on Mr. Duncombe's. This was indeed delightful and I feel that I can breathe again. Thank God!

Sunday, 21st April.—Talked of a very angry letter Uncle Leopold had written to Palmerston and which I saw, and which made Lord M. laugh; Uncle says, as this success of the Conference, in dishonouring Belgium, is mainly owing to England, he hopes they will rejoice in their success; Lord M. thought

[1] The Queen identified herself with her Ministers in these early years, and was in a childlike manner a strong political partisan. It must always be borne in mind that she was not twenty, and a girl. When Peel finally came into power, he received equally strong support from his Sovereign.

[2] See *ante*, p. 149.

H.S.H. Ernest Duke of Saxe-Coburg-Gotha
Father of Prince Albert
from a portrait by Dickinson after Ruprecht

the first part of the letter kind; he saw the Belgians going down to sign the Treaty, and he thought they looked cross and sulky. Lord M. said some allowance must be made, and "if people are made to do what they dislike, you must allow for a little ill-humour."

Talked of Jane Seymour, who Lord M. thinks a bad person, as she supplanted her Mistress, which I said Anne Boleyn did too, and which wasn't their fault. "It's always more the woman's fault than the man's," said Lord M. . . .

Wednesday, 24th April.—At 4 I rode out with Daisy, Lord Uxbridge, Lord Headfort, Lord Alfred, Mr. Byng, Mr. Cowper, and Col. Buckley, and came home at ½ p. 5. I rode Comptroller, who went *quite beautifully*, so safe, never shied or dropped. I rode out through Hyde Park, round Regent's Park and home by Hyde Park; it was a very pleasant evening. I met Lord Anglesey in Hyde Park, and he rode with me the whole time; he rides so well, so gracefully, it is quite wonderful[1]; and he rode a beautiful horse.

Thursday, 25th April.—Talked of Headfort's blundering; of the little Queen of Spain, with Lord Clarendon, who says she doesn't promise well and is very imperious. "I don't mind about her being imperious; if she isn't stupid, all that'll be got over," said Lord M. . . .

Friday, 3rd May.—Talked of this Copyright Bill; of Serjeant Talfourd,[2] whom Lord M. don't very much admire; of Wordsworth, whom Lady Normanby accused him of never having read. "Never read it

[1] He lost his leg at Waterloo. See Vol. I., p. 199.

[2] Talfourd, afterwards Sir Thomas, Judge of the Common Pleas, author of *Ion*, brought in several Copyright Bills. In 1841 he proposed a sixty-year limit from the author's death. Its rejection was obtained by Macaulay.

all," he said, "never read all *The Excursion*; I've gone so far as to buy the book," he continued, "I've bought the book; it's amazing when you leave a book on the table how much you know what is in it, without reading it." "I'm half smothered up with books and papers," he said, and he repeated his wish of having a bedroom with *3* libraries out of it; "I want a *suite*."

Saturday, 4th May.—At ½ p. 1 I went over to the Closet, where I received the Grand Duke,[1] who was introduced by Lord Palmerston and accompanied by Count Orloff and Count Pozzo di Borgo. I made the Grand-Duke sit down; he is tall with a fine figure, a pleasing open countenance without being handsome, fine blue eyes, a short nose and a pretty mouth with a sweet smile. Lord Palmerston then introduced Prince Henry of Orange, who is a timid young man, very like his eldest brother Prince William.[2] I then went out into the Drawing room, where the Grand Duke presented all his gentlemen.

Lord M. then told me that he had been thinking about this Bishopric of Peterborough, for the Dean,[3] and that as he had not seen him he should consider it a little; that Peterborough was a town very much divided, in which the Bishop had always gone against Lord FitzWilliam, and Lord M. fears that the Dean would not have courage to resist the Chapter, and would be carried along by Dr. Turton,[4] a very clever

[1] The Hereditary Grand Duke of Russia, afterwards the Emperor Alexander II.

[2] Prince William married, in June 1839, Sophia, daughter of William I., King of Wurtemberg. The Princess of Orange, mother of the two Princes, was Anna, daughter of the Empress Paul.

[3] The Queen's former tutor, Dr. Davys, Dean of Chester.

[4] Dr. Turton was successively Dean of Peterborough, Dean of Westminster, and Bishop of Ely.

man. I said Lord M. must do as he thought best. Lehzen handed in a letter at this moment from the Dean, in which he expressed a wish to have this Bishopric and that his feelings were *not* against the Government; Lord M. read the letter and wished to take it with him, but I would not let him do so; he said, "I think by this he wishes to have it very much"; but Lord M. said he wished to consider it a little first; he feels the awkwardness of not doing something for him, as it ought to be, he said, and is expected, and at the same time it would be so very awkward were he to go against us, and Lord M. fears, though his intentions may be the best, that he would be carried away by the Bishop of London. The Grand-Duke led me in and I sat between him and Prince Henry; Lord Melbourne sat between Lady Normanby and Miss Anson. I found the Grand-Duke exceedingly agreeable, so good-natured, natural and merry. He is just a year older than I am; Prince Henry is very good-natured, and talks English perfectly; he is not quite 19. The Grand-Duke's other gentlemen came after dinner, and I made them come up to me one by one: M. Tolstoy (a young man and attaché here), Baron Lieven (cousin to Prince Lieven), M. Patkal (a young man of the Grand-Duke's age and brought up with him), M. d'Adlerberg (also brought up with the Grand-Duke, and his father brought up with the Emperor), Prince Bariatinsky (a young man, Aide-de-Camp to the Emperor, who distinguished himself very much in the war against the Circassians and has a ball in his body), M. Zourievitch (an Aide-de-Camp of the Emperor's and who has been with the Grand-Duke for 14 years), and Prince Dolgorouki (an Aide-de-Camp of the Emperor's). They are all pleasing people and rather easy to get on with. I like the Grand-Duke extremely; he is so natural and gay and so easy to get on with.

Sunday, 5th May.—Talked of men being refused, and Lord M. said, "When I was two-and-twenty, I do believe if I had been refused I should have died of it; it would have killed me; I was so very vain." Talked of Orloff, who Lord M. said is "exactly like Henry VIII." I said I thought Henry VIII. was not near so good-natured a man as Orloff. "Oh! he was a very good-natured man," said Lord M., "just read what Dr. Lingard says of him when he first entered life; oh! he was a great man," and added that we owed the Reformation to him. I said his motives for that were not the best; but Lord M. said that didn't signify. Talked of Henry VIII. Lord M. said, "Those women bothered him so." I observed he had ill-treated Catherine of Aragon so. "That was his conscience," said Lord M. funnily; "he thought he was living in a state of concubinage, not of marriage." Talked of Queen Elizabeth and Queen Mary. "Queen Elizabeth was quite Henry VIII.'s daughter," said Lord M., and he never intended she should reign. Talked of Queen Mary and her horrid cruelty. "She thought that was quite right," said Lord M., "and Edward VI. would have done quite the same on his side; he would have killed her; there are letters which show that."

Monday, 6th May.—He then showed me a letter from Lord FitzWilliam about this Bishopric of Peterborough, in which he is anxious the Bishop of Sodor and Man should go there; Lord M. said, "You see what he wants." I said I did, but that at the same time I felt the great awkwardness of the Dean's not getting it; and I gave Lord M. the Dean's letter, which he said he would not show to anyone; there was wrong doctrine in it, he said, viz. that he wished to hold it from the Sovereign and not from the Minister. I said I feared that as he had been so much encouraged last year it would embitter him very much were he not to get it now. "I feel that," said Lord M., and "I feel that they'll say 'The Queen ought to have done something for him.'" I said I did not think he would vote against the Government, as he had refused to join an Address at Chester last year against the Government; Lord M. asked, would he like Sodor and Man, and we agreed he would not. Talked of my ride; of my having met and ridden with the Grand-Duke, and his being so easily pleased with any horse he was put on. "Oh! they're not half as fastidious as these gentlemen," said Lord M. funnily. "There's more stuff and nonsense about horses than there is about anything else."

Tuesday, 7th May.—I awoke at ½ p. 8—and heard from Lord Surrey that we had only had a majority of 5![1] This struck to my heart and I felt dreadfully anxious. Got up; heard from Lord John that we had only had a majority of 5; 294 against 289; and that they must have a Cabinet to decide what was to be done. I wrote to Lord Melbourne expressing my anxiety to hear from him; my box had scarcely gone before I received a letter from Lord Melbourne in which he stated what had taken place, that he had not yet heard from Lord John, but that he feared they had no other

[1] On the Jamaica Bill, *ante*, p. 108. The division was actually on the question of Sir R. Peel's motion, "That the Speaker do now leave the chair," at the end of the Jamaica Constitution debate.

alternative—can *I write it*[1]—but to resign; and he concluded his letter in this *beautiful* way:—"Lord Melbourne is certain that Your Majesty will not deem him too presuming if he expresses his fear that this decision will be both painful and embarrassing to Your Majesty, but Your Majesty will meet this crisis with that firmness which belongs to your character, and with that rectitude and sincerity which will carry Your Majesty through all difficulties. It will also be greatly painful for Lord Melbourne to quit the service of a Mistress who has treated him with such unvarying kindness and unlimited confidence, but in whatever station he may be placed he will always feel the deepest anxiety for Your Majesty's interests and happiness and will do the utmost in his power to promote and secure them." Lehzen, ever kind and good, supported and comforted me under this most heavy trial. I heard again from Lord Melbourne enclosing a note from Lord John, who concurred in his opinion. At 10 m. p. 12 came Lord Melbourne and stayed with me till 25 m. to 1. It was some minutes before I could muster up courage to go in. "You will not forsake me." I held his hand for a little while, unable to leave go; and he gave me such a look of kindness, pity and affection, and could hardly utter for tears, "Oh! no," in such a touching voice. We then sat down as usual, and I strove to calm myself. He said, "I was afraid this would happen." There was a Warrant appointing an Inquiry into the Duchy of Cornwall which he begged me to sign; which I did. "I'm afraid we can do nothing else," he said (but resign). I said I feared he was right. "But we shall see what they say at the Cabinet; I'll put

[1] See *ante*, p. 154, note upon the partisanship of the Queen.

down on paper the course I think you ought to pursue," which I begged he would. He told me when he would come after the Cabinet. Wrote my journal. At 3 came Lord John, who said they had been discussing the whole in the Cabinet very much, but that they could come to no other determination but to resign; and he then thanked me for my kindness—which quite set me off crying, and I said it was a terrible thing for me. He seemed much grieved; he said he hardly expected it, and that the Tories had behaved very ill, and made every exertion to arrive at this end.

At a ¼ p. 3 Lord Melbourne came to me and stayed with me till ½ p. 4. He said, "Lord John has communicated to you the results of the Cabinet," which I said he had; "and I have desired John Russell to make out the Bishop of Peterborough directly,"[1] for which I thanked Lord M. very much, as I said I could not bear to think he should owe it to the others. "And you'll tell the Baroness to write to him to tell him so." And he then said he wished to make either Mr. Cowper or Mr. Anson this Commissioner at Greenwich. Lord Melbourne then said, pulling a paper out of his pocket, "I have written down what I think you should do." He then read to me what he had written down for me.[2] The conclusion of the paper was, "Your Majesty had better express your hope that none of Your Majesty's Household, except those who are engaged in Politics, may be removed." Lord Melbourne said, "I think you might ask him for that." I quite agreed in this and we enumerated

[1] This was the elevation of Dr. Davys to the See of Peterborough. See *ante*, p. 156.

[2] See the memorandum in *The Letters of Queen Victoria*, Vol. I.

who those were;—"Unless you wish to get rid of any," which I said I did not. Talked of my great dislike to some of these people—Sir H. Hardinge—Graham—Peel.[1] "I don't know who they'll put about you," he said. I said it was so hard to have people forced upon you whom you disliked; Lord M. said, "It is very hard, but it can't be helped." I said I thought Lord John was very low. "He was melancholy at seeing you melancholy," said Lord M. Lord M. asked if I had put off the Levée, which I wrote to ask him if I might, and I said I had. The Ball we could reflect about. Lord M. was going to announce his resignation in the House of Lords. I said I was not going out, and I wished Lord M. would come to me. "Yes, Ma'am, I will," he said; and then after a pause he added, "I don't think it would be right"; he said it would be observed; I pressed him and said it would not be, and if he would come after dinner; he said it wouldn't do; and "I'm going to dine at Lady Holland's." But I said he must come and see me. "Oh! yes," he replied, "only not while these negotiations are going on." I said, "For I shall feel quite forsaken," at which he gave me such a look of grief and feeling, and was much affected. He said, "God bless you, Ma'am," and kissed my hand. He said, "I'll come to see you to-morrow morning before the Duke comes," and we settled at 11. I said I would appoint the Duke at one, as Lord M. did not wish to meet him. The whole would be known all over the town in a short time, he said. He then got up, and we shook hands again and he kissed my hand, he said; "God bless you, Ma'am." I fear I

[1] All these "dislikes" evaporated when the Queen ultimately became acquainted with her Tory Ministers.

may have left out much and not placed all rightly; but so much has taken place before I have been able to write this account that I am quite confused. I was in a dreadful state of grief. I received two most kind letters from Lord Melbourne, in the 1st of which he said, "Lord Melbourne felt his attendance upon Your Majesty to be at once the greatest honour and pleasure of his life, and Your Majesty may believe that he will most severely and deeply feel the change." How kind! He further adds that "nothing ever gave him more pain" than to have to tell me he couldn't come to me; but that it was absolutely necessary not to give occasion to any jealousy or suspicion. I wrote once more to him. Wrote one line to the Duke of Wellington to request him to come.

Wednesday, 8th May.—Talked of the Duke of W.'s being so deaf; and Lord M. said, "Mind the Duke understands what you say." "You must try and get over your dislike for Peel," he said, "he's a close, stiff man."[1] Talked of John Russell's being so low. "He was very much affected at seeing you," replied Lord M. "I met him coming away. Rice says he's glad." "I think the Chancellor feels it. Palmerston will feel it, he likes his business so much." I then (10 m. to 1) went over to the Yellow Closet where I found the Duke of Wellington, who was kind; he remained till 10 m. p. 1. Wrote to Sir Robert Peel to come immediately—who came at 20 m. p. 2 and stayed till 20 m. to 3. I saw him

[1] Melbourne had never lost a chance of trying to create good feeling between the Queen and Sir R. Peel. On one occasion, at a Court Ball, he noticed that Peel stood proudly aloof, and going up to him he whispered with great earnestness, "For God's sake go and speak to the Queen." Peel, however, made no move. An episode characteristic of both men.

also in the Closet. He was also in full dress. The best account I can give of these interviews is in the annexed copy of a letter I wrote to my kind friend Lord Melbourne.[1]

BUCKINGHAM PALACE,
8*th May*, 1839.

The Queen told Lord Melbourne she would give him an account of what passed, which she is *very* anxious to do. She saw the Duke for about 20 minutes; the Queen said she supposed he knew why she sent for him, upon which the Duke said, No, he had no idea. The Queen then said that she had had the greatest confidence in her late Ministry, and had parted with them with the greatest reluctance; upon which the Duke observed that he could assure me no one felt more pain in hearing the announcement of their resignation than he did, and that he was deeply grieved at it. The Queen then continued, that as his party had been instrumental in removing them, she must look to him to form a new Government. The Duke answered that he had no power whatever in the House of Commons, "that if he was to say black was white[2] they would say it was not," and that he advised me to send for Sir Robert Peel, in whom I could place confidence, and who was a gentleman and a man of honour and integrity. The Queen then said she hoped he would at all events have a place in the new Cabinet. The Duke at first rather refused, and said he was so deaf, and so old and unfit for any discussion, that if he were to consult his own feelings he would rather not do it,

[1] This letter has already been printed (*Letters of Queen Victoria*, vol. i. 198).

[2] *Sic:* an obvious mistake for "black was black."

Walker & Boutall ph. sc.

The Duke of Wellington and Sir Robert Peel

from the picture by Winterhalter in the possession of His Majesty the King.

and remain quite aloof; but that as he was very anxious to do anything that would tend to the Queen's comfort, and would do everything and at all times that could be of use to the Queen, and therefore if she and her Prime Minister urged his accepting office, he would. The Queen said she had more confidence in him than in any of the others of his party. The Queen then mentioned the subject of the Household and of those who were not in Parliament. The Duke did not give any decisive answer about it, but advised the Queen not to begin with conditions of this sort, and wait till the matter was proposed. The Queen then said that she felt certain he would understand the great friendship she had for Lord Melbourne, who had been to her quite a parent, and the Duke said no one felt and knew that better than he did, and that no one could still be of greater use to the Queen than Lord Melbourne. The Duke spoke of his personal friendship for Lord Melbourne, and that he hoped I knew that he had often done all he could to help your Government. The Queen then mentioned her intention to prove her great *fairness* to her new Government in telling them, that they might know there was no unfair dealing, that I meant to see you often as a friend, as I owed *so* much to you. The Duke said he quite understood it, and knew I would not exercise this to weaken the Government, and that he would take my part about it, and felt for me. He was very kind, and said he called it "a misfortune" that you had all left me.

The Queen wrote to Peel, who came after 2, embarrassed and put out. The Queen repeated what she had said to the Duke about her former Government, and asked Sir Robert to form a new Ministry.

He does not seem sanguine; says entering the Government in a minority is very difficult; he felt unequal to the task, and far from exulting in what had happened, as he knew what pain it must give me; he quite approved that the Duke should take office, and saw the importance of it; meant to offer him the post of Secretary for Foreign Affairs, and if he refused, Lord Aberdeen; Lord Lyndhurst, Chancellor; hoped to secure Stanley and Graham; Goulburn to be the candidate for the Speaker's chair; he expects a severe conflict then, and if he should be beat must either resign or dissolve Parliament. Before this the Queen said how much she was against a dissolution, in which he quite agreed, but of course wished no conditions should be made; he felt the task arduous, and that he would require me to demonstrate (*a certain* degree, if *any*, I can only feel) confidence in the Government, and that my Household would be one of the marks of that. The Queen mentioned the same thing about her Household, to which he at present would give no answer, but said nothing should be done without my knowledge or approbation. He repeated his surprise at the course you had all taken in resigning, which he did not expect. The Queen talked of her great friendship for, and gratitude to, Lord Melbourne, and repeated what she had said to the Duke, in which Peel agreed; but he is such a cold odd man she can't make out what he means. He said he couldn't expect me to have the confidence in him I had in you (and which he never can have), as he has not deserved it. My impression is, he is not *happy* and sanguine. He comes to me to-morrow at one to report progress in his formation of the new Government. The Queen don't like his manner after—oh! how different, how dreadfully so, to that frank, open, natural and most kind, warm manner of Lord Melbourne. The Duke I like by far better than Peel. The Queen trusts Lord Melbourne will excuse this long letter, but she was so anxious he should know all. The Queen was very much collected, civil and high, and betrayed no agitation during these two trying Audiences. But afterwards again *all* gave way. She feels Lord Melbourne will understand it, amongst enemies to those she most relied on and most esteemed; but what is worst of all is the being deprived of seeing Lord Melbourne as she used to do.

Thursday, 9th May.—Wrote to Lord Melbourne; got such a kind delightful long letter from him in answer to my two letters of the day before, approving of my conduct and giving me the most noble, impartial and kind advice as to what I was to do,—begging me not to mind Sir Robert's manner.[1] He said I should urge strongly to keep those of my people about me, who were not in Parliament; he was well, he said; had been at this Scotch dinner of about 40 or 50 members; O'Connell there, and all the speeches very satisfactory. I wrote to him again; signed; wrote my journal. Heard from Lord Melbourne again, about the Members of the Household who were not in Parliament, in which letter he said they had never been removed at any time before,[2]

[1] Peel's manner during his interviews with the Queen was said to have been peremptory and harsh.

[2] Lord Melbourne, in after-years, blamed himself for not having warned the Queen, and prepared her mind for extensive changes in her Household. There was no doubt also some misapprehension as to the extent of Peel's requirement. Sixty years later, in a conversation at Osborne with Sir Arthur Bigge (now Lord Stamfordham), the Queen said, "I was very young then, and perhaps I should act

and that if I said he (Sir R. Peel) pressed me harder than any Sovereign ever had been pressed before,—he thought Sir Robert couldn't refuse. Wrote my journal. At a little after 1 I went over to the Yellow Closet, where I received Sir Robert Peel, who remained till a little before 2. The annexed copy of a note which I wrote in a great hurry to Lord M. will show what took place[1]:

BUCKINGHAM PALACE,
9th May, 1839.

The Queen writes one line to prepare Lord Melbourne for what *may* happen in a very few hours. Sir Robert has behaved very ill, he insisted on my giving up my Ladies, to which I replied that I *never* would consent, and I never saw a man so frightened; he said he must go to the Duke of Wellington and consult with him, when both would return—and he said this must suspend all further proceedings, and he asked if I would be ready to receive a decision, which I said I would; he was quite perturbed. I said, besides many other things, that if he or the Duke of W. had been at the head of the Government when I came to the Throne, perhaps there might have been a *few* more Tory Ladies, but that then if you had come into office you would *never* have *dreamt* of changing them. I was calm but very decided, and I think you would have been

differently if it was all to be done again." In anticipation of the change of Government in 1841, after confidential communications between Mr. Anson and Sir Robert Peel, the Queen waived her right to appoint great officers of State, and also (if in Parliament) lords-in-waiting, equerries and grooms-in-waiting. She also announced that she would mention to the Prime Minister before appointment the names of ladies of the bedchamber, but not those of the maids of honour or women of the bedchamber.

[1] Already printed (*Letters of Queen Victoria*, vol. i. p. 204).

pleased to see my composure and great firmness. Keep yourself in readiness, for you may soon be wanted.

Saw Lord Howick. At ½ p. 2 I saw the Duke of Wellington. I remained firm, and he told Sir Robert that I remained firm. I then saw Sir Robert Peel, who stopped a few minutes with me; he said he must consult those (of which I annex a List) who he had named; and he said he would return in 2 or 3 hours with the result, which I said I should await.

First Lord of the Treasury and Chancellor of the Exchequer	Sir Robert Peel, Bart.
Secretary for Foreign Affairs	The Duke of Wellington
Secretary for the Home Department	Sir James Graham
Secretary for the Colonies	Lord Stanley
Lord Chancellor	Lord Lyndhurst
President of the Board of Control	Lord Ellenborough
Secretary at War	Sir Henry Hardinge
Lord Lieut. of Ireland	Earl de Grey

Received a letter from Lord M. in answer to my 1st; and also to my 2nd, greatly astonished. Wrote to him again and my journal. At 10 m. p. 5 Sir Robert Peel returned, and said that he had consulted with those who were (*to have been*) his Colleagues, and that they agreed that with the probability of being beat the first night about the Speaker, and beginning with a Minority in the House of Commons, that unless there was *some* (I ask *all*; the *Officers of State* and *Lords* I gave up) demonstration of my confidence, and if I retained all my Ladies, "they agreed unanimously they could not go on!" I replied I would reflect; that I felt certain I should not change my mind, but that I should not do anything in a hurry and would write him my decision either that evening or the next morning; he said meanwhile he would suspend all further proceedings. This was *quite* wonderful! The Ladies his only support!! What an admission of weakness! I wrote to Lord Melbourne (from whom I received another note) and begged him to come as soon as possible. Wrote my journal.

At ½ p. 6 came my dear and excellent Lord Melbourne, who stayed with me till 10 m. p. 7. It was a true and real and unexpected happiness to see him again after so much anxiety. I began by giving him a detailed account of the whole Proceeding, which I shall state here as briefly as I can. I first related again what took place in the 2 first Interviews, and when I said that the Duke said he had assisted my Government often very much, Lord M. said, "Well, that's true enough, but the Duke did all he could about this vote." Well, then, I said, when Sir Robert Peel came this morning, he began first about the Ministry; I consented, though I said I might have my personal feelings about Lord Lyndhurst and Lord Aberdeen,[1] but that I would suppress every personal feeling and would be quite fair. Lord M. here observed, "You did say that." I then proceeded that I repeated that I wished to retain about me those who were not in Parliament; and Sir Robert *pretended* that I had the preceding day expressed a wish to keep about me those who *were* in Parliament; I mentioned my wish to have

[1] The Queen became much attached to Lord Aberdeen. See *post*, p. 208.

Lord Liverpool, to which he readily acceded, saying he would offer him the place of Lord Steward or of Lord-in-Waiting; he then suggested my having Lord Ashley, which I said I should like, as Treasurer and Comptroller. Soon after this, Sir Robert said, "Now about the Ladies,"—upon which I said I could *not* give up *any* of my Ladies, and never had imagined such a thing; he asked if I meant to retain *all*; *all*, I said; the Mistress of the Robes and the Ladies of the Bedchamber? he asked. I replied *all*; for he said they were the Wives of the Opponents of the Government; mentioning Lady Normanby in particular, as one of the late Ministers' wives. I said that would not interfere, I never talked Politics with them, and that they were related, many of them, to Tories; and I enumerated those of my Bedchamber Women and Maids of Honour; upon which he said he didn't mean *all* the Bedchamber Women and *all* the Maids of Honour, he meant the Mistress of the Robes and the Ladies of the Bedchamber,—to which I replied *they* were of more consequence than the others, and I could *not* consent, and that it had never been done before; he said I was a Queen Regnant, and that made the difference; not here, I said,—and I maintained my right. Sir Robert then urged upon public grounds only,—but I said here I could not consent; he then begged to be allowed to consult with the Duke upon such an important matter; I expressed a wish also to see the Duke if Sir Robert approved, which he said he did,—and that he would return with the Duke—if I would then be prepared for the decision, —which I said I would. Well, I said, that the Duke and Sir Robert returned soon, and I first saw the Duke, who first talked of his being ready to take the post of Secretary for F. Affairs, which I had pressed Peel to urge upon him (the Duke having first wished to be in the Cabinet without accepting office), and the Duke said, "I'm able to do anything"—for I asked him if it would not be too much for him. Then I told the Duke that I had "been very well satisfied with Sir Robert yesterday,"—and asked the Duke if Sir Robert had told him what had passed about the Ladies; he said he had, and I then repeated all my arguments, and the Duke his,—but the Duke and Sir Robert differed considerably on 2 points; the Duke said the *opinions* of the Ladies were nothing, but that it was the *principle* whether the Minister could remove the Ladies or not; and that he had understood it was stated, in the Civil List Bill, "that the *Ladies were instead of the Lords*," which is quite false, and I told the Duke that there were not 12 Lords, as the expense *with* the Ladies would have been too great. Lord M. said, "There you had the better of him, and what did he say?" Not much, I replied. I repeated many of my arguments, all which pleased Lord M. and which he agreed to; amongst others—that I said to the Duke, was Sir Robert so weak that *even* the Ladies must be of his opinion? The Duke denied that. The Duke then took my decision to Sir Robert, who was waiting in the next room; after a few minutes Sir Robert returned—and I have already related what then took place. I also told Lord M. that I said to Sir Robert that as I had wished him to be frank, he would wish me to be so; and I therefore said that he must make allowance for my feelings, as I had been always brought up in very strong feelings on the other (Whig) side, and that my feelings had always been very strongly with my Government, therefore my feelings could not easily change, though I might be fair; and Lord M. approved all, and saw and said I could not do otherwise. I acted quite alone, I said, and feared I might have embarrassed the Government. "I must summon the Cabinet," said Lord M., "at once; it may have very serious consequences; if we can't go on with this House of Commons, we may have to dissolve Parliament, and we don't know if we may get as good a House of Commons."

I received the following letter from Lord M., written at one o'clock:—"Lord Melbourne presents his humble duty to Your Majesty. The Cabinet has sate until now and after much discussion advises Your Majesty to return the following answer to Sir Robert Peel: "The Queen having considered the proposal made to her yesterday by Sir Robert Peel to remove the Ladies of her Bedchamber cannot consent to adopt a course which she conceives to be contrary to usage and repugnant to her feelings." I immediately wrote a few lines in answer to Lord Melbourne, and copied the letter to Sir R. Peel.

Friday, 10th May.—At 7 m. to 2 Lord Melbourne came to me and stayed with me till 10 m. to 3. He was well; rode here, and asked how I was. I placed in his hands Sir Robert Peel's answer which he read. He started at one part where he says "some changes,"—but some or all, I said were the same,—and Lord M. said, "I must submit this to the Cabinet." Lord M. showed me a letter from Lord Grey about it,—a good deal alarmed, thinking I was right, and yet half doubtful; one from Rice dreadfully frightened and wishing the Whig Ladies should resign; and one from Lansdowne wishing to state that the Ladies would have resigned.

Lord M. had also seen the Duke of Richmond; and Lord M. said we might be beat; I said I never would yield; and would never apply to Peel again. Lord M. said, "You are for standing out, then?" I said certainly. I asked how the Cabinet felt; John Russell strongly for standing out, he said; Duncannon very much so; Holland, Lord Minto, Hobhouse, the Chancellor—all for standing out, Thomson too, and Normanby also; Rice and Howick alarmed.[1] We talked over the whole thing again; I said, in which he agreed, I couldn't wait to hear from him how to act; I was compelled to act alone. Lord M. was very kind, said they must have a Cabinet next day; the Cabinet had come to his house at 10; he would come to the Ball, as it was better he should, and promised to send John Russell to me.—Saw Lord John from a ¼ p. 4 to a ¼ to 5, to whom I repeated the whole; we quite agreed, and I said to him I hoped they would stand by me, as I had stood by them so long and always would, and he said they would as long as they possibly could.

At 10 I went as usual into the 1st Ballroom, where were all my people. Little Adolphus Chichester, poor Lord Templemore's son,[2] kissed hands as Page; a very pretty boy. The Grand-Duke, attended by Count Orloff, Prince Henry of Orange, Aunt Gloucester, and the Duke and Duchess of Cambridge and Augusta, joined us in that room. At ½

[1] But afterwards, when the Queen's letters to Melbourne of 8th and 9th May were read, Lord Broughton (Hobhouse) records that their reading "gave a new spirit to our waverers, and even Howick and Rice owned that it was impossible to abandon such a Queen and such a woman." The "woman" was only nineteen years old.

[2] Lord Templemore had married Lord Anglesey's daughter, and died in 1837. Adolphus Chichester died, aged thirty, in 1855.

p. 10 we went in; it was rather formal, and everybody looked preoccupied; Lord Melbourne was standing near the door of the larger ballroom, and I talked to him for a little while. When I had made the *cercle*, dancing began; I danced 1st with the Grand-Duke; 2ndly with the Prince of Orange (the Grand-Duke and Lady Fanny being my Vis-à-vis), and 3rdly with Lord Mulgrave. After the 1st Quadrille, Peel and the Duke of Wellington came by looking very much put out. All my friends were very kind. Lord Melbourne came up to me and asked me some questions; he assured me he was quite well; I think he went away immediately afterwards. We then went into the other room, where I danced with Prince Dolgorouki, and then with Lord Douglas; at 1 we went to supper. After supper the dancing became much more animated. I danced with Lord March; then with Lord Bruce.[1] We had a Mazurka, which really did very well. Lady Cowper sat near me for some time and was so happy at what had taken place. We then went again into the smaller ball-room, and saw two Reels danced—the Grand-Duke sitting near me—and I concluded the Ball with a Quadrille with the Grand-Duke. I left the Ball-room at a $\frac{1}{4}$ p. 3, much pleased, as my mind felt happy.

Saturday, 11th May.—Lord M. then said, pulling a paper out of his pocket, "Now, Ma'am, for what we have been about; we've had a long sitting of it; from $\frac{1}{2}$ p. 12 till now" (5). "This is what you've

[1] George William Frederick, son of the first Marquess of Ailesbury: he was born in 1804, and married in 1837 Mary, daughter of the eleventh Earl of Pembroke. He was summoned to the House of Lords as Baron Bruce in 1839, and succeeded his father, as second Marquess of Ailesbury, in 1856.

probably never seen, and which is only done on great occasions, a Cabinet Minute." He then read it to me, and was very much affected indeed in reading the part, that they consented to retain office and would support me. I grasped his hand in both mine with real feelings of the greatest gratitude; and he then read what was Lord Howick's opinion, who differs from them, but agrees in their endeavours to support me.

PRESENT

The Lord Chancellor	The Lord John Russell
The Lord President	The Viscount Palmerston
The Lord Privy Seal	The Viscount Howick
Viscount Melbourne	The Viscount Morpeth
The Marquis of Normanby	Sir John Hobhouse, Bart.
The Earl of Minto	The Chancellor of the Exchequer
The Chancellor of the Duchy of Lancaster	Mr. Thomson

Her Majesty's confidential servants having taken into consideration the letter addressed by Her Majesty to Sir Robert Peel on the 10th of May, and the reply of Sir Robert Peel on the same day, are of opinion that for the purpose of giving to an administration that character of efficiency and stability and these . . . [1] of the constitutional support of the Crown which are required to enable it to act usefully for the public service, it is reasonable that the great offices of the Court and the situations in the Household held by members of either House of Parliament should be included in the habitual

[1] In Lord Melbourne's original paper, the words appear to be "*those marks.*"

arrangements made on a change of administration; but they are not of opinion that a similar principle should be applied or extended to the offices held by Ladies in Her Majesty's Household. Her Majesty's confidential servants are therefore prepared to support Her Majesty in refusing to assent to the removal of the Ladies of her Household which Her Majesty conceived to be contrary to usage and which is repugnant to her feelings, and are prepared to continue in their offices on these grounds.

Lord M. said, "That is if Your Majesty thinks proper"; which of course I did, and felt most grateful; he said he would give me a copy of it, when he had copied it. "You know the success of this is doubtful," said Lord M.; I said I felt that, but that I could not apply to Peel again; Lord M. said it would be difficult to pass him over. Lord M. said, "If I had thought that this demand would be made, I would have told you to ask Sir Robert to put his proposition down in writing"; I went and fetched Sir Robert's letter and proved to Lord M. that though Sir Robert *might* deny it, he had stated "the Chief Appointments" of the Ladies, which makes us quite safe. I repeated that I maintained I had the power about my Ladies, else what power had I left!—in which Lord M. agreed.

Sunday, 12th May.—At 12 I went to the Chapel Royal and came back at a ¼ p. 2. I was loudly cheered both going and returning, and expressions of, "The Queen for ever," "God bless Your Majesty," "Bravo," were heard.[1] Talked of my having expressed a wish to Peel that Ireland should

[1] The Queen, at this time, was popular in the streets, but not in the "salons."

be very mildly governed; of Peel's not being sanguine from the beginning; of Lord Winchester's[1] having been with the late King but always having voted with the Government; of Sir H. Taylor being a Tory, but a fair man. Talked of the Grand-Duke and my having told him all, which Lord M. said "was a very good thing"; and his being very much pleased at what had taken place, which Lord M. was almost surprised at. I asked Lord M. if he thought John Russell liked to be out; Lord M. said, "I think he is rather tired, but I don't think he would have liked to have been out *long*; Palmerston is the most ingenuous about it; he says, 'I don't at all conceal that I think it a great bore to go out; I like power, I think power very pleasant'"; and I said Palmerston did it so well, and that how could the Duke of Wellington ever have done it? "They tell me that he never could have done it. It would only be putting it off for a step, for another man (of his Party) couldn't do it; you must come to him," said Lord M. "I myself shouldn't object to leave the Ballot an open question like the Corn Laws." I said, couldn't John Russell do that? "I don't well see how he could," Lord M. replied. I said to Lord M., what he had once told me, that he wasn't very much for the Reform Bill. "I wasn't very much for it," he said, "I saw it was unavoidable. I was for standing firm and doing nothing at all," he said; as he knew when once begun you must go on.

Talked of how they bury people at Venice in some horrid way; Lord M. said, "I'm not well acquainted with the dead; I hate to look on the

[1] Charles Ingoldsby, thirteenth Marquess.

dead; *I* like what is joyous and agreeable; I can't bear what's disagreeable and melancholy." He said, "A Troubadour said once, 'I don't wish to go to Heaven where the Priests and the Monks are; I wish to go where the Ladies and the Troubadours are.'" I then told him Mamma had said Lord M. came too often to me; upon which Lord M. said, "The Duke of Wellington said that was right; and that if he was me, he would establish himself in the Palace," which I said I wished he would. We then talked for some time about Cookery, and Lord M. made us laugh very much about it. "Oh! the French are the first nation in the world; we ought to be eternally grateful to them," he said; for that the art of preparing food was the 1st thing in the world; although the French cookery wasn't as good as it used to be. Lord M. talked of when all this was introduced into France. "Francis I. was the first who introduced that gaiety; he was the first king who had that gay liberty, which has since been so much practised," he said, snapping his fingers and laughing. He also made us laugh about Confectioners, and praised mine.

He then talked of our Army going up to Kandahar, and having gone so prosperously; and he said the Boatmen who brought them along the river, asked them, "Where are you going to?" and when they said to Kandahar, they said, "God! we'll go with you; you pay us, and you don't murder, you don't pillage! God! we'll go with you!"

After dinner, when Lord Melbourne came into the room, he remained talking with me some time before we sat down, near the chimney. Talked of Sir Robert Peel, and my feeling so happy. "You mustn't be sure that you have escaped yet," he said.

Lord M. said, "You must remember that he (Peel) is a man who is not accustomed to talk to Kings; a man of quite a different calibre; it's not like me; I've been brought up with Kings and Princes. I know the whole Family, and know exactly what to say to them; now he has not that ease, and probably you were not at your ease." These are *nearly* his words I think. He said the Marylebone Vestry had voted an Address to support me, in spite of Lord Kenyon's [1] endeavours to prevent it. Talked of the demonstrations towards me, and Lord M. said, "If there's a feeling in the country it's all over with them." Talked of their having quarrelled with the Duke of Buckingham,[2] who Lord M. said is a man of no capacity whatever; the late Duke [3] was very clever, he said.

We were seated much as usual, Lord Melbourne sitting near me. He was very much excited the whole evening, talking to himself and pulling his hair about, which always makes him look so much handsomer. He talked of India, its going on so well, our coming too close (Russia and England), and we talked over what he has often said to me before, of which (if 2 Nations were to govern the World) should be master; and that he meant to talk to Orloff about it before he went. Lord M. asked if I could read the Minute, which I said I could perfectly.

[1] George, second Lord Kenyon, succeeded his father, the Lord Chief Justice, in 1802.

[2] This, the second Duke of the 1822 creation, was the author of the "Tenant at Will," or "Chandos," clause of the Reform Act. Owing to his extravagance, he was compelled to sell the contents of his house at Stowe.

[3] For many years M.P. for Bucks, he supported Pitt and (his uncle) Lord Grenville. He held a small office in the Ministry of the latter in 1806–7. His was the only Dukedom created by George IV.

"I used to write a very ugly hand," he said, "but it used to be a very legible hand; and now I've got to write a hand that almost nobody can read; what I judge from is, that when I read it over myself I can't read it, and so I think if *I* can't read it nobody else can." Talked of handwriting; his brother's; mine; and he said, "The letter you wrote me this morning was beautifully written." I caught his eye when he was frowning very much, and he smiled and rubbed his forehead and said, "Never mind, I was only knitting my brows; I know it looks tremendous," but that one shouldn't judge from expression, that very susceptible people constantly changed expression. I said he was very absent sometimes; "Notoriously so," he said, "particularly when I've a great deal to do."

Talked of Lord Howe's[1] having been allowed to remain, though many wished Lord M. to remove him, but he did not wish it. Lord M. said, one day at Windsor Howe took Lord M. by the arm, led him into the Gallery, and said, "I must vote against you," upon the Irish Bill. "'God!' I said, 'don't,'" continued Lord Melbourne, "'stay away'; 'I must,' he said, 'I've spoken so strongly against it in Leicestershire, I never can show my face at Gopsal again if I don't,' he said; 'Well then,' I said, 'go to the House of Lords, sit on one of the back benches, and vote against us.' He went to the House of Lords, voted against us, and never a word was said about it." Lord M. thought this frank, for he offered to resign, which he says it would have been justifiable to have made him do, but which he (Ld. M.) didn't like to do. "I haven't such a bad opinion of Howe," he said; "he's a wicked hypo-

[1] Lord Chamberlain to Queen Adelaide. See Vol. I., p. 289.

crite,"—which made me laugh. Talked of there being my Balls; of Aunt Gloster's sending me the List and asking me to strike out and put in who I liked. "That's the right way; she's a King's daughter," said Lord M. Lord M. said he was well, but very much excited. Talked of Persia, and these boatmen, and Lord M. said, "An army that *pays* is the greatest blessing a country can have"; that there, where the people were unaccustomed to it, they were quite delighted, and that it made much more effect than it would here.

Monday, 13th May.—Talked of John Russell's having said he wished to resign. Lord M. said, "That would be ruin to us, it would quite ruin the character of the Government." Lord M. had heard from the Duke of W., who did not intend saying anything unless it was begun by others; and consequently Lord M. did not intend either saying anything. Talked of Sir Robert Peel; of what John Russell meant to say; of the lies that were being told of the whole affair. The House of Lords immensely full, Lord M. said. "Must say something one day," he said, "having taken my seat without saying anything after having resigned." He did so on Friday too. "Such a thing never happened before," he said. "He (Peel) spoke very highly of Your Majesty," said Lord M. "He said, nothing could be more gracious than your manner, nor more feeling than the manner in which you mentioned your late Government, and nothing more constitutional than the manner" in which I gave way about the Government. "I hear John had plenty of precedents," continued Lord M., "in the reign of Queen Anne"; and he mentioned Lady Sunderland, who he said was very violent and "known by the name of the

H.R.H. THE DUCHESS OF GLOUCESTER.

From a portrait by Sir W. Ross.

little Whig"; she was one of the Duke of Marlborough's daughters.

Lord Uxbridge had heard part of Peel's speech, and said one part was very vulgar!! I got a box from Lord John after dinner with the following account:—"Lord John Russell has the honour to report that he this day made his statement to the House in answer to Sir Robert Peel. Sir Robert Peel made a skilful and not unfair statement. He however spoke only of his intention of changing some of the Ladies of the Bedchamber. But he did not say that he had made this intention clear to Your Majesty; only that he had so arranged the matter with his political friends. The popular impression is greatly in favour of the course pursued by Your Majesty." I sent this down to Lord Melbourne, and when he came into the drawing-room I asked him if he had seen it, and he said, "That's very satisfactory." I sat down near the fire, and Lord Melbourne sat next to me. I asked him if he liked my dress; and he said he thought it beautiful. Talked of Garcia wishing to bring her mother with her, as she was so young. Lord M. said that formerly that was not allowed in the Green Room, and that they said, "If a girl can't take care of herself without her Mother, she can't do so with her." Lord M. said he remembered one of the actresses told him in the Green Room one day, that there was some woman whose daughter was going upon the stage, who came crying and saying her daughter was too good to come upon the stage, but would have to do so; "upon which Mrs. Siddons and Mrs. Mountain,[1] who were pinks of propriety, drew up" as if it was a reflection upon themselves. . . .

[1] Mrs. Rosoman Mountain (who died in 1841) was an actress of

Thursday, 16th May.—I said he had a much better opinion of Peel than I had. "You must remember he is so very reserved," said Lord M. Lord M. said, "Nobody ever gave up the Household so completely as William IV." [1] I said I did also. "I think you were quite right to reserve your ladies," added Lord M. He said, "that Lord Grey was accused of having said in 1812 that he would ride roughshod through Carlton House; he swears he never said it, but it made a great effect at the time." He meant by that, changing the whole Household, Lord Melbourne said. When Lord Grenville and Mr. Fox came in, in 1806, which they did as there was nobody else, and George III. was obliged to take them "very much against his will, I believe," Lord M. continued, "they asked the King" for some of the Household to be given up as a mark of confidence, and "he scratched out the name of Lord Sandwich, Master of the Buckhounds; only one." "There was some delicacy in that," said Lord M., "as Lord Sandwich left Mr. Fox, and the King knew he would be the one most agreeable for them to remove." I said Peel never came up to me at Gloucester House. "Stupid man," said Lord M. "When I came to the Duchess of Gloucester's," continued Lord M., "I met Lord Fitzgerald, whom I know very well, and I took him by the arm and said to him, 'Now mind Peel goes up to the Queen,' and he nodded his head as if to say, 'I know what you mean.'" Lord M. thought it "natural too."

considerable attainments, especially in musical pieces. She had a large *répertoire*, and made a great success at Drury Lane as Polly in *The Beggar's Opera*.

[1] William IV. allowed his Ministers a very free hand in the selection of his "official" Household.

"I never went near Queen Adelaide, and I believe she was very much annoyed at it. I used to go chattering with the Maids of Honour," continued Lord M., "it's much pleasanter." . . .

Saturday, 18th May.—Lord Morpeth talked of the Horticultural Society, and Lord M. said, "I took my name off about 12 years ago, when a man ran away with £12,000; somehow I hate *societies*, I think they always lead to mischief, they are always for the benefit of the Banker and the Treasurer."

Sunday, 19th May.—Lord M. said he was quite well, and when I said I thought him not well, the night before, he said, "Only sleepy; that's not a sign of being ill; it's right to sleep after dinner; we ought all to lie down all round the room, and sleep," which made me laugh very much. . . .

Wednesday, 22nd May.—Talked of my brother's arrival; I got a box from Palmerston which I begged Lord M. to open for me. Lord Albemarle presented the new Page, Col. Wemyss's son, a dear little boy 11 years old, very small. . . . We then went into the Throne Room, when the Levée began, which was very full,—1,100 people, and lasted till a ¼ to 4. There were a number of Addresses presented, approving my conduct in this last affair. . . . Talked of the Duke of Wellington's and Peel's not having been at the Levée, which I thought very rude. Lord M. said, "I don't think they mean that"; I replied that was all very well for Lord M., who was so kind and good, not to think people could *mean* things, but that there were very few like him (Ld. M.). "I don't like you to have those feelings," he said kindly. I said it was so foolish of Peel to act in this way, as by doing so he has made me dislike him. "That's what his Party feels," said

Lord M., and he said it was very ill-judged of him, as he saw there was a want of confidence on my part, to distrust me, and thus make me distrust him still more.

Talked of Peel's trying to force all. "The only way to gain confidence," said Lord M., "is not to distrust the other person; you must show confidence to gain it; that was how I acted with the late King, and he was very fair; he once or twice did things which embarrassed us a good deal, but upon the whole he was very fair." Talked of what I should say to the Bishops next day, and he promised to write something down for me. Talked of the late King's having made such long speeches so often, "which got the Government into great difficulties," Lord M. said. . . .

Friday, 24th May.—This day I *go out of my* TEENS and become 20! It sounds so strange to me! I have much to be thankful for; and I feel I owe more to *two* people than I can ever repay! my dear Lehzen, and my dear excellent Lord Melbourne! I pray Heaven to preserve them in health and strength for *many, many* years to come, and that Lord Melbourne may remain at the Head of Affairs; not only for my own happiness and prosperity, but for that of the whole Country and of all Europe; and lastly that I may become every day less unworthy of my high station! I said John Russell had been with me, and in very good humour; Peel had sent an excuse, saying he was in the country; Lord M. agreed with me he ought to have come. I said the Duke had been very civil to me at the Drawing-room. Said, John Russell thought there would not be much opposition any more in the House of Commons; that there would be a great deal of opposition about this new Scheme for National Education, and I said John Russell laughed when I talked to him of Lord M.'s doubting the utility of it; Lord M. laughed; J. R. was greatly for it, I said. . . .

Sunday, 26th May.—Lord M. believes Lord Hertford[1] expects the ladies to leave their cards upon him, as he always does upon them. "Whenever he comes to Town," said Lord M., "he always leaves his card on me, and asks the porter how I am; which I'm afraid I never return, and yet he always asks me." . . . Of Bishop Heber's being drowned in a bath. "He was a blundering, awkward fellow," said Lord M. "*All* is awkwardness," said Lord M.; I said not all drowning; "*Every* thing is awkwardness," he continued; "c'est maladroit; c'est les maladroits qui sont malheureux." . . .

WINDSOR, *Monday, 27th May.*—It was a most beautiful, bright day, yet the 1st impression, I know not why—beautiful as it looked and green and bright—is always a triste one. I saw the Grand-Duke arrive at 20 m. to 7; he bowed up to my window. At a ¼ to 8 we dined. The Grand-Duke, Prince Henry of the Netherlands, Count Orloff, Prince Dolgorouki, Prince Bariatinsky, Baron Lieven, Gen. Kaveline, M. Jonkowsky, M. Patkul, M. d'Adlerberg, M. Youriewitch, M. de Bentinck, Captain Amiens, Lady Cowper and Fanny, Lord Albemarle, Lord Erroll,[2] Lord and Lady Uxbridge and Ellen and Constance, Count and Countess Woronzow, and

[1] Lord Hertford (third Marquess, 1777–1842) was the original of Thackeray's Marquis of Steyne in *Vanity Fair*, and Disraeli's Lord Monmouth in *Coningsby*. Nothing can be added to these portraits. See Vol. I., pp. 310, 311.

[2] William George, eighteenth Earl of Erroll, created a Peer of the United Kingdom by William IV. He married the King's natural daughter, Elizabeth Fitzclarence.

Countess Alexandrine Potoska, M. de Tolstoy, the Duke of Argyll, Lord Torrington, Miss Lyttelton, Miss Paget, Miss Anson, and Col. Buckley (Lord Alfred having returned), who are all staying in the house,—and Col. and Miss Cavendish, and Lord Charles Fitzroy, dined here. We dined in St. George's Hall, which looked beautiful. The Grand-Duke led me in and I sat between him and Prince Henry. I really am quite in love with the Grand-Duke; he is a dear, delightful young man. At about a little after 10, we went into the red drawing-room, (next the dining-room), where an Orchestra was raised in which Weippert and his band were stationed; and dancing began. I danced 1st a quadrille with the Grand-Duke, then followed a Valse, during which time I sat down; then a quadrille which I danced with Prince Henry; then again a Valse followed; and I danced after this a quadrille with M. de Tolstoy; this was followed again by a Valse (of course I and also the Grand-Duke sitting down during the Valse); and then I danced a quadrille with Lord Clarence Paget, who came after dinner from Colonel Cavendish's, as did also Mr. and Lady Mary Vyner, Mr. and Lady Louisa Cavendish (who also danced), Mr. and Lady Agnes Byng, Mr. and Lady Fanny Howard, and Mr. and Mrs. Harcourt. At a little after 12 we went into the dining-room for supper; after supper they danced a Mazurka for ½ an hour, I should think nearly; the Grand-Duke asked me to take a turn, which I did (never having done it before) and which is very pleasant; the Grand-Duke is so very strong, that in running round, you must follow quickly, and after that you are whisked round like in a Valse, which is very pleasant. I also had a turn with Prince Henry; I then danced a quadrille with Patkul, which was followed by a Valse. After this we danced (what I had never even seen before) the "Grossvater" or "Rerraut," and which is excessively amusing; I danced with the Grand-Duke, and we had such fun and laughter; Patkul and the Countess Potoska led the way. It begins with a solemn walk round the room, which also follows each figure; one figure, in which the lady and gentleman run down holding their pocket-handkerchief by each end, and letting the ladies on one side go under it, and the gentlemen jump over it, is too funny. This concluded our little Ball at near 2 o'clock. I never enjoyed myself more. We were all so merry; I got to bed by a ¼ to 3, but could not sleep till 5.

Tuesday, 28th May.—The Grand-Duke talked of his very fine reception here, and said he would never forget it. "Ce ne sont pas seulement des paroles, je vous assure, Madame," he said, but that it was what he felt, and that he never would forget these days here, which I'm sure *I* shall never also, for I really love this amiable and dear young man, who has such a sweet smile. I talked to Lord Melbourne of St. George's Hall, which he admired very much. . . . He said, "I don't think the Grand-Duke looks well; he looks rather livid." I talked often with Lord Melbourne. I pointed out Countess Potoska as having £30,000 a year, which he wouldn't believe. He observed upon the great length of the petticoats, which he said gave a suspicion that the feet and ankles are not quite right. He said, "I don't like blue gowns; it's an unlucky colour; no girl ever marries who wears a blue gown."

Wednesday, 29th May.—I said all this excitement did me good. "But you may suffer afterwards," he said; "you must take care of your health,—not to fall into bad health; you complain of that languor increasing, and dislike for exertion; now, it would be a dreadful thing for you if you were to take a dislike for business," which I assured him I never should. "You lead rather an unnatural life for a young person," he continued; "it's the life of a man." I did feel it sometimes, I said.

Talked of the Grand-Duke; of Bariatinsky dancing with that ball in his body, which Lord M. said would kill him some day; of the Russians smoking. . . . Talked of their wearing no whiskers, which Lord M. said was because they thought it was French, and they hated the French; that Orloff said we should one day see Louis Philippe deposed as easily as he had been put on the throne; Lord M. believes there is a good deal of personality in it; that the Emperor says he knows something from his brother Alexander. Talked of Orloff, and Lord M. said Orloff had said when they made him a doctor, at Oxford, he felt as if a new train of ideas filled his mind, as if the spirit had come upon him. . . . Lord M. said, having the Grand-Duke down here in this familiar way was worth any fêtes in London, and an amazing thing for them. After this Valse, which was over at 20 m. to 3, I took leave of all the Grand-Duke's gentlemen, with real regret, as I like them all very much; Patkul and Adlerberg are 2 such merry young creatures, particularly Patkul. I then went to the little blue room next my Dressing-room, where Lord Palmerston brought in the Grand-Duke to take leave. The Grand-Duke took my hand and pressed it warmly; he looked pale and his voice faltered, as he said, "Les paroles me manquent pour exprimer tout ce que je sens"; and he mentioned how deeply grateful he felt for all the kindness he met with, that he hoped to return again, and that he trusted that all this would only tend to strengthen the ties of friendship between England and Russia. He then pressed and kissed my hand, and I kissed his cheek; upon which he kissed mine (cheek) in a very warm affectionate manner, and we again warmly shook hands. I really felt more as if I was taking leave of a relation than of a stranger, I felt so sad to take leave of this dear amiable young man, whom I really think (talking jokingly) I was a little in love with, and certainly attached to; he is so frank, so really young and merry, has such a nice open countenance with a sweet smile, and such a manly fine figure and appearance. Lord Palmerston then brought in Prince Henry (which was not so melancholy), but who seemed in his odd way to be sorry to go too.

Thursday, 30th May.—They played the Grand-Duke's and my favourite quadrilles, called "Le Gay Loisir," which made me quite melancholy, as it put me so in mind of all, and I felt sadly the change. Talked to Lord M. of my feeling the change, and of its being so seldom that I had young people of my own rank with me; of my having so disliked the idea of the Grand-Duke's coming, and that now I was so *very very* sorry at his going. "Very often the case," said Lord M., and of the Grand-Duke's being such "a very good-natured young man." Talked of the strange feeling when all the excitement was over, and that I feared I would feel the difference of not being able to have these sorts of dances; Lord M. said I could have them sometimes in London, though we agreed with difficulty; but certainly here; but I observed there must be many young people then;

"And you had a great posse of them," said Lord M., and so nice, I observed. I said a young person like me must *sometimes* have young people to laugh with. "Nothing so natural," replied Lord M. with tears in his eyes; and I said I had *that* so seldom. Talked of the astonishment of Foreigners, and of Charles, that a person like Lord March should take precedence of the Prime Minister; Lord M. smiled and said, "I think it is better as it is," in which I agreed. He said the Secretaries of State always take rank of the first of their own degree; if a Marquis, the 1st of the Marquises; if an Earl, the 1st of the Earls, &c. Palmerston waives that, he says, as he thinks being in the House of Commons, he loses rank; but the 1st Lord of the Treasury has no rank, Lord M. said, though the Lord High Treasurer ranked very high[1]—but there has been none since Lord Godolphin and Lord Oxford, in Queen Anne's time. . . .

[1] King Edward reverted to the precedent of the Lord High Treasurer when he accorded special precedence to the office of Prime Minister. See *ante*, p. 47, and Vol. I., p. 299.

INTRODUCTORY NOTE TO CHAPTER XV

In June 1839 Lord Melbourne's Government was back in office, shaken by the crisis, but reprieved for another two years. There were inevitable changes in the personnel and some shifting of offices, as is usual on these occasions. Macaulay was appointed Secretary at War, and Lord John Russell, then Home Secretary, exchanged offices with Lord Normanby, and took charge of the Colonies. This enabled the Jamaica Bill to pass. The Ministry had been roughly handled in debate. Although the Duke of Wellington's criticisms were resented by the Queen, her generous instincts responded to the appeal made on the Duke's behalf by her uncle, King Leopold, who laid special stress upon the incurable nature of that disease which goes by the name of "party spirit" in England.

The Queen, for the first time, began to realize the isolation of the Throne. The idea of marriage became less distasteful to her, and when Lord Melbourne asked her whether she desired to agree to King Leopold's suggestion that her Coburg cousin should visit her, she replied in the affirmative. She discussed with Lord Melbourne her uncle's project of marrying her to Prince Albert, and argued in favour of an alliance with a Prince of royal blood rather than with a subject.

The even tenor of the Queen's life had been broken by the Ministerial crisis, and a fresh stage in her moral and political education had been reached and passed. She said in later years that this period of her reign was crucial in forming her character as a Sovereign and as a woman. The excitement of the time upon the mind of a young girl left her in a state only too ready to receive lifelong impressions of good and evil. It was a condition of things full of peril for her, and she afterwards expressed her gratitude that "none of her children have had to run the risk" she believed herself to have incurred. All the talk about the hatred of one Party and the loyalty of the other was highly dangerous from its subjective effects upon the character of a youthful Sovereign. "They wish to treat me like a girl, but I will show them that I am Queen of England," and "I have stood by you (the Whigs): you must now stand by me," were not phrases calculated to strengthen the Throne under a Constitutional form of Government, or to encourage that flexibility of the mind so requisite in a Constitutional Sovereign. By good fortune, the divinity that doth hedge a Queen saved this young Princess from herself, and she agreed to receive the visit of Prince Albert of Saxe-Coburg.

CHAPTER XV

1839

Saturday, 1*st June*.— . . . I had observed him (Lord M.) riding his new horse from the window, which I said seemed very pretty. "Beautiful colour," he said. I said he seemed never to walk. "No, he never walks," said Lord M. I said, "Do you like that?" "Can't bear that," he replied; why did he buy him then? I asked; he couldn't always get what he liked, he said. Of the Duke of W.'s being very fair, for he says Lord M. should go on, and would not meet with so much opposition; I said to Lord M. what could make the Duke so *very* eager at times; "He is an eager man," replied Lord M.; we agreed this Speech was very friendly and likely to displease his own people. Talked of the King of Holland never having been, as Lord M. said, on good terms with England; he quarrelled with the Duke of York during the French campaign. Lord M. remembers the old Stadtholder,[1] who he says was a great favourite of George IV. His wife was a Prussian, he thinks, as Prussians occupied the Netherlands in '82, on account of that relationship, and in consequence thought they might occupy France too, which they could not. Talked of Mamma's Grandmother, the Queen of Sweden, and Frederick the Great's wife being sisters,[2] and of

[1] William VI., who retired on the invasion of the French in 1795.

[2] Daughters of Ferdinand Albert, Duke of Brunswick-Bevern.

how we were all related. Talked of Mary thinking it so wrong that the Saxon Royal Family should have become Catholics, as the Elector of Saxony had been the great patron of Luther.

I rode down Constitution Hill, and as I was crossing over to the Palace I met Lord Melbourne on horseback, stopped him and rode down the Mall and back again with him ; he rode in Col. Wemyss's place. Lord M. said he had sent me a box and talked of its contents which I shall copy hereafter and therefore say nothing here of it ; he then said, "Rather a disagreeable thing happened in the Cabinet," Sir Hesketh Fleetwood,[1] Lord M. said, is going to make a Motion on Tuesday, for the extension of suffrage to £10 holders, and "John didn't wish to throw cold water upon it," but wants to say "he would consider it," and thus conciliate these Radicals a little. "Upon which Howick got up," continued Lord M., "and said if John made any such declaration he must say he was quite against any alteration in the Reform Bill ; so John said, he couldn't go into the House again after that, for he couldn't answer such a declaration. Well, at last we got Howick to give it up and to say nothing on Tuesday, but he says if he isn't satisfied with what John says, he'll resign." Lord M.'s new horse is very pretty and cantered nicely and is better broke, having been a lady's horse. The Cabinet was long.

Sunday, June 2.—I showed him Uncle's letter which made him laugh ; talked of the Grand-Duke's having given £20,000 [2] in charities, and of his

[1] Sir Peter Hesketh Fleetwood, M.P. for Preston. He was founder of the town of Fleetwood, Lancs., and assumed the surname Fleetwood in lieu of Hesketh.

[2] *Sic.* This figure appears in the MS., but it may have been an error for £2,000.

having made a pretty speech about me before he went. We agreed £20,000 was immense; "but it's very popular," Lord M. said. Talked of Howick. "He was not at all vehement," said Lord M., "but doggedly obstinate; John was very much annoyed; I never saw anybody so much annoyed," for he observed Howick was the only one, and all the others (many of whom dislike doing this), said Lord M., were ready to assist. Talked of the Nurse and Tutor calling children by their Christian names,[1] which my brother said was done abroad, and which Lord M. said no one would ever think of doing here, that they always called them Lord, and Mr. We looked at two of my large books of prints; in the 1st there is a pretty print of the Grand-Duke when he was 11 years old, and which we agreed was still so like. There was also a print of Frederick the Great; Lord M. said in looking at it, "A bad man; but we used him very ill," and that that was the origin of the alienation between England and Prussia. We looked at a print of Francis 1st, the late Emperor; and Lord M. said, "Madame de Lieven used to say he was reckoned a stupid and a good man, but I believe that he was neither the one nor the other, and that I take to be the truth." There was also a print of the Duke of Reichstadt, and Lord M. said *his* death was a lucky thing. . . . We talked of titles, that of Zetland, and Dunfermline; and Lord M. said there is no regulation about titles; only subject to my pleasure; and it is not reckoned discredit to take another person's title; "But the Queen might make 20 Earls of Zetland if she liked," he said. There is nothing to prevent

[1] The use of Christian names without a prefix by nurses or tutors is quite modern, and dates not farther back than 1880. See *ante*, p. 145.

anybody from taking a title or wearing a ribbon, and Lord M. said that was Bickersteth's famous answer to Brougham; "Brougham asked, 'What is to prevent a man from wearing a blue ribbon?' 'Nothing but the universal scorn and contempt of mankind, my Lord.'"

Monday, 3rd June.—I asked Lord M. if he thought there would be no objection to my giving Uncle Ferdinand the Bath, as he was a very distinguished Officer; I said I had not mentioned it to anybody; Lord M. saw no objection to it, but would speak to Lord Palmerston about it. Said to Lord M., I shouldn't be surprised if the Emperor himself were to come here one day. "I always expect that," said Lord M. I said the Grand-Duke had said that his father remembered with such delight his visit to England and always hoped to return one day. "And what did you say?" said Lord M. "Nothing," I replied. "That was the best," he said. After the Council, I received in the Closet Prince Esterhazy, Reschid Pasha,[1] and the young Grand-Duke of Saxe-Weimar,[2] who were severally introduced by Lord Palmerston. The young Grand-Duke is just the same age as *the* Grand-Duke; is not at all good-looking, but has a fine tall figure; but after the other Grand-Duke, no one is seen to advantage; he was accompanied by Count Beust and M. Wagner. "I'm afraid we shall get into a scrape about Howick," said Lord M. "I hear he is determined to resign," unless J. Russell declared strongly against any change in the Reform Bill.

[1] Turkish Ambassador in London.

[2] Charles, Hereditary Grand-Duke of Saxe-Weimar (b. 1818), son of the Grand-Duke Charles Frederic, and his wife, Marie, daughter of the Emperor Paul. See Vol. I., p. 125.

I said, would Howick be a loss? Lord M. said he would be no loss,[1] but that "if Howick resigns, Lord Grey would be sure to turn against us, and Lord Dacre[2] too." "It would give a great shake,"—that Lord Grey thought the Reform Bill final, and Lord M. said this extension to £10 freeholders was a great change; "It will lose us a great deal of support," he said, "though it gains it on another side." Talked of my Uncle's and Cousins' arrival.

At about ½ p. 3 I ran downstairs with Lady Lyttelton to receive Uncle Ferdinand. Uncle is grown old, but looking well; Victoire[3]—quite lovely—tall and slender, a skin like lilies and roses, hazel eyes, with beautiful fair hair, an aquiline nose and a very sweet mouth—not shy or awkward; Augustus—grown—but not so handsome as before—the face too fat; Leopold—very short (he is 15, and Victoire 16)—but very clever-looking; large blue eyes, a cock nose, fair hair and a fair skin; Alexander Mensdorff,[4] Charles's height, a very handsome face, very dark, almost Spanish. I took them up to my room; then to their rooms, and then we took luncheon together. . . .

Wednesday, 5th June.—Heard from Lord John "that Sir Hesketh Fleetwood yesterday brought for-

[1] This was no reflection upon Lord Howick's abilities. It was a tribute to the irritation his occasional captiousness excited in his colleagues.

[2] Thomas, twentieth Lord Dacre, sometime M.P. for Herts.

[3] Princess Victoire of Saxe-Coburg married in 1840 the Duc de Nemours, son of Louis Philippe.

[4] Second son of the Duchess of Kent's sister, who married Count Mensdorff-Pouilly. See Vol. I., p. 95. He (Alexander) married Alexandrine, Countess Dietrichstein, and their second son, Albert, is now (1912) Austro-Hungarian Ambassador in London.

H.S.H. Princess Victoire of Saxe-Coburg
Duchesse de Nemours
from a portrait by Sir W. Ross

ward his motion to extend the right of voting in Counties to £10 householders. Lord John Russell felt himself obliged to declare that he could neither support the Motion, nor could he hold out a hope that the Government would concur in the Motion on a future occasion. It must be allowed that this Motion has been looked for with great anxiety by the Radical Party, and that the declaration made on the part of the Government has occasioned great disappointment. The position is a very difficult one and may cause serious embarrassment. The House divided.

Against the Motion . . .	207
For	81
	126 "

. . . At 5 m. to 2 Lord Melbourne came to me in the Closet, and stayed with me till a ¼ p. 2. There was some mistake about the Investiture, which however was set right. Lord Melbourne then said to me, "There's a dreadful ferment." I then said to him, I was rather annoyed at J. Russell's having thus thrown cold water upon the whole at once. Lord M. said J. Russell had seen Howick yesterday morning, who (H.) said he had been thinking very much over it, and that he had asked Lord Grey about it, who told Howick that he ought to oppose it in every way, and that if Government did not oppose it "he" (Ld. Grey) "should come down to the House and make a declaration against it"; upon which J. Russell thought that, considering that he had only a Majority of 22—one of his Colleagues decidedly against it, and Lord Grey and others turning against us,—that he could not act otherwise than he had done, which was that he stated *he* himself was for the measure, but that he could not hold out any hope that the Government could do anything at a future time. It *had* been settled at the Cabinet that J. Russell should say that the Government would consider it next year; Lord M. had not seen J. Russell yesterday before this change and knew nothing of it,—which I said I thought wrong; Lord M. said, "He says, a leader must sometimes act for himself," but that John Hobhouse, Normanby and Thomson were so angry at this, that they were inclined to resign upon it, and Lord M. said their resignation at this moment would break up the Government; so he intends to have a Cabinet next day upon it. "I thought it better to have it to-morrow in order to let them cool a little," he said. Before this, he said, "Duncannon, to whom they always go in such emergencies, advised them" (Normanby, Thomson and Hobhouse) "not to take any hasty step but to consider it first." "But there's a great ferment about it," said Lord M., "and they are very angry." Some of our friends, he says, are very much pleased at what John Russell has done; I asked him, mightn't the Tories be more friendly too, since this; Lord M. said it might have that effect, but that one couldn't depend upon one's enemies; the division against the motion was so large on account of the Tories. This extending the elective franchise to £10 holders "is a very serious change," Lord M. said. I said to Lord M. I had been so angry last night, as both Alfred Paget and Murray had frightened me last night about this affair in the House of Commons. . . . Talked of Sir William Molesworth[1] being such a very odd-looking man, with long

[1] Then M.P. for Leeds. He was one of the first men of the leisured

yellow hair, which Lord M. said he wore to hide the loss of one of his ears; he was at the Levée, as also O'Connell, who brought an Address. "He looked very smug, and very cunning," said Lord M. Talked of Mr. Buckstone[1]; of people looking so odd in Court dresses. "It's as if a man was dressed to act a part"; I said it was such a frightful dress, which he wouldn't allow, and said was from the time of Louis the XIVth. I said the cravats were so ugly, and must be so uncomfortable, and that I should like an open collar so much better. "Why, you wouldn't show a man's neck?" he said; "a man's neck's so ugly, it's so strongly marked,—that's why they hide it; a woman never hides her neck."

Thursday, 6th June.—At 20 m. p. 3 came Lord Melbourne and stayed with me till 4. He asked how I was, and said, "You look pale"; but I said I was well. "Well, Ma'am, we've settled this for the present," he said smiling, which made me very happy. I asked if with much difficulty? "No, not much," he said; "they felt John had done it himself; there was a little attack upon Howick; so it is settled for the present; but I'm afraid it'll not last long before we have new difficulties." That we agreed must always be the case.

Friday, 7th June.—"Esterhazy has been with me this morning," he continued, "he is in a great fright about France, as all the Austrians always are; he has had a long conversation with Peel." I then said I had forced Lady and Miss Peel to shake hands

class to adopt "Radical" opinions. The band of members then holding those views was small but remarkable. In the coalition Ministry formed by Lord Aberdeen in 1852, Molesworth was First Commissioner of Works. He became Colonial Secretary in 1855, the year of his death.

[1] J. B. Buckstone, the manager of the Haymarket Theatre.

with me. Esterhazy told Lord M. she was "in a great state of irritation, and very much annoyed." The Duke, I observed, was very civil; Lord M. said, "Oh! he's in very good humour because he told Esterhazy that you had said to him, he must stand by you, and that you said he had not, but (he said) that Peel was so jealous of anybody else, that he could not." I said I thought Peel saw that I had more confidence in the Duke than I had in him. Lord M. said Peel put forward what happened in 1812[1] about the Household, when Lord Grey came in, as a precedent for what has now happened, which he said was quite different; "That's no precedent whatever," continued Lord M., "and they only put that forward as a pretext," the real truth was, Lord M. said, that George IV. insisted on having Lord Moira[2] at the head of the Treasury; "and he," said Lord M., "was a man who had played the deuce when he was at the Ordnance Office; and they" (Lord Grey and Lord Grenville) "felt they could not go on with him in the Ministry, so they put the Household forward as a pretext to

[1] In 1812 Lord Wellesley was called upon by the Prince Regent to form a ministry in conjunction with Lord Moira. Lords Grey and Grenville were asked to take office but refused, ostensibly objecting to a coalition Government. They also stipulated that the appointments to the Household should be under their control, but this was refused. Lords Wellesley and Moira failed to form an administration, and Lord Liverpool became Prime Minister.

[2] In 1789 Lord Moira (then Colonel Rawdon Hastings) was an intimate friend of the Prince of Wales, and proposed in his favour the amendment on the Regency question. He distinguished himself in the Low Countries in 1794. In 1806 he was Master of the Ordnance in the Ministry of "All the Talents," but resigned his appointment when the Duke of Portland became Prime Minister in 1807. In 1813 he was appointed Governor-General of Bengal and Commander-in-Chief of the Indian Army. Lady Flora Hastings was his daughter.

get out of it." I said some people thought Sir Robert Peel did it only for a pretext; "Just the same thing," said Lord M. "But it must be done," said Lord M.; "*he*" (George III.) "was always very civil." I said *I* was too. "I don't mean by that you are not," said Lord M. laughing; "and he took them in; they said it was all his deceit; I don't believe that; I think that was all their gullibility; *they* thought he really liked them."

"She has got ringlets to-day," he said, looking at Victoire (who had had her hair in puffs the 2 days before), which I said I admired much the most. "I don't like the character," he said, "it gives such a naughty look"; but didn't he think she looked well? He replied, "They are beautiful," but the character the same. "Is Count Mensdorff in good health?" he asked. I replied, Yes, but that he looked pale. "Sallow; that colour is what *I* think beautiful," he said, which it is; and I said he was such a nice young man. "He's a nice fellow." I said his father was a Frenchman. "He looks like a Frenchman," said Lord M.

Saturday, 8th June.—At ½ p. 6 we dined. I sat between Uncle and Alexander. At a little before 8 we went with all but Lehzen, Miss Spring Rice, Lady Gardiner, Lady Flora and Mr. Murray, to the Opera. It was the new opera of *Lucrezia Borgia* by Donizetti; there is a Prologue and 2 Acts; the music is very beautiful, and the story a dreadful tragedy. Grisi looked beautiful; and sang and acted beautifully as Lucrezia Borgia; Tamburini, as the Duke, sang very well; and Ernesta Grisi, very nicely as Orsini. The part of Gennaro was acted by Mario, whose real name is the Marquis di Candia, a gentleman who has taken to the Stage; his voice is very fine and full of feeling, of course not Rubini[1]; he is tall, quite young, and handsome. This was followed by a beautiful Ballet called *La Gitana* in 2 acts; Taglioni danced exquisitely; a very pretty dance with a tambourine; then that peculiar and pretty Russian dance she danced last year, and which I regret so the Grand-Duke has not seen; and a Pas de Trois. We did not stay quite to the end, and came home at a little after 12, much delighted.

Monday, 10th June.—I asked Lord M. what the difference of the Ballot was; that it is done in secret; everybody votes in secret, Lord M. said, and now, everybody knows *who* votes and *for whom* they vote; they think, he continued, the Ballot would prevent Landlords from turning out their Tenants, because they couldn't know *who* had voted. I asked Lord M. did *he* think it would have that effect. "*I* very much doubt myself whether it would," said Lord M. "Now, everything is certainty, and then it would be uncertainty"; and he said there would be great fraud exercised in carrying it into execution; because, if a person asks a man, For whom are you going to vote? he answers, I can't say; then the other says, Oh! I know you are going to vote against me; upon which the man says, Oh! no; thereby telling a falsehood, very probably; and Lord M. continued, you can't then win any election, because you don't know who voted. At the same time, in the other way, the system of oppression and intimidation was very hard, people losing all their customers one way or another; "therefore I don't wonder at *their* wishing to try it," he said. I observed that the 2 brothers, the Duke of W. and Lord

[1] This opinion was not that of the majority. Mario was generally thought superior in every way as a singer and actor to Rubini.

Cowley, were so unlike. "None of the Wellesleys are alike," said Lord M.[1] . . .

Wednesday, 12th June.—I asked Lord M. if he didn't think me very much changed, and much more silent than I used to be. "You are more silent to-night," he said, "but everybody is more silent sometimes; no mortal can always be in the same temper, and then if they are out of humour themselves, they may show it to others. You shouldn't give way too much to personal dislikes," said Lord M., and he alluded to the 2 ladies who everybody knows hissed when I came up the course. "Now, are you sure they did it?" he asked; "quite sure." "They did it at me," he said; "that was just the same," I replied, and that I knew they did it at me also. "I heard it," he said, "some of the women told me." I said I had every reason to be very angry with Peel. "You both say just the same," said Lord M., "he says, 'I feel I can never be the Queen's Minister,' and you say he never can be your Minister." I said that was so. "It's very odd that two such interviews should have produced so much irritation," said Lord M. He asked if I liked Stanley; a little better, but Graham not at all. I said I couldn't conceal my feelings, and couldn't deceive a man; that it might get me into a good many scrapes, but that I couldn't help speaking up my feelings. "Well, *I* should appreciate that," said Lord M., "but everybody not does like that." Lord M. continued, that when he came in again in '35, which was exceedingly disagreeable for the King, "I said to him I hoped he

[1] There were four Wellesley brothers raised to the peerage, Marquess Wellesley, Lord Maryborough, Duke of Wellington, Lord Cowley. The first two successively inherited the Mornington title.

would give me his confidence, and he answered, 'Good God! I wouldn't have sent for you if I didn't mean to do so.'" I said to Lord M., when *Peel* asked me for, or said he hoped I would give him, my confidence, I gave no answer; Lord M. said Esterhazy had told him Peel was moderate. Why should I, I said, mind what was said? "I don't think you should," he said; and I continued that people always made too much of women and that they influenced people. "I dare say they do," he said laughing; "but they don't influence *me*; do you think I talk to them too much?" I said he listened to them too much. "Do I?—better not to talk to them at all? Then one would hear nothing; but I don't talk to them near as much as I used to do," he added laughing. . . .

Friday, 14th June.—Lord M. thinks a boy should leave a Nurse at 4, but he agrees with me that a boy had better have a Governess and not a Tutor till 7. I asked him who had he to take care of him till he went to the Private Tutor's when he was 7. "An old woman who had been my Mother's governess," he replied. "She taught me to read; she was a Jersey woman, a most ill-tempered old woman"; which I said was very disagreeable. "I think it did me good," he continued; "kept one in fear; *I* detested her; my Mother adored her, from having been her governess; she was a sort of Bonne; she married a Swiss clergyman, a M. Bignon, a very gentlemanlike man; he travelled with my eldest brother; he died in my father's family,—he was ill, had an operation performed, and died; he was very much of a gentleman. I was very fond of *him*; *he* lived downstairs with the Family; she did not; people could do that formerly, it can't be arranged now; she lived in the house till she made so much disturbance that they were obliged to put her out. Talked of my having given up my curls (I had plaits), which Lord M. was glad of; though he said curls looked very well. . . .

Sunday, 16th June.—Talked of my Relations having gone, and my liking to live with young people, for that then I felt that *I was young*, which I really often forgot, living so much, if not entirely, with people much older than myself. Talked of my Uncle's asking me if I intended to travel this year; and we then talked for some time about it, I stating very strongly my great dislike to doing so. Lord M. said at first, "You must do it one day; there's no need of doing it now." "You should go to Scotland and Ireland; it would be an immense thing if you could go to Ireland"; though he owned the dreadful trouble and fatigue it would be.

Monday, 17th June.—I went and fetched Lord Melbourne Uncle Leopold's letter, in which he talks of my Cousins, Ernest and Albert, coming to see me, and Lord M. said, "You wish them to come?" which I said I did, and he saw no objection. When Lord M. had finished the letter, he said, "As you say, it is rather stiff; he says nothing about himself." Talked of my having spoken to Palmerston about a Grand-Duchess for Ernest. Talked of making the Throne-room one of the Ball-rooms; Lord M. was going to ride down to the House of Lords. I showed Lord M. the sketch of my letter to the Grand-Duke, which touched him, and he said, "That will do very well indeed; ought you to say *bonne sœur*?" I said he wrote *bon frère*, and Lord M. agreed *I* could do no less. Talked also of there having been such a dreadful piece of work with these two Ladies, who had come quite frantic to Uxbridge, who stopped in the Yard here, denying they had ever done such a thing, and wishing to see me about it, which we agreed never would do.

Tuesday, 18th June.—Talked of the rooms; if I had ever asked Brougham, which I said I couldn't, as he was really too bad; Lyndhurst I had asked; he wasn't quite so bad, I said, though I disliked him very much. Why? he asked. Because he was a bad man. "Do you dislike all bad men?" said Lord M., "for that comprises a large number." Lord M. continued that he was a very agreeable man, which I denied. Talked of Aberdeen, who I also disliked.[1]

Wednesday, 19th June.—Lord M. asked if I had heard from J. Russell, and I went and fetched him the note I had received from J. R. about the Motion on the Ballot; 17 Majority against. At this moment Lord M. received a note from Lord Palmerston about some papers, which Lord M. was to have sent to him, and he had sent the wrong ones; Lord M. was obliged to answer it directly, and I got him paper and pens and ink, and a candle and sealing wax; and he wrote it, sealed it and sent it. Lord M. then asked, "What did Uxbridge write?" to the Duchess; that I was satisfied, I replied. "But the Duke is not at all satisfied with it," said Lord M., and that he (the Duke) had been with him this morning, and wanted to ask for an audience, which we both agreed never would do; and Lord M. said he would write a letter to him, which he would send for my approval. "The

[1] The Queen subsequently showered favours upon Lord Aberdeen. He lived in the Ranger's House at Blackheath, given to him by her, and she lamented his death in very moving terms. See *ante*, p. 170.

Duchess is coming to the Drawing-room to-morrow," he said, "you won't be markedly *unfriendly to her?*" I replied, certainly not, *and that I had never spoken* to her. We both, and *I particularly, suspect that* they did do it. He said these ladies deny having hissed at all; Lord M. said that they couldn't sometimes restrain their feelings; the Duke said that the ladies said to Cantelupe, "We should like to hiss Lord M.," but that they didn't. Now the admission of this comes near the act, and the telling it *to* Lord M.!! "The Duke said it's so unladylike," continued Lord M., "so I said, If you mean by *unladylike*, that it is unlike what a lady *ought* to do, I quite agree with you, but if you mean that it is unlike what ladies *do* do, I cannot agree with you." Lord M. said that Dr. Kay[1] had told him it was extraordinary how the appearance of poor children changed when their education was more attended to; that the system of education hitherto pursued was all wrong, and "that we were all in the wrong box; he filled me with despair," he says that the system of mutual instruction has done no good, and that "it only strengthens the memory." Lord M. sent for this Dr. Kay, as he is the principal person about this new system. "If you will only let them alone and not be always intermeddling with them," he continued. "Walter Scott said to a clergyman whom he was writing to, 'How would you like, if a nobleman was to come into your house and teach you how to make your beef-steak into a ragout?'" Lord M. said that he would have them taught

[1] Afterwards Sir James Kay-Shuttleworth. He was an Assistant Poor Law Commissioner, and on the formation of the Committee of the Privy Council on Education became its first secretary.

to read and write, arithmetic and the first elements of mathematics; and he said that formerly he observed that a *great number* came away from school very ignorant, a *few* tolerably instructed, and only *two* or *three* very well informed. Talked of gardeners, and Lord Melbourne's being such an excellent one; he says he is a great dissenter, and his father also. "Great thing to have a dissenter; they don't go to races, they don't hunt, and don't engage in any expensive amusements." Lord M. said, "*I've* very bitter resentments"; which I wouldn't believe. He said the way the women behaved during the Reform Bill was quite dreadful; the license they gave themselves, calling people liars, and that in general "men are less measured in their expressions than women, but when women once take to strong expressions they are much worse"—which is true. "They said," he added laughing, "'Now let us have a hiss at that blackguard Melbourne'"!!!—which brought the colour to my face.

Thursday, 20th June.—Got up at 10 and breakfasted at ½ p. This day 2 years I came to the Throne. It seems much longer, and shorter, both. At ½ p. 10 I went with Mary, Lady Normanby, the Maids of Honour, Lady C. Barrington, Lord Uxbridge, Lord Albemarle, and the Lord, Groom, and Equerry, to Lord Westminster's. Lord Melbourne arrived just as I did, and followed me in; Lord and Lady Westminster received me. After remaining a little while in the Picture Gallery (which is a splendid room with magnificent Rubens's in it), when Lord Melbourne came up to me for a moment,—we went into the Tent, which was arranged for dancing and which looked beautiful, and dancing began. I danced the 1st quadrille with the Grand-Duke of

Weimar; this was followed by a Valse; I made Lord Melbourne come up the steps to me while they were valsing; talked of the Tent being so handsome. He went away while I was dancing the 2nd quadrille with Lord Wilton; then came a Valse, then I danced with Lord Robert Grosvenor; another Valse followed, and after that I danced with Lord Bruce; which was again followed by a Valse. I sat chiefly near Lady Westminster. Lady Seymour was looking quite beautiful and was twice my vis-à-vis during the evening. Lady Ashley was also in great beauty. At 1 we went to supper; I sat between Lord and Lady Westminster, who were very kind. We then returned to the Tent; and I danced 2 more quadrilles, with Count Valentine Esterhazy (who is very agreeable, and to the button of whose sleeve I clung with my blonde sleeve) and with Prince Doria (who is handsome but tiresome); then followed a long Country Dance which I danced with Lord March. Lady Seymour sat near me a little while during the evening; also Augusta, and the Duchess of Bedford; *Lord Westminster danced* with *the Duchess of Somerset.*[1] This finished the Ball and I came home at ½ p. 3. It was *so* gay and pretty and I enjoyed myself excessively. I was in bed by 4. Heard as I came away that we had had a Majority of 5 on this Education Question.

Friday, 21st June.—Lord M. made me laugh very much by telling me what a row Lord Winchilsea had made at Exeter Hall; there was a Meeting against this new Education System,[2] and people

[1] Lord Westminster was seventy-two. The Duchess, a daughter of Sir Michael Shaw Stewart, had married the eleventh Duke of Somerset, as his second wife, in 1836. She died in 1880.

[2] The Government scheme proposed that a Committee of the Privy

were only to be let in by tickets, but some others got in, and they put a Mr. Savage into the Chair, and Lord Winchilsea knocked him down and he was put in; and then Winchilsea was knocked down by Savage's friends, and they came to a regular fight; upon which Police Men were called in, who with difficulty restrained them and took some prisoners. Winchilsea then got up and made a speech, and said it had arisen from a mistake and they might let the prisoners go. Talked of Lord Westminster's having danced with the Duchess of Somerset. Talked of Mr. Webster,[1] the American, who has come over and who Lord M. saw in the House of Lords; and who was surprised at the House of Lords,—which, Lord M. says, is "the most democratic Assembly in the World." Talked of the Tournament Lord Eglinton is going to have; of the danger of it; of Lady Seymour being chosen "Queen of the Lists." . . .

Saturday, 29th June.—Talked of the report of the Grand-Duke's[2] intending to marry the Princess Mary[3] of Darmstadt, who is only 15, which it seems *he* wished but Orloff stopped on account of her being in bad health. Lord M. says they'll marry him soon, though I doubted his liking to do so. His father did, and thought it right to do so; "and he has con-

Council (the Lord President and five others) be appointed to establish a normal school, directed at four objects—Religious Instruction, General Education, Moral Training, and Commercial Instruction. The Committee should also allocate the grants made by Parliament. The Opposition condemned the scheme as irreligious.

[1] Daniel Webster, afterwards twice Secretary of State in the Federal Government.

[2] Afterwards Alexander II. of Russia.

[3] The Princess ultimately married Alexander II., and was the mother of the Duchess Marie of Saxe-Coburg-Gotha, Duchess of Edinburgh.

ducted himself very correctly ever since," said Lord M.; "it's a very extraordinary thing for a man with supreme power, and in a country not very scrupulous, to have conducted himself so correctly; very few men would do that." . . .

Wednesday, 3rd July.—Saw Lord Uxbridge; Lady Clanricarde (who was very interesting about Russia) and the Duchess of Sutherland with all her children but Stafford.[1] Elizabeth[2] is lovely; Evelyn[3] an immense girl; Constance[4] lovely; and little Frederic[5] much improved. The Duchess looked pale and low; she brought me some beautiful pink coral I had ordered from Naples, and some other little trifles she gave me, which she had brought from Naples.

Told Lord M. I had seen Lady Clanricarde, who had given me many accounts about Russia; Lord M. said he hoped she wouldn't talk too much, for else that would be written back. "I hear she told Palmerston that she couldn't understand how anybody could be afraid of him" (the Emperor). I said that she told me the Grand-Duchess Olga[6] was the most beautiful person she had ever seen,—quite like an angel; the Grand-Duchess Mary also very handsome, the great favourite, and manages the Emperor quite like a Toy; that *really* the Emperor wishes to keep her in Russia and therefore had con-

[1] Afterwards third Duke of Sutherland.

[2] Afterwards Duchess of Argyll.

[3] Afterwards Lady Blantyre.

[4] Afterwards Duchess of Westminster.

[5] Lord Frederick Leveson-Gower, at this time aged six, was afterwards an officer in the Rifle Brigade, and died in the Crimea in 1854.

[6] The Grand-Duchess Olga afterwards married the King of Wurtemberg.

sented to the marriage; that she was desperately in love with the Duke of Leuchtenberg,[1] which surprised her; then that the Grand-Duke was not the favourite, and that the Emperor was jealous of him, which Lord M. said people generally were of their Heirs. I said that she also told me that neither the Empress or any lady were ever allowed to talk Politics—which I said to Lord M. I thought a very good thing. "Did you tell her that?" asked Lord M. laughing; which I replied I could not have done, as that would have aimed at her too much. Talked of Lord M.'s groom, and his not taking as much care of the horses as he ought. "He doesn't take very brilliant care of them," Lord M. said. "He's got a troublesome wife who always tries to get into the stables, which I don't allow." I said, didn't the grooms' wives generally live in the Stables? "Yes, but she quarrels so," he replied, "and whenever a woman quarrels in the house, I always say, shove her out directly." I asked, had he had her shoved out? "I have ordered her out." We talked of the very splendid fruit which Lord M. has, for I never saw such magnificent pines, and he is always sending me such quantities; I said to him I thought he had the finest fruit I ever saw. "I begin to think I have," he replied. He said his former gardener was now his steward; his son is Lord M.'s gardener, and Lord M. says a better one than the father. When they tell the father that his sons are surpassing him, and were cleverer, Lord M. said, he says, "I hope they are; I've taught them all I know, and they have learnt something themselves besides." . . .

Tuesday, 9th July.—There were two plates full

[1] She married Duke Maximilian of Leuchtenberg on 14th July, 1839.

of the most magnificent peaches I ever saw, which Lord M. was so kind as to send me. There never was such fruit as he has got; he got 100 of these peaches in the morning, and had sent some very fine ones to Lord Holland, he said, also. . . .

Thursday, 11th July.—Talked of the Commander of the *Lightning* who took Uncle and Charles to Lisbon, and who they were anxious to get something for; he has been 25 years a Lieutenant and has 5 children. "Oh! 25 years, that's nothing; many have been for 50 years," said Lord M., "and the 5 children, that's his own doing."

Talked of my being so silent, which I thought wrong and uncivil, as I hated it in others. "Silence is a good thing," said Lord M., "if you have nothing to say." I said I hated it in others, and that it annoyed me when he was silent. "I'm afraid I'm so sometimes," he said, "won't say a word." Yes, I said, that nothing could be got out of him sometimes. "And that you dislike?" he said. Yes, I said, it made me unhappy, which made him laugh.

Friday, 12th July.—Talked of my fearing that too many of my relations had come over this year, which Lord M. didn't think, and said there had been no remarks made about it. Talked of my Cousins Ernest and Albert coming over,—my having no great wish to see Albert, as the whole subject was an odious one, and one which I hated to decide about; there was no engagement between us, I said, but that the young man was aware that there was the possibility of such a union; I said it wasn't right to keep him on, and not right to decide before they came; and Lord M. said I should make them distinctly understand anyhow that I couldn't do anything for a year; I said it was disagreeable for me to see him though, and a disagreeable thing. "It's very disagreeable," Lord M. said. I begged him to say nothing about it to anybody, or to answer questions about it, as it would be very disagreeable to me if other people knew it. Lord M. I didn't mind, as I told him everything. Talked of Albert's being younger. "I don't know that that signifies," said Lord M. "I don't know what the impression would be," he continued, "there's no anxiety for it; I expected there would be." I said better wait till impatience was shown. "Certainly better wait for a year or two," he said; "it's a very serious question." I said I wished if possible never to marry. "I don't know about *that*," he replied. . . .

Sunday, 14th July.—Talked of the foliage being in beauty, and I said neither the lime blossoms or the flowers smelt hardly at all in this garden; Lord M. wouldn't believe it, and said, "Everything does better in London; London beats the country hollow in flowers." Talked of the garden being, as I said, very dull; "All gardens are dull," said Lord M., "a garden is a dull thing." Talked of the garden in St. James's Park, and Lord M. said there was a great piece of work about the old Swan being killed, in consequence of their having brought in too many other swans; this swan was called Old Jack, and had been hatched in the year '70!! "They are very angry with me," said Lord M. I asked why; "Because I didn't see that it was taken care of."...

Wednesday, 17th July.—Lord M. said, "J. Russell is very anxious in these arrangements that he should get the Colonies," for that he felt in the House of Commons, when he had to speak so much about them, it made it difficult for him, without having them; but would Normanby give up the Colonies? Lord M. replied he rather wished to do so; "he feels the Colonies are too much for him; but it will never do to put Normanby there." I asked what could they do?—Put Minto in the Home Office, he said, and Normanby at the Admiralty. "It requires somebody in the Home Office who can be respected, and whom the Tory Lord Lieutenants can have confidence in," Lord M. said. It was not necessary for the Secretary of the Home Office to be Leader of the House of Commons; for he, himself, was in the H.O. This Lord M. said some little time before. "Now, they have no confidence in Normanby," he continued; "they have no confidence in his probity, they know he is a Radical; they don't *like* John Russell, but they have confidence in him; they know he is a man of honour." Lord M. fears Normanby wishes to be in the Home Office, as it would raise him and give him power over Ireland, and be a blow against his enemies; but as he has not managed the Criminal part well in Ireland, "they would put their finger upon that." Lord Melbourne, Lord Albemarle, Lord Byron, Lord Surrey, Mr. Macaulay, and Mr. Rice dined here. Lord Melbourne led me in. I expressed surprise at seeing Mr. Macaulay so short; I had expected him tall. After dinner, when Lord Melbourne came up to me, I talked of the heat and being tired, of what I should say to Mr. Macaulay.[1] "Oh! ask him about India and Auckland." Talked of the Play of *Henry V*. "It's a spirited play," said Lord M. Too much of the Welshman, I said. "But that's thought very

[1] Macaulay had been a member of the Supreme Indian Council in Calcutta, 1834–8. He became Secretary at War this year. See *ante*, p. 8.

clever," he replied. The broken French of Catherine at the end, I thought absurd, in which Lord M. agreed. Henry V., he said, wrote in French. I talked to Mr. Macaulay, who had to be presented. We were seated much as usual, Lord Melbourne sitting near me. Talked of Macaulay's being so frightened, and of our having such power abroad, and people looking at us for everything. Talked of the Elsslers, and the Ballets Lord M. saw formerly. Talked of the fate of Edward II. and Richard II. being so alike, and so uncertain; the one by his wife's connivance. Talked of Edward III.'s *seven* sons; of Henry VI.'s widow marrying Owen Tudor, who was illegitimately descended from John of Gaunt. "They didn't mind what a Queen Dowager did then," Lord M. said; "they seldom returned." Anne of Cleves for instance lived and died here. Talked of Henry VIII. behaving very ill to her; he called her "a Flanders mare"; of his using his other wives so ill; Jane Seymour, I said, narrowly escaped being beheaded. "Oh! no, he was very fond of her," said Lord M., which I denied. "She died in child-bed when Edward VI. was born." And poor Catherine of Aragon he ill-used, I said; "He got tired of her," said Lord M., "she was a sad, groaning, moaning woman," which made me laugh. "She had always an idea that her marriage was formed in blood," he said, on account of the poor Earl of Warwick's death, which always hung upon her mind. Talked of Catherine Parr's narrowly escaping death. Lord M. said, "He got to be dreadfully tyrannical; when he began he had every sort of good feeling." Talked of Mary. "She was dreadfully bigoted, she would have sacrificed everything to her religion," he said. Talked of her cruelty

—her having poor Jane Grey, her own cousin, executed. Talked of her (J. Grey's) sister who died in prison, and whom Queen Elizabeth ill-treated because she married somebody without her leave. "Oh! she was dreadfully tyrannical," said Lord M., "just like her father; very stern; she was a Roman Catholic in fact, except the supremacy of the Pope; that she would never submit to." Talked of poor Mary of Scots' execution, which M. said Elizabeth delayed too long, for that her Ministers had been urging it. "When she signed it," said Lord M., "she said, 'I know Lord Walsingham will die of grief when he hears it'; it wasn't right of her to joke at such a moment." Talked of poor Mary. "She was a bad woman," said Lord M., "she was a silly, idle, coquettish French girl." I pitied her; talked of Darnley's brutality about Rizzio; Lord M. fears there's no doubt about her being aware of the intention of murdering Darnley; talked of her unhappiness, and the roughness of the Scotch towards her; of her brother Moray, whom Lord M. admires.

"Macaulay says," said Lord M., "no Christian Prince ever mourned for a Mahommedan; and Mahommedans never wear mourning; they take off their turbans and put ashes on their heads, but never change their garb." "I was speaking to Palmerston about Peel the other day, and he said," continued Lord M., "'The Queen would have liked Peel better when she knew him'; he says that he is much the best of them, that he is a very fair man; that he is not a very *high-minded* man, and has shown himself less so than he thought he had been."[1] . . .

[1] The Prince Consort thought Peel the most "high-minded" Englishman then in the service of the State. His view is not contravened by what has subsequently come to light in reference to Peel.

Wednesday, 24th July.—I said to Lord M., Torrington told me, and several regretted so, that Lord M. called Brougham " his noble friend " in the House, as he always behaved so infamously to Lord M.; Lord M. smiled and said he didn't like *not* to do so, and thought it was only courtesy; but he usen't before, I observed. "No," he said, "but when *he* began," Lord M. didn't like *not* to do so. . . .

Friday, 26th July.—At ½ p. 7 I went into the drawing-room, and received the Queen Dowager and then the Empress[1]; the Queen Dowager was quite shocked at the idea of going in before me, but I insisted on it. The Empress looked handsome; those beautiful expressive blue eyes look so handsome, and she has such a pretty, tall figure. The Duke of Sussex went in first with her; then came Baron Moncorvo with the Queen Dowager, I following with Lord Conyngham. It must have been, I fear, a severe trial for the Queen, seeing all the same servants and the same plate, but she behaved perfectly.

Saturday, 27th July.—" Party went off well ? " he asked. I replied Yes, but that a Concert always dragged, as people couldn't and mustn't talk. "You say the Queen Dowager was rather affected," he said, (I wrote to him last night,) "the same plate, the same servants," he observed (quite touched). I said I had great difficulty in persuading her to go before me, for that she said that really was *too* wrong, that she couldn't think of doing it, but I forced her to do it; she said to me, "I must obey." "I was sure she wouldn't like that," said Lord M. with tears in his eyes, and he was also much affected when I told him that she said she *felt* kind intentions.

[1] The Duchess of Braganza (ex-Empress of Brazil), step-mother of Queen Dona Maria. See *ante*, Vol. I., p. 86.

Talked of my fearing to go to Windsor this year; of my getting tired of the place; of George III. living almost always at Windsor, hunting 6 times a week, which Lord M. thinks he did till 1800; certainly after his 1st illness in 1788. Talked of Lady Tankerville,[1] and he said, "She is a frivolous little woman who doesn't know what she is about; I have known her all my life." Lord and Lady Holland going there; Stockmar, I said, disliked Lord M.'s going to Lady Holland, as he thought she made Lord M. tell her so much. "Well, that may be true," he said, which I said was very wrong of Lord M. "But I don't think I do," he said. Holland tells her all that goes on in the Cabinet, which we agreed was very wrong. . . .

Tuesday, 30th July.—Talked of my being kept so long in London, which when the Opera was over, I should dislike, as I hated *not* going out, and staying at home every day; but Lord M. said in the *country* I must stay at home; *then* I submitted, I said. He said I might go out more next year. I said I felt tired; Lord M. asked why; I didn't know, but that I certainly was tired. Lord M. said, Affairs were not in a very pleasant state. At a little after 7 we dined; and at near ½ p. 8 I went to the Opera with all but dearest Daisy, Lady Charlotte, and Mr. Murray. It was again *Norma*, and oh! more splendid than before. Grisi was perfection; it really is quite a treat to see and hear her; Mario too so delightful; alas! his and *Norma's* last night, for he went away last night to Paris, and this charming opera can't be performed any more.

[1] Corisande, daughter of Antoine, Duc de Gramont. She may have been frivolous, but she possessed undoubted charm, and wrote delightful letters in very pure French. See Vol. I., p. 72.

Wednesday, 31st July.—At 5 I went downstairs with Lehzen and Matilda to the Equerries' room, where Lord Melbourne was sitting to Grant[1] (since a ¼ p. 4) on that wooden horse without head or tail, looking so funny, his white hat on, an umbrella in lieu of a stick in one hand, and holding the reins which were fastened to the steps in the other; he sat there so patiently and kindly, doing just what he was told[2]; but, as Grant said, he is not easy to paint, for he either looks grave and absorbed, or laughs and goes into the other extreme; he is always changing his countenance; I was *so* amused. Grant kept telling him, "Now Lord Melbourne, hold your head in the right position,"—for he kept looking at Islay and trying to touch him with his umbrella; and then, "Now sit up, Lord Melbourne." Grant has got him so like; it is such a happiness for me to have that dear kind friend's face, which I do like and admire so, so like; his face, his expression, his air, his white hat, and his cravat, waistcoat and coat, all just as he wears it. He has got Conyngham in also very like; and Uxbridge, George Byng, and old Quentin ludicrously like. I remained 20 minutes in the room; and I believe Lord Melbourne sat till near 6.

Talked of the news from India, of Sir C. Metcalfe, his being so odd-looking; his being quite tired, as Lord M. said, of one year in the Oak Plantations at Fern Hill;[3] Lord M. told Lady Normanby (who has taken an unjust dislike to Sir C. Metcalfe on account

[1] Sir Francis Grant, elected P.R.A. in 1866.

[2] The sitting was for a picture which now hangs in the corridor at Windsor. The Queen is shewn riding out from the Castle accompanied by her Court.

[3] A place at Cranbourne, on the outskirts of Windsor Forest.

of his ugliness) that he went from Eton to India, and got to be Governor-General; Lady Normanby observed, only *ad interim.* "But he *was* Governor-General," said Lord M. Talked of these famous Musk Melons which they have in Kandahar, and which he wishes to get some of. "We never were in Kandahar before," he said, "we *are* in it now." Talked of the Empress,[1] and her Cousin Louis Napoleon, who, Lord M. said, "has a good many friends" and "is living very quietly."[2] Talked of the Empress's child, of the numbers of relations the Empress has; of her being such a nice person and my liking her so much. "She's a very nice person," said Lord M., "a very fascinating manner." Talked of our fearing the Harvest would suffer from this weather; of the beautiful pictures in the Gallery here, for some time; of their being all Dutch, which we agreed was a low style; our preferring the Italian Masters. "There is nothing like the Italian style," said Lord M. Of my wishing in time to buy some Italian pictures, which he said I might. Talked of Lord M.'s having had his umbrella in the room, and I said he always took it about with him. He replied laughing, "You should never quit your umbrella when it rains." What use was it in a close carriage? I said. "Might be upset," he said, "I might want to get out; suppose I might be stopped and put out of the carriage, which may happen one of these days,—at least leave me the umbrella to go on with," he said laughing so much himself and making us all laugh too. Talked of where Lord M. had been reading about the lean and fat kine. "It's Joseph's dream," he said, and as he was thinking

[1] Ex-Empress of Brazil. See *ante*, p. 220.

[2] He was living at this time in London, in Carlton Gardens.

of famine, he read it. I thought it difficult, which he does not. "All the history of Abraham is very beautiful and very clear," he said; "it's the history of an Arabian Tribe." The Prophets, he agreed, were very difficult. . . .

Saturday, 3rd August.—He asked if I had heard the news from Alexandria from Palmerston; I replied none except those which he had written me in the morning (which were that "The Capitan Pasha had taken the Turkish Fleet to Alexandria,[1] and Mehemet Ali says that he will not give it up to the Sultan until he dismisses the Grand Vizier and acknowledges the hereditary right of the Pasha to the countries which he at present governs. This is to make the Sultan his subject and his Vassal.") What could make him do it? I asked. "He disagreed with the Vizier," said Lord M. "Stopford is to be written to, to force him to give back the Fleet." Talked of there being so few marriages; I named 4, and mentioned March's paying great attention to Sarah Mary. Lord M. observed he was too young, and said, "A man shouldn't marry before 30." *He* did at 26, I observed. "Yes," he replied, "I wasn't fit to be married; a man oughtn't to marry before he can lead the life of a married man; I was always ashamed of it." I said a man might be fit before 30, and a man *needn't* marry. "No," he said, "but you don't

[1] War had been declared between the Viceroy and the Porte, but the Turkish Admiral, Achmet, under whose command the fleet had been despatched to Syria, treacherously sailed to Alexandria, and the Ottoman troops under Hafiz in Egypt were severely defeated. On 1st July the Sultan Mahmoud II. died after a reign of thirty years, and was succeeded by his son, Abdul Medjid, a youth of seventeen. Admiral Sir Robert Stopford commanded the British fleet. The French fleet was under Admiral Lalande. See *post*, p. 257.

marry out of reason; you marry because you fall in love."

Sunday, 4th August.—Talked before this of one's disliking things which one had been made to learn by heart when a child; and Lord M. talked of its being unnecessary that a child should *understand* what it learnt. "I don't mind their pottering about explaining things." I said I thought they should always understand. "Then you would teach them nothing at all," he continued, "if you only taught them what they understand." But if they asked? I said. "Oh! if they ask," he said, "then I would explain." But I said nothing I hated so much as explaining anything to a child. "Now that I must say is very wrong," said Lord M., and when I observed that one often did not know what to say to them, he said, "It doesn't do to show ignorance, you must explain it in some sort of way." Talked of Governesses, and the English ones generally being so bad, and he said, "Emily was very unfortunate; I really think they" (Lady Ashley and Lady Fanny) "are the two best brought up girls in England, but their education was shocking." Talked of the Pagets being so well brought up. I observed Lord M. had the new glasses again, which are of ebony inlaid with gold, and which he has had some months; I thought some years, as there is W. L. upon one side. "The person who gave them to me had that done," he said; "I don't know why that was put." He thinks them "very pretty," but I told him I preferred the old ones, as these did not look like him.

Tuesday, 6th August.—Talked of Uncle Leopold; my Cousins Ernest and Albert's coming, which we agreed would create observation. Lord M. said there had been a paragraph about it the other day in one of the papers, which the Editor of the *Observer* sent to him, asking Lord M. if he should contradict it. "I told them they had better not contradict it; I thought it better not," he said. I repeated to him that he had said he did not like the connection; he laughed, and hesitated to say anything, but upon my urging it, he said, "I don't like it very much." But he agreed with me, a great deal depended upon what sort of person he was; and I said much as I loved my Country, and was ready to do what was for its good, still I thought my own liking was one of the principal things. "I think you have a right to expect that," he said. "It's a very difficult subject; I don't think a foreign Prince would be popular." But I said I *couldn't* and wouldn't like to marry a subject, and whatever family he belonged to, Lord M. said, they would be the object of jealousy. "No, I don't think it would do," he added. I said I heard Albert's praises on all sides, and that he was very handsome.

Wednesday, 7th August.—When I returned from the Opera at a ¼ p. 12, I found a box from Lord Melbourne containing the following intelligence: "Lord Brougham spoke for 3 hours and a ½, as usual a most powerful, and also as usual a most violent and acrimonious speech.[1] Violent against Normanby,

[1] Brougham was exasperated at not being asked to resume in 1835 the Lord Chancellorship, which he had held in Lord Grey's, and Lord Melbourne's first, Administrations. He never forgave Melbourne, and on 6th August, 1839, he attacked the Government for their administration of the criminal law in Ireland. Lord Melbourne said that a more inveterate and criminatory speech had never been heard in that House. He moved the Previous Question, which, however, was negatived. See Vol. I., p. 244.

but still more violent against Sir Michael O'Loghlen, at present Master of the Rolls and formerly Attorney-General. Normanby is now replying and the debate will probably be late. Lord Melbourne apprehends that the Duke of Wellington will vote for the resolutions and in that case they will be carried." I wrote to Lord Melbourne asking for more news, and sat up till a little after 1, when I received the answer dated a ¼ to 1, in which he says, "He" (Ld. M.) "has spoken and also Lord Wharncliffe and Lord Plunket. Lord Roden is now speaking; there is no doubt that most of the Opposition will vote for the resolutions and they will of course be carried. It is as Your Majesty says, very awkward." At a ¼ to 9 this morning, my Maid woke me, and brought me another box from Lord Melbourne in which he says: "The House divided at a little after 3; for the resolutions, 90, against, 53." I went to sleep again and got up at a ¼ p. 10. Wrote to Lord Melbourne; breakfasted at near 11. At 20 m. p. 4 came Lord Melbourne and stayed with me till 10 m. to 5. I asked if he wasn't very tired; "I'm better now," he replied, "I was very tired." He only got to bed at 5, having had his dinner when he came home at 4. I said that was very bad, which made him laugh very much. "Must eat," he said. He should eat before he went to the House, I told him. "I've no appetite before a Debate." Talked of Brougham having been very violent, and its having lasted longer than Lord M. expected. "Normanby is in a dreadful state," said Lord M.; he had not spoken to him at the Cabinet, but Duncannon told Lord M. so. I said Lord M.'s speech was so fine that it must have annoyed Brougham a good deal. "Very much," said Lord M. I asked how Normanby spoke;

"Pretty well," he replied, "he was very much annoyed, and it was rather a difficult case, not very tenable." I said Lord M.'s always read so well, and asked if he didn't read them afterwards to see how they were well reported. "Never look at them afterwards," he replied laughing. I rode *Pegasus*, a grey horse whom I had never been on before; he is very quiet and easy in his paces, but rather heavy and not quite action enough. I rode between Col. Buckley and Lord Headfort. We rode only in Hyde Park; it was a pleasant evening. At 8 we dined. Lord Melbourne, Lord Surrey, Charles Howard and William Cowper dined here. I asked what he had had for his dinner *this morning* at 4; a pike, chicken, peas, a raspberry tart, and a bottle of madeira, he said, which quite surprised me. He told me in the morning that he had slept till 12.

Talked of another Lord, and Lord M. said Duncannon had mentioned Lord Lurgan, but that he didn't think he would be the man for it. "He's a man of great abilities," he said, "and of great oratorical powers"; and I added a good sort of man. "Very," said M., "he's an enthusiastic, excitable man." Talked of Lord M.'s not looking over the reports of his own speeches. "Never care about them afterwards," he said; "nothing I like less," he continued, making a face of disgust, "than to read the report of my own speeches; it makes a bad publication." . . . Talked of the Italian opera, which Lord M. agreed could only be kept up by the Manager's asking a great deal of money. "It has a very factitious existence," he said; he continued that it was only introduced about 100 years ago, in Queen Anne's reign, and that there was a terrible row about it then. His ancestor, Mr. Coke, was Vice-Chamberlain, and therefore, Lord M. said, he has a number of papers relating to the commencement of it; the first singers were the Marguerite (who married a Frenchman of the name of Le Pine), a Mrs. Tofts, also an Italian by birth, Nicolini Hayimes (a man); and he said the opera was half English, half Italian, the Italians only singing in Italian. Addison, who wrote very violently against the Italian opera, said, "We are so tired of understanding half, that better understand none of it, and have it all in Italian." Talked of George III.'s love for Handel, and my disliking him. Lord M. said so funnily, "There are no good voices in England, no good *voce di petto,*" which I denied. "You should sing from the chest,—walk from the hip—not from the knee and ankle." He said the English voices being all "Saxon nasal voices," that singing and speaking was in fact the same thing, and that both could be taught; and that singing should be always taught. "I've a great deal of latent music in me," he said, which made us laugh much.

Thursday, 8th August.—The Duchess of Sutherland and her 2 daughters there. Talked of the Duchess caring for Politics, that I could not bear women mixing in Politics, and that I never talked to my Ladies about them. "That's quite right," he said; and that I thought it very wrong in the Ministers telling their wives everything, in which Lord M. quite agreed, but said everybody told everything to somebody. I never did, or wish to do so, I said. "But that's very rare," he said.

Friday, 9th August.—The Band played some of my favourite Quadrilles during dinner, which I said made me quite frantic when I heard them. "Those Quadrilles are dangerous," said Lord M., "if they produce that effect on you." We had great fun about the fir plantations at Windsor; some were set fire to, which Lord M. said was a very good thing, as there were too many. "Everything works for the best," said Lord M. in his funny way, "even the worst intentions." Talked of the fir plantations at Swinley, which Lord M. dislikes but which Lord Duncannon said were in order to nurse up the young oaks with firs. "I don't believe anything about *nursing up* with firs," said Lord M. Lord Duncannon laughed and said there was no doubt about it. "There is no doubt, is there?" replied Lord M., "*I* believe there is the *greatest*. If the oaks have to be nursed up by firs," he continued, "I don't think they are worth planting at all; nobody knows so much about planting as I do and as my man does." We laughed at this. Lord Melbourne when he came in after dinner, asked Miss Anson very funnily about her family, and when I asked him what he was saying, he said, "You should always ask people about their families, else you never know anything about *them*." We talked for some time about the possibility of my hearing a Debate in the House of Lords some day, as I had been expressing my great wish to that effect to Lord Duncannon at dinner, and he thought there was the possibility of a grille being made in some place, so that I could *hear* it without being seen. Lord M. said, "It's a very serious question; think if it was known, of the allusions there would be made." We all agreed that if it was *known* it never would do; but Lord Duncannon said I meant it *not* to be known; and that I could get down without its being known. "I have much doubt about the secrecy of a thing," said Lord M., which we denied; he talked of there being no doubt whatever of the

Sovereign's having the *right* to go. If it were to be known, he said, "Brougham would talk for half the night." We then talked of this Church in Hyde Park, to be built near the Cavalry Barracks, which Lord M. did not see so great an objection to, as he said it was a vile piece of ground; but Lord D. said great pains had been taken to open all that ground, and therefore that it would never do to build it all up again. Lord M. said, "Well then, you must stick to that" and allow no other building to be put there, "no playhouse"!! The difficulty in refusing this Church is, that the King consented to it. Talked of the trees in the Park, and Lord M. said, "I don't like trees, I don't like trees in a town"; and he rather thought he should like the Park "a plain"!! Talked of the late King's strange ideas of architecture; and Lord M. said, "He said that all pictures of sacred subjects were improper and ought to be destroyed"!! We talked about the garden here, and Lord M. said *he* would make a large flower garden on the lawn, and would cut down the elms and the oaks and plant rare exotics. Talked of Brighton, the impossibility of sailing there, the burden the Pavilion was, and what to do with it. . . .

Sunday, 11th August.—Talked of this Tournament being such folly; he understands there is a lady who has paid £1,000 for 3 dresses; "Lady Seymour's is only to cost 40, I was *told* to-day," he said. Talked of old Mrs. Fox,[1] who is past 90, having a tooth taken out which was quite sound. Talked of washing dogs being a bad thing for their coats; and washing the hair being as he said a very bad thing, but which he used to do formerly, and which he thinks makes

[1] The widow of Charles James Fox. She died in 1842 in her 93rd year.

people bald. Losing the hair came from the vessels of the skin not being in good order, he said. "I think a man looks better without hair than with it, if he has a fine head," said Lord M.

Monday, 12th August.—I then showed Lord M. Uncle Leopold's letter, in which he says he is desired to sound me, whether I should object to the *King of the French's coming over to see me* at Brighton from Eu, for one afternoon and one night, with the Queen, Mme. Adelaide, Clémentine, Aumale, and Montpensier ! ! in the beginning of September. We talked of this, and of people never believing Kings or Queens travelled merely for friendship. Lord M. said he would speak to Palmerston about it, and I gave him part of the letter to take ; I would have to go down to Brighton to meet him.

Tuesday, 13th August.—I then talked of what I should write to Uncle Leopold about the King of the French's coming over ; (Lord M. sent me yesterday afternoon a note from Lord Palmerston about it, in which he says amongst other things, "The Visit would no doubt set people a-talking, and give rise to many conjectures and surmises, but all the speculations which could be founded upon it, would go upon the assumption that the visit indicated a tendency towards a closer union between England and France ; and good rather than evil is likely to arise from the propagation of that notion throughout Europe"). Lord M. then asked if I should like it ; I said I certainly should, and that I had a great friendship for the King of the French ; but I begged Lord M. to inquire if I could go down to Brighton for a night. I said I thought Palmerston disliked the King of the French, which Lord M. denied[1] ; he said

[1] The Queen was right, for, on the death of Louis Philippe, Lord

H.M. MARIE AMÉLIE.

QUEEN OF THE FRENCH.

From a portrait by Dalton, after Sir W. Ross.

that Palmerston thought he had behaved ill about Spain, "but he is very much for the French alliance; no one more so." I asked Lord M. what *he* thought of the visit. "*I* agree with Palmerston," Lord M. replied.

Wednesday, 14*th August*.—They are going to have the Portuguese Slave Trade Bill to-morrow, and *16* other Bills, and on Friday those Bills which they cannot get through to-morrow. Talked of how they had got to such a number this year, many having arisen out of circumstances having lately taken place, he said, and also the business of the country increasing. I said if it increased every year, Parliament would end by sitting all the year round. "That's what I always expect it will come to,"[1] said Lord M. Talked of Normanby, and his coming down to Windsor, which Lord M. thought he would not try to do often. Talked of his (Normanby's) not seeming happy, of his having been much attacked; and Lord M. said the fact was, that a much greater expectation had been raised of him than he deserved, that he had got a factitious renown, Lord M. knew not how—and that there had been "a good deal of disappointment,—not that he's the worse," but because a factitious expectation had been raised. All which is so true. "It's very easy for a man to be Lord Lieutenant of Ireland" (and I observed Lord Ebrington did it well; "much better," Lord M. replied), "but when you bring a man over to be Secretary of State, you see what he is." "Normanby

Palmerston wrote to his brother William Temple, "The death of Louis Philippe delivers me from my most artful and inveterate enemy, whose position gave him in many ways the power to injure me" (*Life of Palmerston*, iv. 229).

[1] Prophetic (1912).

is a very clever man," he said, "but he has no public ability, no power; very fluent, but not impressive." Talked of Lady Fitzalan,[1] and Lord Surrey's praising her, which Lord M. said was quite right, now that the thing was done. . . .

Saturday, 17th August.—At a little before 2 I set off with Mamma, Lady Charlemont, dearest Daisy, all my ladies and gentlemen, for Windsor, where we arrived at 4. We had a deluge of rain on the road. Quiz was in our carriage, and Islay was in the next. At 5 it ceased raining. We set off in the pony carriages for Virginia Water. Mamma, Lady Cowper and Lady Charlemont drove with me; and all the ladies except dearest Daisy, Lady Fanny Cowper, Lady Uxbridge, Ellen and Constance, Lord Uxbridge, Lord Morpeth, Lord Leveson, Lord Torrington, and Mr. Cowper, who had all arrived at the Castle, followed us in others. When we got to the Fishing Temple we had refreshments there; after which we went on the water in the Barge, for about a ¼ of an hour, and it was a delightful evening; all the ladies, and Lord Morpeth, Lord Leveson, and Lord Uxbridge, were in the barge with us. We returned home at 7, and it rained the whole way almost coming home. At a ¼ to 8 we dined. Soon after 10 we went into the Red room and dancing began; the 1st Quadrille, which I danced with Lord Torrington, was beyond everything funny and full of confusion; my Band, from not being accustomed to play for dancing, made every sort of confusion,—1st played too slow, then stopped too soon, or went on too long. Talked with Lord M. of my being unable to bear tea, and he,

[1] Lord Fitzalan (see Vol. I., p. 190), grandson of the Duke of Norfolk, had married, on 19th June, Augusta, youngest daughter of Sir Edmund Lyons, afterwards Admiral Lord Lyons.

coffee; he thinks Parliament may be up by Tuesday week. He had, to my astonishment, a large fire in both his rooms. I asked if he had had one also at home; he said yes; and "I always have a fire if I am annoyed or worried; it's astonishing how it dissipates that"; and he always has one when he comes home late from the House. We stopped dancing at 3 minutes to 12, but remained in the room till 10 m. p. 12. . . .

Tuesday, 20th August.—At 20 m. p. 2 came Lord Melbourne and stayed with me till 3. Talked of the rainy, bad weather; of my having a fire; and he said, "Always should have a fire when it rains." He was quite well. He said, "We have had a Cabinet," and he laughed when I said he had told me the day before there would be none. "I said there was none settled; we were sent for at 11." Who summoned it? "Rice," he replied, "we've got him to give up his Bank of Ireland Bill; and the Bank of Ireland have behaved very well about it." [1]

Wednesday, 21st August.—I then showed him a very long letter I had received from Aunt Gloster, which he read out to me; she proposes I should give the Lodge at Richmond, which I gave in reversion to Mamma, to the Duke of Cambridge, and settle Bagshot Park on Mamma, letting Aunt G. have old Kew House, and she adds Lord Sidmouth could easily be asked to leave the house. I said I knew Mamma never would hear of Bagshot, and it never would do to move Lord Sidmouth out of the house where he lives, at his age.[2] "You can't propose it to him," said Lord M.; that he was an old man, and

[1] The practice of a Minister, other than the Prime Minister, summoning a Cabinet has fallen into disuse.

[2] Lord Sidmouth was then 82.

that it would be very hard, "and it was given him under very peculiar circumstances by George III. as a mark of favour." Lord M. continued, "He was Prime Minister 3 years,[1] and Secretary of State for many years; George III. was very fond of him, much fonder of him than of Mr. Pitt." Was he clever? I asked. "No, not a clever man," said Lord M. "George III. didn't like clever men."

Thursday, 22nd August.—"The Emperor is going to send you a present," Lord M. said; "haven't you seen that?" I said No, and he continued, "A Malachite Vase[2]; they say it is the finest in the world; it stands in his Palace at present." Lord M. said the Emperor was exceedingly angry at the proposition of the Fleets going up to Constantinople, and that if that had taken place he should have desired his Minister to leave Constantinople immediately. "It's the French he hates," Lord M. added. "Ponsonby has always been wanting our Fleet to come up to Constantinople; it would do no good." He then said John Russell had begged him to ask my leave[3] to go out of Town on Saturday. "I believe he wants it," and that all would be over in the House of Commons on Saturday, and in the House of Lords on Monday, so that the Prorogation would be on Tuesday. At 20 m. to 8 I went with Mamma, dear

[1] Mr. Addington was Prime Minister 1801–4. He had been Speaker of the House of Commons; and was commonly called "The Doctor" in reference to his father's profession. He died in 1844.

[2] This vase now stands in the State Drawing-room at Windsor Castle.

[3] The Principal Secretaries of State, the Lord Chancellor, and the First Lord of the Treasury never left town, when the Sovereign was at Buckingham Palace, without leave. Up to the end of Queen Victoria's reign they never left England without the permission of the Sovereign. This rule has been considerably relaxed of recent years; although it is not customary of the Prime Minister to go abroad without leave of the King.

Victoire, Lady Lyttelton, Uncle, my 3 Cousins, Lady C. Dundas,[1] Thérésine, and the Lord and Equerry, to Stafford House, where we were received by the Duke and Duchess of Sutherland, and were taken into a pretty drawing-room downstairs, full of fine pictures. Dinner was announced soon; the Duke of Sutherland led me in and I sat between him and Lord Melbourne to my right. The dining-room, downstairs, is not large, but pretty; many fine pictures; fine plate. The Duke seemed much better. The House had been up very early; only the Bolton Police Bill; Lord Melbourne pale and ill, said he was not well, and ate almost nothing. I said to him it was all that Fish dinner. After dinner I found my other ladies and gentlemen, Mary Howard and Elizabeth, Evelyn and Caroline in the drawing-room; the Duchess then showed us all the pretty rooms downstairs, and then took us up to see her beautiful bath-room,[2] bed-room, dressing-room, and sitting-room, all full of such pretty things and pictures; and then we came downstairs again, and the gentlemen came in. I observed to Lord Melbourne how pretty the room was; he said, "But this is only the Vestibule"; and that upstairs was all the finery. We then went upstairs, and the Hall and Staircase, lit up, with a Band in it, was really the handsomest thing I ever saw. We sat in the pretty room where the Christening had been; I sat between Victoire and the Duchess, all on chairs; Uncle and my Cousins behind us; Lord Melbourne, Evelyn, &c. opposite to us. We remained sitting here for some time, having tea and ice. We then

[1] Lady Charlotte Dundas, daughter of first Earl of Zetland. Lady of the Bedchamber to the Duchess of Kent.

[2] Bath-rooms are a modern luxury.

went into the Gallery, which is quite unfinished, to see the effect of some lighting. After that we sat in the room where we lunched last year; I sat on a large sofa with dear Victoire; and then Lord Melbourne came and sat down there. "This is a beautiful room," said Lord M., "that Gallery will always be a dingy room," which I denied.[1]

Friday, 23rd August.— . . . Talked of there being such a complication of Visits; Uncle Leopold having written, in short, quite a confusion—and that I hoped the King of the French would not come.

Saturday, 24th August.—At a ¼ to 6 came my excellent Lord Melbourne, who asked how I was; I said better. He, quite well. They were kept till 11 in the House of Lords. "I've brought you this speech," he said, pulling it out of his pocket, and he read it to me in his usual beautiful manner; it is rather long; written out by William Cowper, Anson being gone, and he feared not well written. Talked of there being so few flowers at Windsor; he admired some in my bouquet; of what Nursery Gardens my Uncle could go and see; of a rail-road going through Lee's garden; of rail-roads going through gardens and places; and I asked him if he would like it if one was to go through Brocket. "I couldn't bear it," he said, "must abandon the place." Talked of Lyndhurst. "What Campbell, the Attorney-General, says," said Lord M., "is very true; he says when Lyndhurst wants to say anything that isn't law or that he doesn't like to say, he gets Brougham to say it." Follett, Lord M. says, is certainly very clever and much the same sort of talents as Lyndhurst; "as to what sort of man

[1] The word "dingy" could not be fairly applied to-day to the gallery at Stafford House.

he is," said Lord M., "I'm sure I don't know." Talked of Miss Fox, who Lord M. says always looked the same; he saw her 1st in '90, 49 years ago. Talked of her, and Lord Holland's being very like their Uncle; though Lord M. said Lord Holland was not like C. Fox in conversation; that the latter was not near so talkative as Lord Holland; that Miss Fox had that great good-nature which they all had, and that she was very much beloved. Lord M. said, "That great good-nature is apt to degenerate into facility, so that people will do almost anything; I'm afraid Morpeth will have that; he's so very soft that I think he can never hardly say No to anyone; a very bad thing for a public man." They all tried to play at the Cup and Ball, and the Bandelore, after dinner. Lord Melbourne tried them also, and succeeded with the former. He said the only way to do it was "perfect steadiness, patience, perseverance, and tranquillity,—which is the only way to do anything." I sat on the sofa with Uncle Ferdinand, Lord Melbourne sitting near me and Victoire and some of the young people being seated round the table, playing at games, at draughts, and at a game of tee-totums in a bowl, in which I also joined occasionally. Lord Melbourne talked of the Pictures in the room; of the room. I said to Lord M. it must be so tiresome to hear German always spoken before him,[1] which he didn't understand. "Oh! not at all," he said, most kindly. Talked of going to church next day. "You should always attend wherever you are," he said, "should always read the Psalms." Talked of proroguing Parliament in person, which he said was not necessary, but was right; that formerly

[1] The Queen here alludes to the practice of the Royal Family at that date and for many years afterwards.

the Sovereign was obliged to go down and give the Royal Assent in person, and that the first time it was done by Commission was when the Bill of Attainder of Anne Boleyn had to be passed, and Henry VIII. had not the nerve to go down. I asked Lord M. if he wasn't very tired; that the House of Lords must be dreadful. "It is not the House of Lords," he said, "there's some fun in that; I like that; I don't mind those attacks; it's those *internal* dissensions that vex me." I said to Lord M. I was very childish with all my Cousins. "That's a very good thing," he said kindly. I added I often forgot I *was* young. "That's a capital thing to be reminded of it," he said so kindly.

Sunday, 25th August.—Talked to Lord M. of his being tired, and I said to him he mustn't go to sleep before so many people, for that he generally snored! "That proclaims it too much," he said, in which I *quite* agreed.

Talked of Hampton Court, its great size, none of the Sovereigns having lived in it since William III.,[1] of William III.'s being killed in coming from Hampton Court, the spot was well known, Lord M. said. "He broke his collar bone and drove it into his lungs; but anything would have killed him a'most, he was a weakly man;—a great man, who kept Louis XIV. in fear." A cruel man, I said. "Oh! no," said Lord M., "not cruel, not cruel in Ireland; he was the most tolerant monarch that ever sat on the Throne." And he said the only thing he ever did that was cruel, was that affair at Glencoe, when they told him by mistake there was a band of ruffians whom he ordered "to be knocked on the head." . . .

Tuesday, 27th August.—Lord M. then showed me

[1] A mistake. Queen Anne, George I., and George II. occupied the Palace.

a letter from C. Wood,[1] also resigning in consequence of Howick's resignation; he was to have been Secretary to the Treasury, what Baring was, but will keep on in the Admiralty till a successor can be found. Lord M. said he had sent Howick a long letter from John Russell (which he had not read) and which he concludes is to try and persuade him not to resign. "I don't think it'll have any effect," he said. I observed it would be a good thing if Howick resigned. "We shall have all the Greys against us," he said, which is a bad thing; and he thinks "it will not be long before Howick is in the Opposition," which would be too bad. No one knows of his resignation, and Lord M. has not yet mentioned it *formally* to me, he said. He said Howick was very much disliked at the Horse Guards; talked of Howick's disliking Lord Hill. "Lord Hill *is* a very dull man," said Lord M., "quite accustomed to the old routine." I asked how would he fill up Howick's place? He must take some time to consider it, he said. . . . I then showed him a letter from Uncle Leopold in which (by a curious coincidence) the King of the French has also given up coming over. "It's a very good thing," said Lord M., "and a very good thing also that you have mentioned you didn't wish it."

Wednesday, 28th August.—Talked of Lord M. and his being well; I said I should certainly not ask the Duke of W. this time when Uncle came. "Why not?" said Lord M. Because he had behaved very ill. "You must recollect that people have particular feelings," he said. There was no other Party; the Radicals themselves had quite given up the idea of being able to form a Government, which they had *once* thought possible; and that there could be only

[1] See Vol. I., p. 99.

2 Parties in England. I said, as for the Tories, I never would apply to them; I must, in some shape, he said; I never would submit about the Ladies; that must be arranged, he said. But why speak of all this *now*? I said, there was no fear *now*? "I don't know," he said. I said, as the others (the Tories) admitted *themselves* they could not stand, they ought to help and not to oppose every reasonable measure, as they had done, and not behave as they had done in the House of Lords. "They didn't behave so badly in the House of Lords," said Lord M. (This is admirable fairness.) "They didn't throw out many bills." But altered a good many, I said. "But I don't know that those alterations didn't do them good," said Lord M. laughing. The only outrageous thing they did, he said, was their throwing out the Admiralty Courts Bill, and that was "a very wanton thing." He thinks of offering Howick's place to Macaulay. I observed that some of Palmerston's despatches were rather severe. "I was looking over those Portuguese papers," said Lord M., "and they are very bitter; that does no good; on the contrary, 'a soft word turneth away wrath.'" Talked of Lady Granville, who Lord M. said was "a shrewd clever woman."

Thursday, 29th August.—Talked of the Tournament, and Lord M. had written to Wilhelmine that she ought to have gone to attend on the Queen of Beauty. Of there being no doubt in my opinion about her (Lady Seymour's) beauty. "I think her funny," he said. "Helen[1] is very clever too," said Lord M., "but she is always very nervous." "I've seen Howick to-day," said Lord M. (since Lord M. had been with me). "He was very civil;

[1] Mrs. Blackwood, afterwards Lady Dufferin. See Vol. I., p. 192.

said he was very sorry," but that what with his own opinions and his father's he couldn't have remained. "Lord Grey has done it," said Lord M., "he said he couldn't show his face again at Howick, if he was to remain; that his life would be intolerable; and that's what made Charles Wood resign; Charles Wood is wretched to leave office." Howick said to Lord M. *that he had been a sacrifice* to the opinions of others, that he had been quite "*a slave*" to J. Russell, that "no soldier ever obeyed his Commander" as he had done. "It is idle to talk to people of their faults," said Lord M., "for if they knew them, they wouldn't commit them"; which is so true. He then said that Sheil[1] had been very much agitated when I saw him. "I found him labouring under very great emotion when I went out to him," said Lord M., so much affected as to stifle his voice a little, and he continued so while he said that this was such an immense thing for Sheil, raising such a man to office, that it drove such people "quite mad." "I said to him," Lord M. continued, "'Now mind what you say when you get down into your county of Tipperary, for your election; mind not to get into any scrapes.' 'I know I'm a terrible character for indiscretion,' he said, 'but you needn't be afraid; I've not been tried *in office* before, you'll see I'm discreet.'" Lord M. said, much affected, that he understood Lady Howick[2]

[1] Richard Lalor Sheil was M.P. for Tipperary, and Vice-president of the Board of Trade. In early life he had been a dramatist, but he was more successful as an orator, in his exertions, in co-operation with O'Connell, for Catholic emancipation. He entered Parliament in 1831, and made a great speech in April of this year (1839) in support of the Irish policy of the Ministry.

[2] Maria, daughter of Sir Joseph Copley of Sprotborough. See Vol. I., p. 210.

had fought a most severe battle with Howick to try and prevent him from resigning. "It is right that you should know," said Lord M., "these things are of more consequence than you may think for, I fear George Grey won't remain," also for fear of Lord Grey. I said that was not what I called right. "But the last thing people think of," said Lord M. laughing, "is doing what is right." "Lord Grey is very hostile," said Lord M. But he resigned, I said. "Yes, and recommended me to the King," said Lord M.; "but it caused immediately a comparison to be drawn between his Government and mine, in disfavour of his,—which nearly drove him mad." I asked Lord M. did he really think Brougham was sincere. "I may flatter myself," said Lord M., "but *I* think he likes me." I said no one but Lord M. would speak so of Brougham. "I haven't the slightest animosity against Brougham," said Lord M. This is a truly angelic disposition and worthy of eternal record.

Friday, 30th August.—Talked of Victoire's sitting to Landseer; of a picture Leslie has done of Holland House, which I said I would send for. I rang the bell and ordered the picture to be brought in; I said to Lord M., "Don't get up," when I did to ring the bell, and he smiled and sat down. The picture was brought in; it is very pretty, not large; the interior of the Gallery at Holland House; Lord Holland and Lady Holland sitting at a table; old Allen [1] standing, and a young man standing in front, who Lord M. said is one of her Pages; the other Page is seen quite at a distance; Lady Holland *calls* them *Edgar* and *Harold*, but their real names are John and Thomas,

[1] John Allen (1771–1843), an intimate friend of Lord Holland and constant inmate of Holland House, where he acted as librarian.

Lord M. said. Lady Holland very like, he says, though flattered in size and put in a black velvet gown; "Allen the least like; too smart," he said; Lady Holland *had* a very fine skin. Lord M. pointed out where the various doors in the Gallery led to.[1] . . .

[1] Many years later, under the gentle dominion of another Lady Holland, the Queen went to Holland House.

INTRODUCTORY NOTE TO CHAPTER XVI

A VISIT to England of the French King, planned by her Uncle Leopold, was not welcome to her Ministers, and the Queen managed to obtain its postponement. King Leopold and Queen Louise, however, visited Windsor early in the month of September, and the final arrangements were completed for the reception of the young Coburg Princes. They were expected on 30th September, but the Queen, finding that all her Ministers were to be at Windsor on that date, feared that it might be too readily assumed that her marriage was settled, and asked that her cousins' arrival should be postponed until 3rd October. She then found that they could not set off until the 6th, and was undoubtedly piqued at what, in a letter to her uncle, she called their want of *empressement.*

When, however, the meeting took place, the impression made on the Queen by Prince Albert was immediate. "Albert's beauty is most striking," she wrote to King Leopold; "and he is so amiable and unaffected—in short, very fascinating."

Three days later she told her uncle that her mind was made up, that she had told the Prince, that the last few days had passed like a dream, that she was so bewildered she hardly knew how to write, but that she was certain of a prospect of very great happiness before her.

"My feelings are a *little* changed," her letter concludes, "I must say, since last Spring, when I said I couldn't *think* of marrying for *three or four years*; but seeing Albert has changed all this."

King Leopold expressed his deep satisfaction in the words of Zacharias. He had laboured hard and unswervingly to bring about this marriage. It was the crowning act of his educational policy; it was the coping-stone of the regal edifice he had been so carefully engaged in rearing. He told the Queen that she would find in Prince Albert the very qualities and dispositions that were indispensable for her happiness, and would suit her own character, temper, and mode of life. The result, in after-years, was a fine tribute to the sagacity of King Leopold. He also told the Queen that Lord Melbourne had, in all this affair, exhibited that amiability and disinterestedness with which he was rightly credited. Many another man might have looked to his own personal views and imaginary interests. Lord Melbourne had but one idea, the happiness and security of the young Queen.

On 23rd November a special meeting of the Privy Council received from the Queen herself the intimation of her engagement to Prince Albert. She noted that Lord Melbourne was deeply moved. She was loudly cheered by immense crowds when that afternoon she left the Palace for Windsor Castle.

H. S. H. Count Alexander Mensdorff Pouilly
from a portrait by Sir W. Ross

CHAPTER XVI

1839

Monday, 2nd September.—We then went downstairs to look at the enormous Vase which the Emperor of Russia has sent me; it is not yet unpacked, but is the most enormous thing to be imagined. Went upstairs, and played in the Gallery with dearest Victoire and Leopold, at Battledore. . . .

Thursday, 5th September.—Talked of my grief at my Cousins' going; and Alexander going on Saturday to Paris. Told Lord M. that his father was a French émigré who took the name of Mensdorff but whose real name was *Bouillée.* Talked of Alexander's mother.[1] . . . "Nice hair *he* has," he said, looking at Alexander. "I'm glad he's a Frenchman; I knew no German could have such hair." I said I admired his eyebrows so. "Beautiful eyes and eyebrows," said Lord M., and I said I had been drawing him.

Friday, 6th September.—George IV., he said, was a famous man for finding reasons for doing a thing he liked; the recognition of the Independence of the South American States was, Lord M. said, one of the worst things possible; "and the King disliked doing it very much," continued Lord M., "but Mr.

[1] Princess Sophia of Saxe-Coburg and Gotha, sister of the Duchess of Kent and aunt of the Queen. See Vol. I., p. 95.

Canning knew the way how to do it; he knew the King disliked Lord Ponsonby; and Mr. Canning proposed Lord Ponsonby should be sent to recognize the South American States; that was just the way,—the King gave way immediately." Lord Melbourne rode almost all the time in our row. We heard on returning that Uncle Leopold and Louise would be here in an hour's time; I waited till a ¼ p. 8 in my habit, and no one arrived; (dearest Victoire had been sitting with me ever since ½ p. 7, dressed;) and I read Despatches. I then took off my habit and was only half dressed when I heard they were coming; I rushed down half dressed, with Victoire, and received my dear Uncle and dear Louise at the door; Uncle F. and my Cousins were also at the door. I took Uncle and Aunt to their rooms, and soon left them; none of their things being come, they did not wish to come to dinner. Louise and Victoire came and sat with me while I was dressing. At 9 we dined.

Saturday, 7th September.—Talked of Uncle L.; their baggage not being come; of Louise having only one pair of stockings. Lord M. said Madame de Campan was so angry, when Marie Antoinette ordered so many things before they fled from Paris, and thus excited observation, and said to her, "On peut trouver des chemises et des bas partout." . . .

Wednesday, 11th September.—At 20 m. p. 11 we set off in open carriages, Louise, dearest Victoire and dearest Augustus were with me in the carriage; in the 2nd, Uncle Leopold, Mamma, Uncle Ferdinand, and Leopold; in the 3rd, Lady Lyttelton, Lady Charlotte, Thérésine, and Lord Fingall; and in the 4th, Lord Surrey, Col. Wemyss, Sir Robert Otway, and Col. Cavendish. We changed horses 3 times, at Staines, the Stud House, and Kennington Green. We got to Woolwich at a ¼ p. 2, and drove into the Dockyard immediately; we had only 2 steps to walk to the Boat; the Band of the Rifles played *God save the Queen*, and the guns fired, but it was all very quiet. I got into the boat with Louise, my 2 Uncles, Mamma, and Vecto; all the others going in another boat; we were rowed to the *Lightning* steamer, which was a little way off, and went on board her; I climbed up the side ladder with ease,[1] all my nautical feelings and recollections returning again; and we walked about the deck a little while. I then went down with Victoire in the cabin; it is very small but neat; she and Thérésine and Résy sleep in the same cabin. I made dearest Victoire take off her little handkerchief and give it to me; and I gave her mine. I gave Leopold a little pin, which I had also worn, a little Knight kneeling. It was heart-breaking to see the steamer go away from us—for she set off as soon as we were clear of her, and we remained on our oars to see her go; dearest Victoire looked *so* pretty standing near her father, and waved her handkerchief to the last.

Thursday, 12th September.—Talked of the Windsor Uniform,[2] and formerly the full dress of the uniform being red Pantaloons!! Lord Melbourne sat near me for a few minutes, and talked of Bats, and their

[1] As the Queen was about to leave the ship the captain and officers betrayed some anxiety and a desire to help her down the tall side of the vessel. The Queen looked up with the greatest spirit, and said quite loud in her silvery voice, "No help, thank you: I am used to this," and then descended, as an eye-witness observed, "like an old boatswain." She was enthusiastically cheered by the sailors.

[2] The Windsor Uniform was instituted by George III. It was copied from the uniform of the Household of Lady Pembroke. It is only worn by the King and his household at Windsor, and by such persons as are specially privileged to wear it by command of the Sovereign. See *ante*, p. 65, and Vol. I., p. 351.

settling in people's hair, and Lord M. said, "It is always so, if a thing happens once, it is said to happen always." Mme. Sebastiani said she knew it to be a fact. "Has she ever seen it?" asked Lord M. She replied No. "Then I don't believe it," he said.

Friday, 13th September.—I missed my dearest Cousins, alas! Saw Louise. Wrote to Ferdinand. Read despatches. Signed. At 8 we dined. After dinner we were seated as the day before—only that Lord M. sat near me the whole evening.

Saturday, 14th September.—We talked of the dreadful weather, pouring with rain the whole day. "I'm quite muzzed with reading so many despatches," he said; that *I* need not read them all through; talked of asking young Werther down; of my missing my dear Playfellows (which I *did* most dreadfully); Lord M. asked if I hadn't heard from any of them; I said no. Talked of Alexander, and Uncle's having told Lord M. he was "a very nice fellow"; I said *I* thought him exceedingly handsome. I sat between Uncle Leopold and Lord Melbourne. Talked to Lord Melbourne of Fanny; of his sleeping and its being too bad. "It's a sign of a composed mind," he said, which I admitted. Talked of my Cousins having had a good passage; of Lord M.'s and my being quite muzzed with reading; of Lord M.'s going to church next day, which we said he ought to do 3 times; he would go, he said, "though it's against my creed; I'm a *quietist*; it's the creed which Fénelon embraced, and which Mme. Guillon taught; you are so perfect that you are exempted from all external ordinances, and are always living in God." I said that the use of church was, that it made one think of what one would otherwise *not* think of; that I had often doubted him; that I had often suspected him; "What about?" he asked; he said of all things he could be the least suspected of having heterodox opinions. . . .

Sunday, 15th September.—Talked of the weather, its being fine but cold; of the Eton boys, and Lord M. said Seymour had been down to Eton and had asked one of the boys if they saw much "of the Queen," upon which the boy had replied, "Oh! no, she considers us a Nest of Tories."

Monday, 16th September.—I danced 5 Quadrilles; (1) with Van de Weyer; (2) with Baron Werther; (3) with M. de Kisseleff; (4) with Count Moerkerke; and (5) with Lord Uxbridge. Louise danced each quadrille. How sadly different it was from last Monday, when I had my beloved Cousins with me! . . .

Thursday, 19th September.—Got up at 9 and breakfasted at ½ p. Wrote to Alexander, and my journal. Played on the piano. Fanny brought up the 2 dear boys at a ¼ p. 1, and we took them to the room where Louise was sitting; and then we went into the Gallery. After 2 we lunched with all. Lord Melbourne also lunched with us. The 2 little boys[1] came in and were very funny. Mitty, who has beautiful dark brown curls, is I think a little like Lord Melbourne; Dimitty like Spencer Cowper. Lord Melbourne was very funny with them.

Friday, 20th September.—I got up at ½ p. 4, put on a dressing-gown and a bonnet, and went to Louise's sitting-room, where I found her and Uncle at breakfast by candle-light; they were much pleased to see me. I took some bread and butter and an egg; poor dear Louise was so sorry to leave me; so kind;

[1] The two eldest boys of Lord and Lady Ashley.

she is so fond of me, which I really don't deserve. I went with them to Mamma's room, and then took leave of them on the top of the staircase, with much regret, for they are both *so* kind to me; Uncle is so amusing and funny. I watched them from my window; day was dawning and it looked grey and melancholy.

At 10 m. to 3 Lord Melbourne came to me, and stayed with me till ½ p. 3. He asked how I was. He gave me a warrant to sign about a Banner. He gave me the return of the revenue, which is most satisfactory. He said, "The King was quite astonished at the large sums; I showed him one of these." "I have had Brunow[1] with me this morning," Lord M. continued; "he says they only wish to do what we like; that they would act with France if we wished it, but they would rather without France; that the Emperor 'can't bear the King of the French'; 'he has a Crown that don't belong to him'"; that he sent an Ambassador there, but that he never would call him "mon frère" in a letter; that he (the Emperor) has a great contempt for the Carlists, and a pity for the elder branch (of the French family); that he would not meddle with it, "he left that in the hands of Providence," who would not allow it to go on. Brunow, said Lord M., went on to say that it was useless to speak to the Emperor of Russia of the opinion and will of the people; then he said to Lord M. that Persia in their eyes was of much more importance than this Oriental Question; that we should upset the Shah, which would be very dangerous, and in which case Russia must interfere. He desired Lord M. to express on his (Brunow's) part his great feeling at his recep-

[1] The Russian Ambassador.

tion here, and also the great affection the Emperor had for me.

Saturday, 21st September.—When I came out of my room I saw Lord Melbourne on the top of the staircase, and I asked him if he was going to drive out. "No," he said, "I'm come to see you go out." He went downstairs with me and said, "Macaulay will take this; I have had a very satisfactory conversation with him; he doesn't wish it to be mentioned directly." Talked about these gentlemen having intimated their wish to remain. "I didn't think it would create so much clamour," said Lord M. . . .

Monday, 23rd September.—Talked of Uncle's disliking any great gaiety. Lord M. said to him, the life of Kings and Queens was not very amusing, and they must have some amusements. "'You are quite right,' he said, 'it is very tiresome.' This seemed to tickle his fancy very much," said Lord M. laughing, "for he repeated it to me several times afterwards." Then Uncle wanted me, Lord M. said, to ask the great people of the Country, which Lord M. thought I had; Lord M. wished some Tories, and mentioned Lord Liverpool. Perhaps Lord Sandwich, I said. "That would be a good thing," said Lord M., and that the Beauforts were great personal friends. I said, I wished to ask none of the Tories this year. "If you do that," said Lord M., "you, as it were, cut them off." I observed John Russell disliked them; Lord M. said, "I think J. Russell has a good deal of bitter personal feeling," which he didn't show, but which extended towards the Tories pretty generally. "*I* don't dislike the Tories," said Lord M., "I think they are very much like the others." We agreed J. Russell disliked being supported by them. "I don't care," said Lord M., "by whom I am supported; I consider them all as one; I don't care by whom I'm helped, as long as I *am* helped," he said laughing.

Tuesday, 24th September.—Talked of the very curious account which he sent me (and which I read when I came home) of Runjeet Singh's last days and death. Lord M. said the account of the Women burning themselves was very curious. "They said, 'What we want is name and reputation, and therefore we will burn with the Maharajah'"; and of the Prime Minister repeatedly trying to do the same. Talked of its being a good thing to keep up the army a little; of the great expense of it for this country. Of Howick and his coming to see me next day; and Lord M. said he would probably state to me the causes of his resignation, and I asked what I should answer. "Say you are very sorry," said Lord M., "very sorry to lose his services, that you have every reason to be satisfied with the manner in which he performed his duty, that you had always heard he did it very well." I asked was he sorry; Lord M. replied, "I think he is," but that he was so influenced by his father. Talked of Lord Grey's hostility, and Lord M. said, "I know why he is angry with *me*; because I don't go and talk to him." Then, he continued, he consulted Lord Grey upon the drawing up of that Answer to the Address from the House of Lords, when Lord Grey gave very valuable service; "and he says I never thanked him for that. That is his forte," continued Lord M., "in drawing up papers of that kind; he is quite unrivalled for that."[1]

Wednesday, 25th September.—Talked of my having

[1] It was the natural envy on Lord Grey's part (felt by many men) of his successor; of the older for the younger man!

seen Howick, whom I thought rather irritated; that he had said he thought the Government was getting weaker, and was not going on well, either to my satisfaction or to that of the country. "That's always his tone," said Lord M., "and those are the two difficulties we have to contend with,"—on one side people say that we are going too much towards the Radicals; on the other hand that we lean too much towards the Tories and lose "the popular support." It is very difficult to please both. I told Lord M., Howick said he would always support the Government, which Lord M. thinks he will, coupled with a great deal of opposition; his last grievance, we agreed though, was his not being made Chancellor of the Exchequer. I said I had said to him just what Lord M. had told me. "Now you don't like having all these people down here," said Lord M., "because of these young Princes."[1] But I replied I didn't mind it. Lord M. said it might excite remarks, all the Ministers being down here just when these young people came here; but as there must be a Council it would be as well to have them here. I could stop my Cousins for a day, I said; but he didn't mind it; however, just before the audience ended we settled I should write to Uncle to keep them till Thursday. Being made Under Secretary of State does not vacate your seat, as it is not made by the Crown; a seat is only vacated by an Appointment made by the Crown. "Macaulay said," Lord M. went on to say, "he had no fear about his election; 'Indeed I think I should lose in Edinboro if I was to refuse to join you'";—also very satisfactory. Lord M. said Howick fretted so; was so eager about everything,

[1] The young Coburg Princes, Ernest and Albert.

which Lord M. believed was from conscientiousness. "But that won't do in public service," said Lord M.; "you must sometimes do things you don't like, and sometimes you mustn't press things you think right."

Thursday, 26th September.—Lord M. observed the rooks flying in a manner which indicated rain; I said I disliked them *so.* "How very odd," said Lord M., "I could sit looking at them for an hour; those are rural habits," he used to be always in the country formerly, shooting all day. Talked of my disliking this meeting of Ministers; my disliking to hear nothing else but Politics and always Politics.[1] "Nothing so disagreeable," said Lord M., "very tiresome; and that's the worst of Holland House; you hear nothing else, which is very tiresome, particularly when you are at it all day. Holland thinks of nothing else." Mr. Fox, on the contrary, Lord M. said, was always talking of poetry and literature, which he liked much better than Politics; people seldom liked, Lord M. said, what they did best. . . .

Saturday, 28th September.—I told him the Monkey was better; that I had finished Guizot, and thought it such a pretty book; the end Lord M. said was very curious, and I said melancholy, in which he agreed. I said I meant to finish Walpole, but that the sinking fund and all that alarmed me. "I wouldn't trouble myself with that," said Lord M., "I would give it up"; and I begged him to recommend me another book. Talked of the orange lilies in my hair being in Ireland the emblem of

[1] After her marriage the Queen used often to lay stress upon the relief it was to her that she could shift the burden of "politics" on to the Prince.

Orangeism; of William III., my not having descended from him but from James 1st and Mary Queen of Scots, and from Henry VII.; of Elizabeth's beheading Mary, which Lord M. said *she* didn't *wish* to do but was forced to do so; of Elizabeth always refusing to name her successor (which was then thought necessary), and saying, Lord M. said, "'I remember Hatfield,'" when *she* was her sister Mary's successor and they all came and courted her; of her being wretched when James 1st was born. "She didn't like it" (marrying), said Lord M., "and I think she never really intended it; but she liked all the courtship and flirtation." Lord M. then asked if I had ever read Hallam's *Constitutional History of England*, which I said I had not, and he recommended me to read it. "I think it's a good book to read," he said, "as you know the History well."

Sunday, 29th September.—Islay was much noticed; he (Islay) has a very odd trick of liking to lick and play with anything bright, and he remembers Lord M. giving him his glasses, and he sits begging before Lord M. the moment he sees them; and Lord M. said, "How very odd; it's quite a subject for the reflection of Philosophers; must be considered at the next meeting of the Philosophical Society." . . .

Tuesday, 1st October.—He then said that Russia's proposition relative to these Eastern Affairs[1] was to

[1] After the Battle of Navarino the general attitude of Europe towards Turkey underwent a change, and the desire to turn the Turks out of Europe gave place to a policy of bolstering up the Sick Man. The defeat of the Turks by Mehemet Ali at Konieh in 1832, and the danger thereby caused to Constantinople, led Mahmoud II. to appeal to the European Powers for protection. Russia alone was ready to come to his aid, and in 1833 Turkey concluded the Treaty of Unkiar Skelessi with Russia; by it the Dardanelles were closed to all but

act with us, rather *without* France, but *with* France if we wished it; and in case of Ibrahim Pasha's marching upon Constantinople, that it should be allotted to *them* to defend Constantinople; but *no* other fleet to come up the Dardanelles. Russia is bound by the Treaty of Unkiar Skelessi to defend Constantinople. "Now we think it very important to carry Russia along with us," said Lord M., "but also France," and that it was likewise *very* important to bind Russia by *convention* to do what she would otherwise do of herself; but would France agree? I asked. Lord M. said they thought France would not agree to anything of such magnitude and importance being done without her; Lord M. said more, which I cannot sufficiently recollect to put down. "So we have settled to return a favourable answer to Brunow," said Lord M., "to say that we are ready to act with Russia, and to act quickly, but that we think it very important also that France should go with us," and thus not state specifically *what* we shall do.

Wednesday, 2nd October.—I talked to him of Sir J. Hobhouse, and Lord M. said, "Hobhouse is a man of immense knowledge and acquirements; there's nothing he don't know"; and we agreed, a very agreeable man; of Macaulay, who Lord M.

Russian vessels. The death of Mahmoud in 1839 and the feebleness of his successor, Abdul Medjid, induced Mehemet Ali to attempt further encroachments, and this time the Powers determined to intervene, and ensure the integrity of the Ottoman Empire. France, however, stood aloof, and was greatly disgusted when in 1840 a treaty with Turkey was signed by England, Russia, Austria, and Prussia. By it Mehemet Ali was called upon to restore Syria and Candia to the Porte. He refused, and was thereupon compelled by English and Austrian forces to submit, after a defeat in Syria and the bombardment of Beyrout and Acre. See *ante*, p. 224.

said was "a man of immense learning; I think you'll see he'll make a great man some day,"—Lord M. continued. I observed he was odd-looking. "Uncouth, and not a man of the world," Lord M. replied, "he has studied a good deal; his father was a great Saint; and that restrained him a good deal." I regretted *I* knew so little. "Oh! you know quite enough," Lord M. replied, "and you will have plenty to learn as you will have a great deal to read." Talked of the odiousness of having everything repeated that I said, which he said was "irremediable."

Talked of horses, my grey one being so perfect; mine this year being so much steadier than they used to be; Tartar making Lord M. always uncomfortable. Lord Holland bought once a carriage and 4 horses for £100 at Calais, drove them to Naples and back, and for some time here afterwards! Talked of this Proposition of Russia to Lord M., and my fearing their getting alone to the Dardanelles, which he thought wouldn't signify if they were made to agree to leave it. "I don't doubt the Emperor's word," he continued. "Now mind me, if he ever breaks his word——" Stayed up till ½ p. 11.

Thursday, 3rd October.—Talked of Uncle's thinking I ought to play at cards, which Lord M. thought quite a mistake; of George III.'s playing at Commap[1] and at Backgammon on a Sunday, which Lord M. said would *now* be thought very wrong; George III. was very religious, Lord M. said, but against everything puritanical. "When Bishop Porteus[2] came

[1] Commap, a popular game in the eighteenth century.

[2] Beilby Porteus (1731–1808), famous as a sermon writer. Bishop successively of Chester and London.

to remonstrate with him," he continued, "about his going to Windsor on a Sunday, he received him with his carriage at the door."

Friday, 4th October.—Lord Melbourne said, "Here's a letter from my sister[1] about domestic affairs," and when I had read it, he gave me a letter from Sir Fred.[2] to her. "Now this is what has never been mentioned to any one about Palmerston; he's always wanting to marry her." Sir Fred. writes in order that if the letter were seen, no one might know what it meant, and talks of *Henrietta*, by which he means her. He advises her, if she likes it, to do it, not to potter about it. "I wrote to her she must do what she liked," said Lord M., "I couldn't advise her. The thing is," Lord M. continued, "what his (Palmerston's) circumstances are; some say he is very much indebted; and then they might both be very poor together" were he to be out of office; a very nice place in the country,[3] with a nice house, something like Holkham, Lord M. said. "He (P.) presses her very much, she says," continued Lord M. "You'll not mention it to anybody?" which I said he might rely on. I talked to him whether people were ever happy who married so late in life, and whose habits were settled, as Lord M. observed. "It would be a great change for him," said Lord M., "accustomed to run about everywhere; she says her own family like it. I said to her, 'You mustn't deceive yourself about it; if you do this you must take the consequences.'"

Saturday, 5th October.—Talked of asking Lady

[1] The Dowager Lady Cowper. See Vol. I., p. 242.

[2] Sir Frederick Lamb. See Vol. I., p. 253.

[3] Broadlands, in the New Forest, near Romsey.

Clanricarde,[1] which he again urged; of how the Granville's came to care so much about her. "Why, they, as the adherents of Canning," said Lord M., "naturally look to her; Lord Granville, Lord Morley, Lord Seaford, and also Lord Carlisle were very much attached to Mr. Canning." I observed Canning was no Whig, in which Lord M. agreed, but also no Tory. "He followed Mr. Pitt," said Lord M., "he began with Mr. Pitt, and Mr. Pitt was certainly not a Tory, though he was generally supported by the Tory party; he was called so, as he was in opposition to the Whigs." Then, when Mr. Pitt died, Lord M. said, Canning "took a line of his own." These, like Granville and the others, "are our best friends," Lord M. said, "but they are not Whigs; he (Canning) acted with the Whigs, and they followed him," and have remained with *us*; Lord Haddington was also one of his followers but went over. "They are very much mixed," said Lord M., "there are many on the Tory side who have not Tory opinions, and many amongst the Whigs who have not Whig opinions," and these, like Granville, consider Lord Canning as quite a Tory, and look to Lady Clanricarde instead. . . .

Wednesday, 9th October.—After dinner we were seated much as usual, Lord Melbourne sitting near me, but both he and I were sleepy, and I very tired. Talked of my having over-walked myself. "You'll be better to-morrow," he said, "after a deep sleep"; and when I said it was reckoned a bad thing to sleep immediately after eating, he said, "Reckoned?

[1] Lady Clanricarde was daughter of Mr. Canning and his wife Viscountess Canning in her own right. She was a sister of Lord Canning, Viceroy of India, who inherited the title from his mother. See *ante*, p. 75, and Vol. I., p. 318.

who reckons it so ?" and that he thought it a very good thing.

Thursday, 10th October.—Got up at ½ p. 10 and saw to my astonishment that a stone, or rather 2 stones, had been thrown at my dressing-room window and 2 glasses broken; the stone was found under the window; in the little blue room next the audience room another window broken and the stone found in the room; in the new strong room another window broken, and in one of the lodging rooms next to this, another broken and the stone found in the middle of the room. This is a very strange thing, and Lehzen told Lord Surrey of it. We stopped and got out at the gate of the Terrace, and walked on the Terrace and new walk; Lord Melbourne walking near me the whole time. He thought it cold; he had met Brunow in the Quadrangle, who directly said he was ready to play at cards with Mamma after dinner. As we were returning along the new walk, one of my pages came running with a letter from Uncle Leopold, saying my cousins would be here very soon; they sent on the letter announcing their arrival. I said to Lord M. I was sure they would come this day, but he would never believe it. At ½ p. 7 I went to the top of the staircase and received my 2 dear cousins Ernest and Albert,—whom I found grown and changed, and embellished. It was with some emotion that I beheld Albert—who is *beautiful.* I embraced them both and took them to Mamma; having no clothes they couldn't appear at dinner. At 8 we dined. Besides our own party, Lady Clanricarde, Lord and Lady Granville, Baron Brunow, Lord Normanby, the Hon. William Temple,[1] and Mr. Murray (who returned), dined here. I sat between

[1] Brother of Lord Palmerston.

Baron Brunow and Lord Melbourne. Talked to Lord Melbourne of my cousins having no baggage; I said I found my cousins so changed. Talked of my cousins' bad passage; their not appearing on account of their *négligé*, which Lord M. thought they ought to have done, *at* dinner and certainly after. "I don't know what's the dress *I* would appear in, if I was allowed," said Lord M., which made us laugh. After dinner my Cousins came in, in spite of their *négligé*, and I presented them to Lord Melbourne. I sat on the sofa with Lady Clanricarde, Lord Melbourne sitting near me, and Ernest near us and Albert opposite—(*he* is so handsome and pleasing), and several of the ladies and gentlemen round the sofa. I asked Lord M. if he thought Albert like me, which he is thought (and which is an immense compliment to me). "Oh! yes, he is," said Lord M., "it struck me at once."

Friday, 11th October.—Got up at ½ p. 9 and breakfasted at 10. Wrote to Lord Melbourne. Signed. My dear Cousins came to my room and Albert gave me letters from Vecto, Louise, Uncle Ernest, and Uncle Ferdinand. They remained some little time in my room and really are charming young men; Albert really is quite charming, and so excessively handsome, such beautiful blue eyes, an exquisite nose, and such a pretty mouth with delicate moustachios and slight but very slight whiskers; a beautiful figure, broad in the shoulders and a fine waist.—At about ½ p. 10 dancing began. I danced 5 quadrilles; (1) with Ernest; (2) with dearest Albert, who dances so beautifully; (3) with Lord Alfred; (4) with Ernest; and (5) with dearest Albert again. After the 1st quadrille there was a Valse; after the 2nd and 3rd Gallops; and after the 4th another Valse; it is quite a pleasure to look at Albert when he gallops and valses, he does it so beautifully, holds himself so well with that beautiful figure of his. Lord Melbourne sat near me during the intervals and during the valses. He was quite well, he assured me, and not tired; he talked of Kolowrath and Alvensleben. I praised him for not sleeping. Just before I began the 4th quadrille, I asked him if he was going or staying; going, he said; and when I began he went away, at 10 m. p. 12.

Saturday, 12th October.—At 20 m. p. 3 I rode out with my cousins, Mamma, Lord Melbourne, Daisy, and the same party as the day before with the exception of Lord Granville, Lord Normanby, Lord Surrey and Mr. Byng; and came home at ½ p. 5. I rode Friar, who went beautifully. I rode the whole time between Albert (with whom I talked a good deal) and Lord Melbourne, who, out of anxiety lest I should suffer from his horse shying against me, rode his white-faced horse, which he has not ridden since he came down with him, and which isn't half as easy as the other, nor so safe; it was so kind and I felt it so much, but it grieved me; luckily the horse went safe and quiet.

Sunday, 13th October.—At 11 I went to church with Mamma and my beloved cousins (in my carriage) and all the other ladies (except Daisy) and gentlemen, to St. George's. Besides Mamma and my 2 Cousins, Lady Sandwich, Lord Melbourne, Lord Palmerston, Lord Falkland and Alvensleben were in the Closet with me. Dearest Albert sat near me, who enjoyed the music excessively and thought it quite beautiful.

Lord M. said he had a gossiping letter from Lady Holland, which he read to me; as he thought I couldn't read it. Talked of Spain; Alava's pleasure at being asked, and his saying in a letter he did not wish to change his name for any other. Talked of my cousins having gone to Frogmore; the length of their stay being left to me; and I said seeing them had a good deal changed my opinion (as to marrying), and that I must decide soon, which was a difficult thing. "You would take another week," said Lord M.; "certainly a very fine young man, very good-looking," in which I most readily agreed, and said he was so amiable and good tempered, and that I had such a bad temper; of my being the 1st now to own the advantage of beauty, which Lord M. said smiling he had told me was not to be despised, in spite of what I had said to him about it. Talked of my cousins being religious. "That strong Protestant feeling is a good thing in this country," he said, "if it isn't intolerant,"—which I assured him it was not. I had great fun with my dear cousins after dinner. I sat on the sofa with dearest Albert; Lord Melbourne sitting near me, Ernest playing at chess, and many being seated round the table. I looked at some drawings by Stephano della Bella and Domenichino, with Albert, and then we gave them to Lord Melbourne. Lord M. was quite well; he talked of a letter they had sent him from Charles Napier,[1] on Sir Robert Stopford's station. Lord M. looked at the drawings. Eos[2] came in again and yawned. I played 2 games at Tactics with dear Albert, and 2 at Fox and Geese. Stayed up till 20 m. p. 11. A delightful evening.

[1] Charles Napier (afterwards Admiral Sir Charles Napier, K.C.B.) had commissioned the *Powerful* early in the year, which was sent out to the East when it became necessary to reinforce the fleet under Sir Robert Stopford.

[2] A favourite greyhound of the Prince Consort's.

Monday, 14th October.—Went to Lehzen's room where Lady Sandwich[1] was with the baby whom I nursed and petted, for he is a darling. Wrote letters to the Duchess of Gloucester and Princess Augusta. At 1 came Lord Melbourne and stayed with me till 10 m. p. 2. He was quite well. He said, "Here's a letter from my sister," in which she talks again of her intended marriage, and she contemplates with horror—and very naturally—her surviving Lord M. and Sir Fred. She advises Lord M. to *marry* again, if he was out of Office!! which made us both laugh, and proposes one of the Hardys!! All Lord M.'s property "goes to her by my Father's will," he said.[2] I thought it a pity Sir Fred. didn't marry.[3] "I'd just as much wish Fordwich[4] had it, as anyone else"; before this he showed me a letter from Lord Morpeth about Lord Cremorne. Talked of so many families becoming extinct. Then she wanted Sir Fred. to marry Theresa Villiers. "She was always wanting me to marry Olivia De Ros," said Lord M. I observed that they had said also he (Ld. M.) would marry Lady Boyle, Emily Seymour that was. "There was a good deal of report about it," he said.

Talked of my Cousins' having gone out shooting. After a little pause I said to Lord M., that I had made up my mind (about marrying dearest Albert).—"You have?" he said; "well then, about the time?" Not for a year, I thought; which he said

[1] Formerly Lady Mary Paget. See Vol. I., p. 349.

[2] The whole of Lord Melbourne's property, Melbourne and Brocket, passed to Lady Cowper and her children.

[3] He eventually married, at the age of sixty, the young daughter of Count Maltzahn. See Vol. I., p. 253.

[4] The second title in the Cowper family, and the name by which Lord Melbourne's nephew was known before his accession to the Peerage.

was too long; that Parliament must be assembled in order to make a provision for him, and that if it was settled "it shouldn't be talked about," said Lord M.; "it prevents any objection, though I don't think there'll be much; on the contrary," he continued with tears in his eyes, "I think it'll be very well received; for I hear there is an anxiety now that it should be; and I'm very glad of it; I think it is a very good thing, and you'll be much more comfortable; for a woman cannot stand alone for long, in whatever situation she is." Lord M. said then that he wondered if I didn't wish to have it directly (which I said I didn't), as in that case Parliament would have to be assembled before; but if I didn't, that it had better be in January or February, after Parliament met; not later; upon which I observed, "So soon." "You are rather alarmed when it comes to be put in that way," he said laughing; which I assured him I was not. Then I asked, if I hadn't better tell Albert of my decision soon, in which Lord M. agreed. How? I asked, for that in general such things were done the other way,—which made Lord M. laugh. That Uncle Leopold and Uncle Ernest should know it; of settling my own time; and then for some time of what should be done for him; George of Denmark would be the person to look back to; he was Lord High Admiral, Lord M. said; of making him a Peer—my being against it. A Field Marshal he ought be made, just like Uncle; and anyhow a Royal Highness; of how I should say it to Albert; Lord M. thought there was no harm in people's guessing the thing; he said that he would mention it to John Russell and Palmerston, and perhaps the Chancellor. When we got up, I took Lord M.'s hand,

and said he was always *so* kind to me,—which he has always been; he was *so* kind, *so fatherly* about all this. I felt *very* happy. Read despatches. Wrote to Ernest and Albert sending them things. Wrote my journal. At 8 we dined. Prince Esterhazy, Lord Uxbridge and the Ladies E. and C. Paget dined here. Prince Esterhazy led me in, and I sat between him and my dearest Albert, with whom I talked a great deal. Lord Melbourne sat opposite between Lady C. Dundas and Ellen. Talked to Lord Melbourne after dinner of my hearing Albert couldn't sleep these last few days; nor I either, I added; that he asked a good deal about England, about which I tried to give him the most agreeable idea. "I mentioned it to J. Russell," said Lord M., but that J. Russell was very anxious it should be told to very few, as it was so difficult to *deny* such a thing when it was really settled; and that if I could talk to Albert about it and settle it with him but no one else, which I said I would. "I'll talk to you about it more fully to-morrow," Lord M. said.

Tuesday, 15th October.—Saw my dear Cousins come home quite safe from the Hunt, and charge up the hill at an immense pace. Saw Esterhazy. At about ½ p. 12 I sent for Albert; he came to the Closet where I was alone, and after a few minutes I said to him, that I thought he must be aware *why* I wished them to come here,—and that it would make me *too happy* if he would consent to what I wished (to marry me). We embraced each other, and he was *so* kind, *so* affectionate. I told him I was quite unworthy of him,—he said he would be very happy "das Leben mit dir zu zubringen," and was so kind, and seemed so happy, that I really felt it was the happiest brightest moment in my life. I told him it was a great sacrifice,—which he wouldn't allow; I then told him of the necessity of keeping it a secret, except to his father and Uncle Leopold and Stockmar, to whom he said he would send a Courier next day,—and also that it was to be as early as the beginning of February. I then told him to fetch Ernest, which he did and he congratulated us both and seemed very happy. I feel the happiest of human beings.

At 25 m. p. 1 came Lord Melbourne and stayed with me till 20 m. p. 2. He was well and had slept well. Talked of the weather; he read me a letter about this Lord Huntingdon,[1] who seems to be very proud and tenacious of his rights and rank, as Lord M. already knew, and as his Uncle-in-law Lord Carew writes. Talked of that, of William Cowper's coming down, and George Anson; I then began and said I had got well through this with Albert. "Oh! you have," said Lord M.; and I continued that he had said he would let no one perceive that anything of the kind had taken place; that he seemed very happy, and his brother as happy as him, only that *he* (E.) said he was the only loser by it, as his brother had been everything to him. Lord M. then said—if I had wished to have it immediately—that Parliament must be assembled. He said there was a great deal of talking going on about it; Lady Holland had written about it. Before this Lord M. said, "You can then (when married) do much more what you like." "Normanby wishes it," said Lord M. "He wishes the thing should be done and thinks it the best." "John Russell said," continued Lord M. with tears in his eyes, "his only wish is

[1] Francis Henry, twelfth Earl.

that you should be happy," which I said I hadn't a doubt of.

Wednesday, 16th October.—Talked of Albert's behaving so wonderfully, so that no one could imagine that anything had taken place; Ernest's saying *he* couldn't bear it, if he was in such a situation. "I find you must declare it in Council," said Lord M., when it is to be announced; "it is quite done by you; you assemble the Privy Councillors and announce it to them; that is what George III. did." Talked of making him a Peer, which Lord M. said he should like to take other people's opinion upon; but I talked of the necessity of his having precedence of everyone else. "There'll be no difficulty about that," said Lord M., "as everybody will see the propriety of that." . . .

Saturday, 19th October.—Signed. Wrote my journal. Went into the little room and began a letter to the Duchess of Northumberland; my dearest Albert came to me at 10 m. to 12 and stayed with me till 20 m. p. 1. Such a pleasant happy time. He looked over my shoulder and watched me writing to the Duchess of Northumberland, and to the Duchess of Sutherland; and he scraped out some mistakes I had made. I told him I felt so grateful to him and would do everything to make him happy. I gave him a ring with the date of the ever dear to me *15th* engraved in it. I also gave him a little seal I used to wear. I asked if he would let me have a little of his dear hair.

Later.—Talked to Lord M. of Col. Brown; of Palmerston being so poorly; of Saxons, and who were descended from Saxons or Normans. I asked what he was; Saxon, he said; and Palmerston, Saxon; Cowper he wasn't so sure of; and Paget

I thought sounded Norman; and Lord M. told me a curious anecdote about the Pagets. "Their ancestor asked to have a *patch* of land, which was this great Beaudesert, and it was given to him, but they said to him, 'You must call yourself Patchet.'" The first Lord Coke, Lord M. said, was accused of acquiring so much property, and he asked leave to buy *one acre* more, and that was the great estate of Castle Acre. Talked of this Patchet. "I remember her very well," Lord M. replied, "she was nurse to some of them; to Lord Hertford, Lady Louisa Murray and me." I told Lord M. I had another present for him, which I feared would bore him. "Oh! no," he said; and I told him, as he had said to me his writing-case was too old, I begged he would let me offer him one. "I'm very much obliged to you," he said, "you may depend upon it I shall always keep it."

Sunday, 20th October.—At ½ p. 2 both Ernest and Albert came to my room and stayed with me till 20 m. p. 3, talking about many things. At ½ p. 3 my kind excellent Lord Melbourne came to me and stayed with me till 4. He was quite well.

Monday, 21st October.—Talked of my cousins hunting, and Lord M. said, "William Cowper said *the Prince* (Albert) rode like an old hand." Heard from Lord Melbourne that there was a report in London that Brougham had been killed by falling out of a carriage. When I came out of my room into the Gallery, Lord Uxbridge told us he had seen the letter from a Mr. Shafto (who had been in the carriage with Brougham) to Mr. Montgomery, saying Brougham was killed; and Lord Uxbridge said there could be no doubt; and Mr. Leader so hurt (who had been also in the carriage) as not thought likely he would live. The gentlemen came out with us. I talked to Lord Melbourne about Brougham, and how it had happened—his having been kicked on the head by the horse and then driven over; I observed it was a very striking thing. "Oh! very; I've a great feeling about it myself," said Lord M., greatly affected. "I have known him 37 years; and somehow or other he always stood by me"; which I observed I thought he had certainly *not* done, and that it was all Lord M.'s excellent kind heart. Lord M. thinks he would have come round to us, and that the death of "a man of weight" was always a bad thing. Talked of his wife being ill left.[1]

Tuesday, 22nd October.—Talked of the accounts of Brougham and how he had been killed. "I've seen the Chancellor," said Lord M., "and have told him" (about Albert). We heard before we went out that Brougham was *not* dead, and that it was all a hoax. Too monstrous this is!

Wednesday, 23rd October.—At 12 Lord Melbourne came to me and stayed with me till 1. Talked of the weather; of a letter of Count d'Orsay's, denying that *he* had spread the report about Brougham, which he was accused of having done. "If Shafto has really written this letter," said Lord M., "nothing on earth will ever make them believe it isn't Brougham who has written it." I said I heard D'Orsay and Brougham said they knew for certain I wouldn't marry Albert. . . .

[1] On Tuesday, 22nd October, the *Morning Post* and *Morning Chronicle*, assuming that the report was well founded, published eloquent and generous obituary notices, but *The Times* discredited the rumour. There had indeed been a carriage accident, but the servants alone had been injured. It has been assumed that the rumour of his own death was originated by Brougham himself.

Tuesday, 29th October.—I then said that both Albert and I were very much against his being made a Peer, that he didn't like the idea. "Well," said Lord M., "if he is against it and you have a leaning that way we needn't press it." At 6 dearest Albert came to me and stayed with me till 7. Part of the time we sat in the Closet, and Albert gave me a ring just like the one I gave him with the date of the 15th in it. . . .

Thursday, 31st October.—After this Lord M. gave me some more extracts to read, which Anson had sent him, about Queen Anne and George of Denmark, by which it seems he always led the Queen in and sat on her left hand; which Lord M. said I could settle respecting Albert as I liked. They don't seem certain if George of Denmark had the Garter, which we both thought very odd.[1] Talked of Albert's being made a Privy Councillor; of how the Declaration should be made; about the end of November in an open Council, which I thought disagreeable, but which Lord M. said must be. Of when the marriage should be; about the 6th of February—not later.

Friday, 1st November, 1839.—After this Lord M. took up the *Annual Register* of the year 1761, and read me an exact and minute account of George III.'s Declaration to the Council of his Marriage; of Queen Charlotte's coming over, her reception, the marriage, the procession to and from the Chapel Royal, and all the entertainments that followed it, which must have been awfully fatiguing. Talked of the whole being in state, and I said laughing to Lord M. I thought he said it was *not* in state, in order to get

[1] He was made a K.G., and in his portraits is represented with the ribbon of the Garter. See *post*, p. 276.

out of it, which made him laugh much. "It must be just the same," he said, of course; and my train borne by young ladies; two of those who carried Queen Charlotte's train were Lady Sarah Lennox and Lady Susan Strangways.[1] Talked of my not being obliged to have so many Fêtes as they had; of sending two of my gentlemen to bring Albert over; the Duchesses of Ancaster[2] and Hamilton[3] (the Duke of Argyll's mother) went over to fetch her[4]; the former was her Mistress of the Robes, and the latter her Lady of the Bedchamber, for there is an account of her Household in this same book.

Saturday, 2nd November.—Read in Hallam, which I thought very interesting. Played on the piano. Wrote my journal. At 20 m. to 12 dearest Albert came to me, and he went and fetched Ernest. Lord M. talked of the Duke of Devonshire saying grace before dinner. "He asked my sister," said Lord M., "if she thought it looked odd; she said not, if he liked it." The Duke said, that as it was always done when a Clergyman was there, why should it not be done when a Clergyman was not there?—but Lady Cowper said the Foreigners couldn't make out what it meant. Talked of the marriage and my insisting *he* (A.) should lead me out, which George III. had not done Queen Charlotte; of whether we should go to Windsor *after* it or not, which Lord M. said was for us as we liked; of Albert's having George Anson[5] about him, which Lord M. thought a good plan. I asked what Lady Cowper had said

[1] The friend of Lady Sarah Lennox. She married the actor, William O'Brien.

[2] Wife of the third Duke of Ancaster. See Vol. I., p. 313.

[3] Elizabeth Gunning. See Vol. I., p. 215.

[4] *I.e.* Queen Charlotte.

[5] See Vol. I., p. 69.

H. S. H. Prince Ernest
afterwards Duke of Saxe-Coburg-Gotha
Brother of Prince Albert
from a portrait by R. Thorburn

about Albert. "She thinks him very good-looking," he replied; of which I said *he* had no idea. . . .

Monday, 4th November.—Lord M. said to me, his sister had told him she had written to old Mr. Henry Cowper about her marriage, and had received a very kind letter from him saying that he quite approved of it; and she intends to have it in December after the Cabinets are over. "'The only person I fear now,' she said, 'is the Queen,'" said Lord M., "'as she may think it foolish in a person of my age marrying.'" . . .

Friday, 8th November.—At 25 m. p. 6 came Lord Melbourne and stayed with me till 20 m. to 7. He was in a strange costume, that is to say, light white and grey striped calico trousers with very large shoes. I feared I had interrupted him in his sleep, which he wouldn't allow, but which I think *was* the case. . . .

Sunday, 10th November.—At 11 I went to St. George's with dearest Albert, Ernest and Mamma (in my carriage) and the ladies and gentlemen, and came home at ½ p. 1. Lord M. made us laugh very much by telling us that when they were making a noise at the dinner in the City,[1] when he got up to speak, a woman came behind him and said, "There are a few men against you, but never mind, all the women are with you." I sat on the sofa with Albert and we played at that game of letters, out of which you are to make words, and we had great fun about them. Albert gave "*Pleasure*," and when I said to the people who were puzzling it out, it was a very common word, Albert said, But not a very common *thing*, upon which Lord M.

[1] At the Lord Mayor's Dinner on 9th November, Lord Melbourne, on returning thanks for Her Majesty's Ministers, was received with considerable uproar.

said, "Is it truth, or honesty?" which made us all laugh. . . .

Tuesday, 12th November.—At 20 m. to 1 Lord Melbourne came to me and stayed with me till 20 m. p. 1. I then told him Uncle Leopold had written to Albert urging very strongly his being made a Peer,[1] which I said we were both so against; and that Uncle said he refused it because he could not have voted with the King's Government. Lord M. said he had never heard *why* Uncle refused it, and *why* they afterwards refused to give it him when he wished to have it. Uncle says George of Denmark was Duke of Kendal[2]; even if he was, said Lord M. (which he doubts), he never was called so; and we agreed that if A. and I didn't like it, there was no reason why the thing should be pressed; for that it could always be done hereafter. I said Albert wished to see Lord M. and wished to know if he might say to Uncle that Lord M. was against it. Lord M. agreed to this, but said he was anxious it shouldn't be said he opposed it.

Wednesday, 13th November.—He read me a letter from Normanby, about Col. Thomas[3]; one from

[1] King Leopold's reason was that he thought the Prince should have an English name and title. The Queen wrote to the Prince about this time: "Lord Melbourne told me yesterday that the whole Cabinet are strongly of opinion that you should *not* be made a Peer. I will write that to Uncle."

[2] In 1684, the year after his marriage, Prince George was made a K.G. In 1689 he was naturalised, and created Baron of Ockingham, Earl of Kendal, and Duke of Cumberland.

[3] Colonel Thomas and the officers of the 20th Regiment were present at a dinner of the Conservative Association of Ashton-under-Lyne, at which a speech was made by a Mr. Roby containing expressions most insulting and disrespectful towards the Queen. For not promptly repudiating these sentiments, Colonel Thomas and the other officers present were severely censured by the Commander-in-Chief, Lord Hill.

Lord Minto about our having plenty of large ships; and one from Lord J. Russell about who should be Solicitor-General; he says he cannot consent to Austin,[1] for that the Queen's Crown lawyer must not be a Radical, in which Lord M. quite agreed; J. R. mentions Serjeant Talfourd,[2]—which Lord M. didn't quite like. "He writes plays," he said, "and I don't think a man who writes plays is ever good for much else; and he is a great friend of Wordsworth's." . . .

Wednesday, 20th November.—He had seen his sister at Lady Holland's; talked of the reports the Cambridges told me of Fanny's marrying either Charles Gore,[3] Frank Charteris,[4] or Frank Sheridan, all which Lord M. thought unlikely. Talked of various things; of George III.'s marriage having been kept so secret, which Lord M. said was on account of keeping it from Mr. Fox, on account of Lady Sarah Lennox. . . .

Saturday, 23rd November.—We were seated as usual, Lord Melbourne sitting next me. Lord Dun-

[1] Charles Austin, the friend of J. S. Mill, Macaulay, and Romilly, was now in large practice at the Bar. Though mentioned for the Solicitor-Generalship, he was not then or at any other time in Parliament.

[2] See *ante*, p. 155. Talfourd was now M.P. for Reading. He was sponsor of a Copyright Bill, which caused Dickens to dedicate *Pickwick* to him.

[3] Hon. Charles Alexander Gore, brother of the fourth Earl of Arran, married in 1845 Augusta Lavinia, widow of Lord Kerry and daughter of the 4th Earl of Bessborough. Their third son is now (1912) Bishop of Oxford.

[4] Mr. Charteris, who entered Parliament in 1841, and was (as Lord Elcho) long and nobly associated with the Volunteer movement, is now (1912) Earl of Wemyss. His recent speeches and letters to *The Times* upon questions of National Defence display a vigour of mind and physical powers which the seventy-three years that have elapsed since the Queen wrote these lines have scarcely dimmed.

cannon near him. Lord M. played with Islay; talked of Brougham, and Lord Duncannon believed *what* he said to one, he *always meant* at the *time*.

Sunday, 24th November.—Talked of the *Gazette* having arrived; of what the Courier had said of the Coburg family being true, except Uncle Ferdinand's having turned Roman Catholic; and all about Albert's being a staunch Protestant being well done. Talked of the people outside the Palace having made a great noise when the Ministers went away; but Lord M. said more cheering than otherwise. Talked of who the 10 young ladies should be, and showed him a list of Queen Charlotte's. I sent for the Peerage, and Lord M. read through *all* the Dukes, and we decided besides Car Lennox to have Lady Augusta Somerset, the Duke of Beaufort's daughter. Then through all the Marquises, and we thought of Lady Marianne Compton [1]; and then through all the Earls,—Elizabeth Howard [2] decided upon, besides Fanny, Wilhelmine, and Mary Grimston, and Ellen; and then Sarah Villiers,[3] which Lord M. said he could find out through his sister. Mary Lambton [4] we then thought of, instead of Lady Marianne Compton, as it would please Durham.

Thursday, 28th November.—Talked of having good news from my Cousins, and their thinking Uncle so well; Albert's having talked to Uncle Leopold

[1] Daughter of the Marquess of Northampton, and afterwards well known and deeply respected as Lady Marianne Alford.

[2] Daughter of the sixth Earl of Carlisle, afterwards wife of the Rev. and Hon. F. R. Grey.

[3] Daughter of Lord Jersey, and afterwards wife of Prince Nicholas Esterhazy, eldest son of the diplomatist Prince Paul Esterhazy. See Vol. I., pp. 77 and 190.

[4] Afterwards wife of the eighth Earl of Elgin.

about his being a Peer, Uncle's giving many reasons for having it, but Albert's saying it was best to wait and see. Lord M. said he had seen Sir William Woods, who told him the Garter could easily be sent at any time; he had shown Lord M. some very curious precedents of former Royal Marriages, of Queen Mary's and Philip's [1]; and that George III.'s [2] was the scene of the greatest confusion that ever took place; he has notes which show that *none* of that procession took place, and that we must make this different; and there was one curious thing, Lord M. said; I had observed that George III. didn't lead the Queen out; well, it was settled they should go separate, but by these Notes it says the King insisted on leading her out and did so. Talked of the Chapel Royal; Uncle Leopold's being married at Carlton House in private. Talked of the possibility of Parliament having to meet as early as the 9th of January on account of this Breach of Privilege [3]; then I would *not* open it myself, I said. "Oh! you must," he said, "that never would do." I wouldn't, I said, and always wished to get out of that. "You mustn't do that," he said kindly and gently. After dinner when Lord Melbourne came in we talked of the cold. I again teased him about not opening Parliament in person. "Oh! you will

[1] Philip and Mary were married with great pomp in Winchester Cathedral, 25th July, 1554.

[2] George III. was married in the Chapel Royal, St. James's, at 10 o'clock in the evening of 8th September, 1761.

[3] The Courts of Law decided that the report of a Committee of the House of Commons printed by order of the House was not privileged from being the subject of an action for libel. The House, however, imprisoned the Sheriffs of Middlesex for executing a judgment obtained by the plaintiff, one Stockdale, in such an action. An Act was then passed conferring the privilege for the future.

do it," he said earnestly, with his good kind face expressing anxiety I should. "Not to do so would not be right when it is necessary for Public affairs," he replied. Talked of the Marriage Ceremony, the impossibility of all the Peers and Peeresses attending; Sir William Woods[1] intending to draw up a Programme; its being right that Albert should stand to my left, as Philip had done at Mary's marriage; George of Denmark had only rank after the Princes of the Blood Royal; but I observed there were none. Talked of the Marriage Service being sometimes shortened. Lord M. played with Islay, who, he said, was "a Campbell."[2] He then said, "The greatest compliment that ever was paid to me, was by an old Mrs. Campbell at Inveraray; she said, 'If I didn't know who you were, Mr. Lamb, I should have taken you for a Douglas'; now that for a Scotchwoman!"

Friday, 29th November.—"I've got all these papers," he said, and he read me a letter from Sir William Woods to Anson, and then a very curious account of Queen Mary's marriage to Philip, who was only *Prince* of Spain then; and it was announced in the Cathedral at Winchester, where they were married, that his father gave him the Kingdom of Naples; Queen Mary was given away by 3 of her gentlemen in the name of the *realm.* Lord M. then showed me the Act of naturalization of George Prince of Denmark; and read me an account of the marriage of the Princess Royal to the Hereditary Prince of Wurtemberg.[3] Lord M. said

[1] See Vol. I., p. 356.

[2] Islay being one of the Western Isles near Inveraray.

[3] The marriage of George III.'s eldest daughter to Frederick Charles, Duke and afterwards King of Wurtemburg, took place in 1797.

he would get these papers copied for me. Talked of my marriage; of the Chapel Royal; of the possibility of having it at Buckingham Palace; *not* at Westminster Abbey, as that would be like a 2nd Coronation. Lord M. read a note from a Mr. Pennington of the Treasury about Albert's income. . . .

Friday, 6th December.—Talked of the attacks against the omission of the word "Protestant" in the Declaration. "You mustn't think it belongs to the Party,"[1] said Lord M., "now you'll see not one word will be said about it in Parliament"; that he heard Lyndhurst deplored it very much; I thought it was Croker's doing, as he had asked Lord M. about the word Protestant being left out. Lord M. said he *on purpose* left out what was put in George III.'s Declaration, which was, that the Princess was a lineal descendant of a House which had always been warmly attached to the Protestant Religion, as that didn't say anything about *her* religion; and Lord M. said he left that out on purpose *not* to attract attention, as else they would have said that wasn't true, and that many of the family had collapsed into Catholicism. . . .

Saturday, 7th December.—Talked of Philip, Queen Mary's husband, having been Titular King of England, which however Lord M. said he disliked so much, and that he disliked her. Talked of Princess Charlotte having always said she would make Uncle King if she came to the Throne. Talked of William III. having insisted on being King *de facto*, which Bishop Burnet settled with Queen Mary for him, and William said he (Bp. B.) had settled in an hour what he had been contemplating for years. I said she (Mary) was a cruel woman, which Lord

[1] The Tory Party.

M. wouldn't allow, and said, "She had been the handsomest woman in Europe."[1] He said William always left her to settle his affairs while he was abroad; she died in '93 or '94, he thinks. Talked of Queen Anne, who he said had also been handsome, which I said couldn't be the case, and that the Bust of her in the Gallery here was very ugly. "That was done when she was old," said Lord M., "when she had had 15 or 16 children."

Sunday, 8th December.—Uncle is also full of the necessity of a Marriage Treaty. "I think the best, Ma'am, would be," said Lord M., "if you approve, for Stockmar to be instructed with all they wish to be done, and to be sent over here directly, so as to settle it here before the Meeting of Parliament," which I quite agreed in. Lord M. observed Uncle thought a Treaty safer, and perhaps it might be, though he thought an Act of Parliament equally so. Talked of my letter from Albert being from Coburg. Talked of sending a drawing of these Arms to Albert, and how we should settle about the Seal. "The Arms[2] are rather a ticklish thing to meddle with," said Lord M., "as they are not *your* arms but the arms of the Country,"—which is very true. . . .

Tuesday, 10th December.—Talked of those papers of the late King's, which I begged Lord M. to speak to Wheatley about, and which we agreed ought to have been kept in the Family.[3]

[1] It is difficult to imagine the source from which the Queen had gathered this impression of Queen Mary. It was probably the unqualified inference from the fact that she never showed much tenderness towards her father, James II.

[2] The Queen had sent a little drawing of the Arms made by herself to the Prince at Coburg.

[3] There is some misapprehension here, as there is no reason to suppose that the papers of William IV. were ever in the hands of Sir H. Wheatley.

Wednesday, 11*th December.*—"Here's the Chancellor's answer about this bill of naturalization," said Lord M. "I wrote to him to consider it," and Lord M. then read it; he thinks the same course as that pursued in Uncle Leopold's case should be followed; and agreed that Albert should certainly have precedence[1] over the Royal Dukes. "And now he mentions what I never thought of when I talked of it to Your Majesty, 'and even I think before the *Queen's Children,*'" Lord M. read. Lord M. then said he thought he never could go before the Prince of Wales, before the Heir-Apparent; but *I* said *they* never could go before their father. The Chancellor concludes by saying, it would be very disagreeable if the Parties concerned were not to concur; I said I felt certain both the Duke of Sussex and the Duke of Cambridge would *not* object to this, and that otherwise Albert's position would *not* be bearable. He talked of Mrs. Hamilton (Margaret Dillon), and Lord M. asked, "How many children? Why, the measure of married happiness is to have a great number of children," said Lord M. . . .

Wednesday, 18*th December.*—Then he talked of a mistake there was in those "points" they had written from Coburg, viz. that I had the right to appoint my Husband Regent, which I have not. Lord M. says he must consult the Chancellor about many other things. George IV. bought a good deal of property, he said. There was a bill brought in, in George III.'s reign, Lord M. continued, enabling him to make a will, which till then no King could. . . .

[1] Lord Melbourne ultimately advised the Queen that it was unnecessary to say anything about the Prince's precedence in the Bill, as she could, by her own Sovereign Act, grant him any precedence she pleased.

Sunday, 22nd December.—I continued Albert's position would be too difficult if he must go after *all*, that he *ought* to have the title of King, that power wasn't worth having if I couldn't even give him the *rank* he ought to have. "You can't give it him but by Act of Parliament,"[1] said Lord M. "Here's the Chancellor's answer to that letter" (those questions and propositions from Coburg), which Lord M. then read to me, and which are very clear and good. Respecting the Succession to Coburg, he says *they* may settle *there* what they like, to which we shall not dissent but agree; but that *we* cannot *legislate here* about a Foreign Succession. He states likewise that I cannot appoint Albert Guardian to my children—for that if my son was of age when I died, he, as *King*, would be Guardian of his brothers and sisters, and if he were *not* of age, then there would be a Regency. "These are our laws," he said, and he added laughing, "I don't know if they are right." He wished me to send a copy of these answers to Albert, and he would send one to Uncle Leopold.

Monday, 23rd December.—Lord M. said how singular it was, that since William the Conqueror, that there had only been 3 Queens, and that those were only Queens by extraordinary circumstances; the title of Prince of Wales only belongs to a man, he said, there can be no Princess of Wales (in her own right). Talked of Queen Mary having been a good deal persecuted and ill-used by Edward VI., and Lord M. said, as a proof, Edward said he hoped he should not be obliged to proceed to violent measures against her. Talked of Hallam's not having

[1] This refers to the Title of King. Any other rank the Queen could bestow by her own act.

a good opinion of Cranmer; saying what he had done when he became Archbishop, but that as he was burnt, everybody thought him a Saint. Lord M. said he was "very shuffling," and that he heard that somebody was going to publish a life of Cranmer, tending to lower him very much in the eyes of the world,—upon which the Archbishop of Canterbury wrote to say he had better not do it, "not rake all that up," for that "after all he is our first Protestant Archbishop."

Lord M. was very well and in high spirits; talked of the long Paper I had sent him (a Historical Sketch of our Saxon Ancestors, which Albert sent me, and which I sent off immediately to Lord M. without reading it). "I've read it," Lord M. replied; "it told me a good deal, though I knew a good deal before." Talked to Lord M. of Albert's being anxious of who he should have about him. . . .

Wednesday, 25th December (*Xmas Day*).—Got up at ¼ p. 9 and breakfasted at 10 m. to 10. Read one of Arnold's sermons and part of another; they are so fine. At 11 I went to church with Mamma and all the ladies and gentlemen. Besides Mamma Lord Melbourne, Lord and Lady Normanby, Lord and Lady Albemarle, Lord and Lady Kinnaird, Lord Byron and Lady Fanny were with me in the Closet. They sang a beautiful anthem by Handel, "There were shepherds"; I never heard anything so beautiful as the boy's voice. We stayed upstairs during all the prayers in the Communion Service, and then went down, and we all knelt before the Altar; that is I, Mamma, Lady Normanby, my 3 ladies, Lord Melbourne, Lord Normanby, Lord and Lady Albemarle, Lady Fanny, and Lord Byron. It was a fine and solemn scene in this fine old Chapel. I felt for one, my dearest Albert,—and wished he could be by my side,—also dear Lehzen,—but was *very* glad Lord Melbourne was there, the one whom I look up to as a father, and I was glad he took it with me.

Thursday, 26th December.—Talked of a violent speech of O'Connell's I had seen in the papers, announcing war against the Tories.[1] . . .

Sunday, 29th December.—Talked of the Provost of Eton,[2] his having looked so ill at church. Lord M. always liked him, and said he taught so well. "Very clever man," said Lord M., "he wrote Latin verses as quick as he could speak; I think he made his house gentlemanlike, which was rather wanted when I was there; he was what is the worst thing for a schoolmaster, a timid man; he was a very good-natured man. Schoolboys certainly are the greatest set of blackguards," he continued; "sure sign of a shuffling blackguard at school, is to have no hat, and a great-coat without another coat under it, and no book." . . .

Tuesday, 31st December.—Talked of Lady Ailesbury's[3] sending me something from Paris, her wishing to be about me. "*I* like her," said Lord M.;

[1] At Bandon, after an outburst of sentimental loyalty over the Queen's engagement, O'Connell observed: "The moment I heard of the daring and audacious menaces of the Tories towards the Sovereign, I promulgated, through the press, my feelings of detestation and my determination on the matter. Oh! if I be not greatly mistaken, I'd get, in one day, 500,000 brave Irishmen to defend the life, the honour, and the person of the beloved young lady by whom England's throne is now filled."

[2] Dr. Goodall. See Vol. I., p. 119.

[3] Maria Elizabeth, daughter of the Hon. Charles Tollemache, wife of the first Marquess of Ailesbury. A well-known figure in London society throughout the reign of the Queen, she was held in high and affectionate esteem under the sobriquet of "Lady A."

"she is one of my sort of women." Talked of Miss Pitt[1] having behaved very well about her brother, and her brother regretting the life he led. "Most people are sorry," said Lord M., "except me, I never was sorry"; which I said was very wrong. Talked of Albert's having such a fear of our not putting people of good character about him. Lord M. said, "Lady William" (Russell)[2] "said the Prince's character is such as is highly approved at a German university, but which would be subject to some ridicule at ours"; as Lord M. said formerly, any attention to morality in universities was ridiculed, which I said was too shocking. I said funnily I thought Lord M. didn't like Albert so much as he would if he wasn't so strict. "Oh! no, I highly respect it," said Lord M. I then talked of A.'s saying I ought to be severe about people. "Then you'll be liable to make every sort of mistake. In this country all should go by law and precedent," said Lord M., "and not by what you hear."[3]

[1] Miss Pitt's two brothers were the fourth and sixth Lords Rivers. She married in 1841 Mr. Charles Dashwood Bruce. See Vol. I., p. 211.

[2] Lord William Russell (elder brother of Lord John) was sometime British Minister at Berlin. Lady William was a niece of the first Marquess of Hastings.

[3] It must be remembered that the Prince was little over nineteen years old, and that his standards of right and wrong, always high and noble, were tinged at this time with the uncompromising severity of youth. In after-years he adopted to the full Lord Melbourne's formula, and never acted upon hearsay.

INTRODUCTORY NOTE TO CHAPTER XVII

At the beginning of 1840, a year pregnant with changes vital to the Queen as Sovereign and to her happiness as a woman, Lord Melbourne, her Minister and friend of long standing, was still at her right hand.

The political fates had been kind. It was to Lord Melbourne, and not to a comparative stranger, that the girl-Queen announced her intention of asking Prince Albert of Saxe-Coburg to become her Consort; and it was not from formal lips, but from the heart of a devoted mentor and friend that the words of approval and congratulation flowed. No one but Lord Melbourne could have said to her in homely language, "You will be very much more comfortable, for a woman cannot stand alone for any time, in whatever position she may be"; and no one during the trying months that followed, in which the joys of a love-match were blended with the irritation caused by displays of party spirit in Parliament, could have filled Lord Melbourne's place in the eyes of the fatherless girl, who stood without a male protector of any kind.

Lord Melbourne took leave of the Queen with his usual cheerful and kindly smile. "For four years I have seen you every day; but it is so different now to what it would have been in 1839." This allusion to the political crisis of the previous year, and to the difference between ceding his place to Peel or to the Prince, was the note of parting. He was about to feel the quality of the difference in his daily life. The fragrance had been too pungent. From this hour Lord Melbourne's vitality began to fade. He was only sixty-three, a young Prime Minister, as years are now counted in the lives of statesmen. His place remained unfilled throughout the reign of the Queen. A virile personality had stepped between her and all men. Prince Albert was a mere boy, but he grew rapidly in the sight of all, and from Prince in name he became King in fact, and the "Permanent Minister" of the Queen. She was soon to determine that if he could not be, as she wished, King-Consort, he should never play the "subordinate part played by the very stupid and insignificant husband of Queen Anne." These were her words, and they covered an intention from which she never swerved and which the Prince more than fulfilled.

It is upon the threshold of twenty-one years of supreme happiness that the last words of these published Journals leave her. Their concluding phrase dramatically rings down a curtain, which may never be lifted, upon a love-story interwoven with the fate of the country that Victoria and Albert ruled together and the Empire that grew apace under their auspices.

No one living is ever likely to see much more of the inner life of Queen Victoria, or the secret working of our political institutions, viewed from the standpoint of her Throne.

These Journals show a Queen in the making, and a Queen whose imperishable fame is engraved, with that of Elizabeth, upon the hearts of her people.

CHAPTER XVII

1840

Wednesday, 1st January.—Lord M. asked if I had read the Paper for Nesselrode about sending a Russian Minister to Brussels, and stating the reasons why they couldn't do so,—on account of the Poles, which I said was only an excuse. Talked of the danger for us of an alliance between France and Russia, when the former might say Russia might take Constantinople, and Russia would let France go up to the Rhine; on the other hand, Lord M. said, France dreaded an alliance between England and Russia, when *we* might let Russia take Constantinople, and they let us take Egypt and Syria. The *only* country sincerely *friendly* to England, Lord M. says, is Austria. Stayed up till 20 m. p. 11. I feel *most grateful* for all the blessings I have received in the past year, the acquaintance and love of dearest Albert! I only implore Providence to protect me and those who are most dear to me in *this* and many succeeding years, and to grant that the *true* and *good* cause may prosper for *this year* and *many* years to come, under the guidance of my kind Lord Melbourne!

Thursday, 2nd January.—Talked of Hallam, and his account of Jane Grey's having 2 sisters. "He tells it very clearly," Lord M. said; "that was a sad scene" and not poor Jane's fault. Talked of Elizabeth's imprisoning that unfortunate sister of Jane's, Catherine, for marrying; Lord M. said, "When the Princess Elizabeth" (our Queen) "was sent to the Tower, she inquired very particularly if Jane Grey's scaffold was still up." I begged Lord M. to take great care of himself.

Friday, 3rd January.—Talked of Pozzo's not returning here; his being violent against the Coburg Family, and we couldn't think why. Lord M. said he wondered what the feelings of the Russians were about Princess Charlotte's marriage with Uncle Leopold; George IV.'s wishing for the Prince of Orange; Lord M. said he knew nothing about it; his (George IV.) disliking Uncle Leopold and also his daughter. I said Lord Anglesey told me he had a great hand in persuading the Regent to let Princess Charlotte marry Uncle Leopold. "That may be true," said Lord M., but he had never heard it before. Talked of George IV.'s disliking Uncle Leopold; Lord M. said it was just like George IV. Lord M. talked of Queen Charlotte's excusing her son; George IV. being fond of his mother. Talked of my being surprised that as George III. and Queen Charlotte were so strict and demure, the sons should all run so wild. Talked of the Spaniards being very sober, and Lord M. said quite seriously, "Somehow or other those sober nations don't get on well amongst other nations," which made us laugh exceedingly. Lord M. said there was no doubt that a *sober man* got on better than a drunken one, but not so whole nations. . . .

Monday, 6th January.—Received another delightful letter from Albert written on the 31st; it is written in such spirits too. He sent me (which I begged him to do) Ernest's pretty verse which E. made for me about *Die Orangen-Blüthe*, set to music by dearest Albert; I sang it twice over and it is quite *beautiful*; longer than any of his others, and quite lovely.

Tuesday, 7th January.—Lord M. was funny about Ellen and Constance,[1] and said, "Young ladies like to be looked at from head to foot." He said his sister was "very happy," "she looked uncommonly well," Lord M. said, "rather a dashing gown; she would beat any of these now." I said I didn't use to admire her formerly, and didn't think she dressed so well as now. "She was always like a pale rose," Lord M. said. Lord M. assured me he was very well; of franking being nearly over—on the 9th is the last day[2]; and I said I wished so much to have one of Lord M.'s franked on the last day, and if he would frank one to me. He said he couldn't *frank* one to me; "people would say that was a very odd thing to do"; but I begged him then to frank one to one of the Ladies for me, which he said he would. I showed Lord M. a lithograph of Albert after Ross's (in large) just finished, which he said was "very like."—I wish Lord Melbourne could have remained till I went. Having him *here*, is so different to seeing him in London. I have the greatest affection for him. I trust and hope and *feel confident* all will do well. . . .

Friday, 10th January.—At 20 m. p. 2 I left Windsor with Mamma and Lady Charlemont, and

[1] Daughters of Lord Uxbridge. Lady Constance afterwards married the Earl of Winchilsea, and Lady Eleanora Sir Sandford Graham.

[2] The Penny Postage, which incidentally abolished franking, came into operation on January 10th. The idea emanated from Rowland Hill, and the work of initiating the new system was entrusted to him.

Islay, all the others following in other carriages, and reached Buckingham Palace at 20 m. p. 4. It is all so changed, fresh painted and gilded; my rooms fresh painted and the doors altered, and the ceiling gilt; and beautiful chintz curtains and furniture; it looks like a new house and so pretty. Received a letter from dearest Albert dated 3rd of January. At 10 m. p. 5 came my good Lord Melbourne and stayed with me till 5 m. to 6. He asked how I was and if I was just come. I said to Lord M. wasn't he surprised at the change? "Is this the same room?" he asked; I said it was; and he observed the gilding of the ceiling. He and Islay seemed equally pleased to see one another again.

Talked of Stockmar's saying it was much better to settle as much as possible verbally with Albert when he came, which Lord M. quite agreed in; of Stockmar's not saying where he lived, and Lord M. having sent all over the Town to find him out. "He said," said Lord M., "which is no great comfort to me, 'I've known 3 Ministers, Canning, Liverpool, and Castlereagh, and they all sank under it, and I shouldn't be surprised if your mind was to affect your digestion.'" He asked if "the frank" arrived safe, which I said it did, but that I thought it wasn't his best writing. "I took great pains," he replied. "Minny wrote to me for 2, for Lady Charlotte Sturt[1] and Lady Emma Pennant[2]; and Lady Georgina Codrington[3] wrote to me for one." Talked

[1] Wife of Henry Charles Sturt, M.P. for Dorset, and daughter of the sixth Earl of Cardigan. Her eldest son was the first Lord Alington.

[2] Second wife of David Pennant, junior, of Bodfari, and daughter of Robert, sixth Earl of Cardigan.

[3] Wife of Christopher George Codrington of Dodington, and daughter of the seventh Duke of Beaufort.

of my thinking this new Penny Postage was disliked by the higher classes. Talked of Albert's not quite understanding about his Household, and about the Treasurer, which however, I said, I should make him easily understand. "Don't let any difficulty stand in the way about George Anson,"[1] said Lord M. kindly, but I said G. Anson was the fit person and that I should easily make him understand it. "If I had thought of it," Lord M. continued, "it would have been best if Stockmar had come over directly. He didn't like to press himself," Lord M. said. Talked of Stockmar's thinking Uncle Leopold so very ill; "I'm very sorry for that," said Lord M. I said independent of the great loss he would be for us all, what a dreadful thing it would be for the country. "Would throw us all into confusion," said Lord M.; that there must be a Regency then, and who could it be? they might name *her*, he said, but I replied she would not have the nerve for it. "Perhaps she would if she was put to it," he said. "That was the great thing about Queen Mary," he continued, "when he (William III.) was in Ireland he could leave her with perfect safety and confidence,—and she managed so well."

Saturday, 11th January.—"We have nearly settled upon the speech," said Lord M. as he unlocked a box and took the Speech out of it. "This is the amount of it," he said, showing it me; and he then read it in his usual fine way; I said it was rather long; "I told you it would be so," he re-

[1] George Anson (see *ante*, p. 37) was private secretary to Lord Melbourne. At first the Prince resented the selection of Anson to act in a similar capacity for him; but they became ultimately firm friends. Anson was a faithful and most judicious servant to the Prince until his premature death in 1849.

plied, "there is so much to say; we have not quite settled that end; there may be some alterations; it'll do if you get it Tuesday morning?" which I said it would. Talked of the Penny Postage—there were 112,000 letters last night, Lord M. said. Talked of the marriage of my Aunts; of the Duke of York (George III.'s brother). The Duke of Cumberland (his brother) Lord M. remembers; he came down with George IV. to Brocket, a little man, also in the Navy, and gay; he and the Duke of Gloster were great Whigs, and the Duke of Cumberland hated the Clergy.

Sunday, 12th January.—Talked of the new Postage. "My Tutor at Eton was the best person I ever knew for folding up letters," said Lord M. They asked him if he learnt it of him. "Oh! no," he replied, "I'm a very blundering fellow at it," which made us laugh. "When Lord North was at school," Lord M. continued, "his Tutor told him, 'You're a blundering blockhead, and if you are Prime Minister it'll always be the same'; 'and it turned out to be so,' Lord North said"; Lord M. told this so delightfully. We were seated as usual, Lord Melbourne sitting near me. They were talking of Paget[1] who is studying at Edinburgh. "They never taught him anything before," Lord M. said, "and now they've launched him at Edinburgh, and God knows what he may learn." The Paget system is never to learn anything, and this they steadily adhere to; "I don't mean *her*," he said, looking at Matilda.[2] Talked of the Universities in Scotland having gone down excessively. I showed him the Duchess

[1] See Vol. I., p. 363.

[2] Miss Paget, the Maid of Honour, niece of Lord Anglesey. See Vol. I., p. 230.

of Gloster's letter giving a better account of the Landgravine. Talked of Albert's people; Lord M. heard Lord Colborne[1] recommended; talked of that; Stockmar's saying Albert had no idea how high parties ran here; of its being worse within these last 2 years, and that I was sure it couldn't go on so. "Oh! it will,—it'll lumber along," Lord M. answered. "You mustn't mind those speeches,[2] that'll never do if they hear you mind them; it's giving them your head, as they say in fighting, to pound upon; dear me! if I chose to go and make abusive speeches," he continued, "I could kill a great many of these people." He said the attacks on George III. were atrocious; and he agreed with me it was a shocking thing. He said Uncle Leopold was very right in saying that character was everything, and that therefore the attempt of one's enemies was to do everything to ruin that character, "which is a horrible practice." I told him I heard he had been cross with Lady Holland the last time he dined there and had told her she hated all her friends. "Who told you that?" Lord M. asked. "It's true," he continued, and that he told her she had a spite against J. Russell, Duncannon and Minto, whom she had known as children. "I wonder at your hearing that," he added.

Monday, 13th January.—I asked if on the Wed-

[1] Nicholas William Ridley-Colborne (second son of Sir Matthew White-Ridley) was for over a quarter of a century an M.P. on the Whig side. At Lord Melbourne's instance, he was created a peer, as Lord Colborne, in May 1839. He was a patron of art, and bequeathed several pictures to the National Gallery.

[2] The Tories, at this time, were raising vexatious objections to the Queen's marriage, and doing what they could to minimize the importance of the Prince.

ding day, as I should *not drive* in full state, and Albemarle said he did not make a point of going with me, I should take Mamma with me. "Yes, I think so," said Lord M. "I think it would be a very right thing to do on that day." Talked of the Treaty being settled easily; of the Cabinet dinner at the Chancellor's in the evening. "We shall settle the Speech to-night," he said, "and let you have it to-morrow morning." I said I felt very nervous about reading it and beginning with my Marriage. "If you say it to 20, or 20,000, it's the same thing," he said, which is true enough.

Tuesday, 14th January.—Talked of other things; of absurd reports in the papers of Lord M.'s resigning after my marriage; he said he *never* dropt a word which could give rise to such a report. "I'm afraid it's our own people who spread these reports," he said, "Bannerman and Ellice" (who always go together). "When people say a report prevails it generally makes me suspect that they spread it," Lord M. said. Talked of Stockmar, and how he was, and Lord M. said, "I should like to see him when he has seen people and made his estimate of the state of things; I think he is about the cleverest man I ever knew in my life," he added, "a little misanthropic"; and a good man, I said. "An excellent man," Lord M. replied, "he has rather a contempt of human affairs and means; a bad digestion." I said to Lord M. I could not help thinking William C. did not seem quite happy at his mother's marriage. "Can't help being a feeling," Lord M. replied; "Lord Cowper was a man whom people so loved and admired."

Wednesday, 15th January. — Talked of some

H.R.H. The Duchess of Kent
from a portrait by F. Winterhalter

people wishing this Precedence should be limited to *my* life, which I said I never would do. "It wouldn't be handsome," Lord M. said. The Act of Parliament, Lord M. says, only gives me power to give him precedence as I please, and then the actual precedence is done by an Order in Council. At a ¼ p. 3 Lord Melbourne came to me upstairs and stayed with me till ½ p. 3. I feared I had let him wait; talked of his being tired. I asked what was the opinion of the Government about my going to the House or not. "There was a little difference of opinion, but upon the whole they think it is better you should go," said Lord M. I wished it, I said; Duncannon and Clarendon doubted about my going in person.

Thursday, 16th January.—At ½ p. 1 I set off in the State Coach, with Lord Albemarle and the Duchess of Sutherland, and the whole procession just as usual, to the House of Lords. The House was very full; my good Lord Melbourne just as usual standing close next to me. Wonderful to say, I was less nervous than I had ever been. The Duke of Cambridge was there. There was an immense crowd of people outside, and both coming and going I was loudly cheered, more so than I have been for some time. Uxbridge told me the Duke of Wellington had made a sad mistake by moving that the word *Protestant* be put into the address, and saying[1] it was left out to please O'Connell!! and that Lord Melbourne had replied beautifully to it. Then that

[1] The Queen wrote to the Prince that "The Tories make a great disturbance, saying that you are a Papist, because the words *a Protestant Prince* have not been put into the Declaration—a thing which would be quite unnecessary, seeing that I *cannot* marry a *Papist*."

Sir John Yarde-Buller[1] had given notice in the House of C. of a Motion on the 28th of want of confidence in Ministers!! I was so angry. Immediately after dinner I wrote to Lord M. begging he would come. Meanwhile I received a letter from him giving an account of the Debate; and very soon after a note saying he was undressed, but would dress and come directly. At ½ p. 10 my good Lord Melbourne came and stayed with me till 5 m. to 11. I saw him upstairs as of a morning. I said I was shocked to have made him come out, but that I hadn't then received his box, and Uxbridge had alarmed me. He was quite dressed,—really so *very, very* kind of him to come. The Duke of W. had been very foolish, he said; Lord M., however, consented to the word being inserted. "J. Russell sent to say he wished it should be put in," Lord M. said, "as he thought there might be an awkward division about it in the House of Commons." Lord M. asked if I had heard from the H. of C.; I replied I had about this Notice of Sir J. Yarde-Buller's, but that I thought there could be no alarm about it. "No, I hope not," Lord M. replied, and we agreed this was the best shape they could put it into for us, as our people will be sure to go with us upon this. "They say they wish to see which is the strongest," Lord M. said. Talked of a General Election. "We have always lost (by that) hitherto since the Reform Bill," he said.

Friday, 17th January.—After dinner Lord Mel-

[1] Disraeli in his *Life of Bentinck* calls Sir John Yarde-Buller Peel's "choice and pattern country gentleman, whom he had himself selected and invited to move a vote of want of confidence in the Whig Government, in order, against the feeling of the court, to instal Sir Robert Peel in their stead."

bourne and I looked at the picture of Albert. "The head is like," he said, "very good—fine expression—melancholy" (as it is), "which is good for a picture." Lord M. don't like a *fine hand* or a *fat* hand for a man. He made me laugh by saying, "The arms are one of the principal points in a woman." He looked at the picture of Queen Mary (which with one of William III. and 2 other portraits have replaced those 4 landscapes), and he said, "She was the handsomest woman in Europe; I consider her as the first of the Stuarts; she managed everything so well, and the perfect confidence he had in her." We looked at William III., whom he again praised very much and said wasn't cruel. "It was only that accident at Glencoe," he said. . . .

Sunday, 19th January.—Talked of Albert's indifference about Ladies, and Lord M. said, "A little dangerous, all that is,—it's very well if that holds, but it doesn't always," Lord M. said. I said this was very wrong of him, and scolded him for it. "It's what I said at Windsor; I think I know human nature pretty well." I said not the *best* of human nature. "I've known the best of my time," he said, "and I've read of the best."

Monday, 20th January.—Talked of Mr. Wakley[1] attacking the Tories for disloyalty. Talked of Hallam and my liking it so much; his giving an account of the persecutions in Elizabeth's reign; of Queen Mary

[1] Mr. Wakley was Radical M.P. for Finsbury and founder and editor of *The Lancet.* Sir E. Knatchbull had complained of the want of notice; Mr. Wakley said not one in a hundred of the members who went with the Speaker was a Conservative, whereupon Mr. Blackstone retorted that not only was he there, but to his surprise had seen the brother of a Cabinet Minister in the Queen's presence "dressed in a cut-off green coat with brass buttons," although the Court at the time was in mourning.

of Scots and her innocence. "All the ladies take Queen Mary's part," Lord M. said, "all those who reason like Hallam do quite admit her to be guilty, and all those who consult their feelings, do not." Talked of Darnley's murder, which I maintained her not to have knowledge of, but which Lord M. says she *did* know of. "I think she was quite right to have him knocked on the head," Lord M. said funnily, which made me laugh. Talked of Rizzio's murder, and poor Mary's cruel fate. Lord M. said Elizabeth was very reluctant to have her executed, and that the whole country demanded it. I said Hallam says that Walsingham and Leicester urged Elizabeth to persecute the Roman Catholics; Lord M. said, as I know and Hallam says, that Leicester was a bad man. "Whenever he (Lord Burleigh) put anything before her," Lord M. continued, "he always put the reasons on both sides in 2 columns, which may have been a very good way, but I think a way to puzzle," in which I quite agree; I couldn't bear it, I'm sure. Talked of Essex—his being a fine character—his conduct in Ireland—his sudden return—his unfortunate death, and the possibility of his having been saved if it had not been for the Countess of Nottingham. "It killed her" (Elizabeth), Lord M. said. Talked of Hallam containing so much knowledge which one hadn't before known, and Lord M. said he couldn't recommend a better book. I observed to Lord M. he didn't seem at all low. "No, I'm much better," he replied, "but still I'm not well." I entreated him to take some good advice about his health. "That won't do any good," he said, "it's age and that constant care"; which alas! alas! is but too true. "I'm nearly 61," he continued, "many men die at 63, and if they get over that, live till 70." I told him he mustn't talk in that way. "People like me grow old at once, who have been rather young for their age." I said he still was that. "Still, I feel a great change since last year," he said.[1] I feel certain his valuable health and life will be spared yet many a year. His father lived to be 83, but was very feeble, he said, for many years, and that it was not worth living then; his mother died at 66. "She had been a very strong woman till then," Lord M. said, "but she declined and sank rapidly." I begged Lord M. to take great care of himself, as he belonged to all of us; and he promised he would.

Tuesday, 21st January.—I showed him Uncle Leopold's letter. I also showed Lord M. Stockmar's letter, in which he talks of a Clause in the 2nd Article of the Marriage Treaty, which Stockmar had taken upon himself to agree to; it's about Albert's having no other Claims besides the £50,000[2] settled on him. "It's the same which was put in to Queen Mary's with Philip," Lord M. said. "It is impossible to say what claims a man may have who marries a Queen, over the property of the Crown; I'm afraid there'll be a good deal of observation about the Prince's Provision; they'll say it's too much"; which I said would be wrong. The Prince's position was disagreeable enough as it was, I said, but this would make it too bad; that I wouldn't

[1] He died aged sixty-nine, but, like his father, much enfeebled.

[2] This was the amount proposed by the Government. Mr. Hume proposed to cut it down to £21,000, but this was negatived by a large majority. The whole Conservative party, however, supported an amendment of Colonel Sibthorp to make the Prince's income £30,000 only, and this was carried by 262 to 158.

do it for the world. "You wouldn't do it," Lord M. said laughing; "still, if he is a man of discretion he may make it" (his position) "a very considerable one," he added.

Wednesday, 22nd January.—I then said I was so vexed and distressed by poor dear Albert's letter yesterday; that I feared they made him believe abroad that we wanted to degrade him here.[1] His letter to Lord M., and also to me, were misapprehensions about his Household, and about Lord M.'s letter. "We can't proceed to form his Household now," Lord M. said. I said, Oh! yes, for that I would be answerable for it[2]; that I thought Albert didn't quite understand the difference between "standing by" and "acting." "I don't quite *understand* his letter," Lord M. said; therefore, I replied, Stockmar and I would let Lord M. have the letter back again. "At the same time, 2 Households are very awkward," Lord M. said, and that there had been great trouble about the Queen Dowager's. We think the number of Albert's ought to be reduced. Talked of my being vexed about the whole; of all that; of its being unfair that the *Queen's husband* should have so much less than the *King's wife*, in which Lord M. agreed. Talked of various things, and German being so difficult. "So everybody says," Lord M. said. "Is it possible to be so diffi-

[1] The Prince was naturally much annoyed by the attacks and criticisms in Parliament and in certain organs of the Press. They were of a purely party character, and although plainly understood here, were misapprehended abroad, where the match was believed to be unpopular among the English people. This was not the case.

[2] See *Letters of Queen Victoria*, pp. 254–62, for all the little troubles which arose in connection with the formation of the Prince's Household. In after-years the distinction between the Households was purely nominal.

cult ?" "Oughtn't to know more than one language," he continued. "You can't *speak* one purely if you know a great many,—you mix them. They say you needn't know more than Latin and French"; Greek, Lady Lyttelton mentioned. "There's no necessity for it," he said; its being difficult; "a very copious language," he replied. I observed learning much as I did at once, prevented one from learning anything very well, and bewildered one. "That's very true what you say," Lord M. said, "that's the fault now, they teach too much at once." Talked of teaching being a dreadful thing, the poor children being more eager to learn than the higher classes, and Lady Lyttelton saying the Irish children were so very much quicker in learning than the English. "It's that quickness that leads to that disregard of truth," Lord M. said, "for when you ask them anything, they don't think of what you *say*, but of what they think will *please* you. He told me at dinner that he was having a new *full-dress* coat made, for the *great* occasion, which was "like building a 74-gun ship" in point of trouble and work, and that he had had the man with him in the morning, trying it on and pinning and stitching. He asked how Stockmar was, and wished much to see him. "I am always ready to see him, he is such a very clever man, and he don't stay long." "He is one of the cleverest fellows I ever saw,"—"the most discreet man, the most well judging, and most cool man."[1] I said I told him I thought he (Stockmar) ought to stay a little while after the Marriage, as it would be of use. "Of infinite importance," Lord M. replied. "And

[1] This opinion was subsequently endorsed by Sir Robert Peel.

the King," he said, "in his last letter to you, wished to be remembered to me, and hoped I had some recollection for him; pray say everything you can of respect and affection." I told him Uncle was, and very naturally, very fond of him. After this some new *Assam* Tea, which Sir J. Hobhouse had sent me, was brought in, and I gave Lord M. a printed paper which had been sent me with it, which he read out loud and so funnily; there was the opinion of a *Dr. Lum Qua* quoted, which name put him into paroxysms of laughter, from which he couldn't recover for some time, and which did one good to hear. After this I said to him he had been so very kind about all that matter which vexed me so yesterday. "The advantage of Monarchy is unity," Lord M. said, "which is a *little* spoilt by 2 people,—but that must be contended against." "I've no doubt," he continued, "that is what kept Queen Elizabeth from marrying; but you mustn't think that I advocate that; I think that's not right, it's unnatural, and nothing's right that's unnatural." I said I was certain that Albert wouldn't interfere. "Oh! I haven't the slightest doubt that he won't interfere," he replied warmly; and I added that that was the very reason why he might run into the other extreme. "My letter may have appeared dictating," he said, which I said was not the case; "that's my way of writing, I write so to you, and did to the King." I said I was sure it would all do very well in a little time. "*You* understand it all," he said, "you have always lived here"; and I had had three years' experience, I said. "But you had just the same capability for affairs," Lord M. said, "when you came to the Throne, as you have now,—you were just as able; I'm for making people of age much sooner." He again went into an amazing fit of laughter about *Dr. Lum Qua.* Talked of children having the measles, his having them, about which he was very funny, as also about children learning, as he said, everything from the nurses and servants,—which he talked of for some time. "I'm sure, all I have learnt that's useful was from the nursery maid," which made us laugh so. Talked of the H. of C. and the Provision. "I can't think there can be any real difficulty," he said; "one can't tell; a Legislative Assembly is as capricious as a woman."

Thursday, 23rd January.—Talked of my having ridden in the Riding House; of the new Steward in Feltham's place; of my having heard from Albert, and my thinking he seemed fearful he had vexed me; of the Queen Dowager's health; of a novel by Miss Martineau[1] called *Deerbrook*, which Lady Lyttelton was praising very much, and which she said was about the Middle Classes. "I don't like the Middle Classes," Lord M. said, "they say that the Upper and Lower Classes are very much like each other in this country; the Middle Classes are bad; the higher and lower classes there's some good in, but the middle classes are all affectation and conceit and pretence and concealment." I said to Lord M. he so often kept one in hot water by saying *such* things before, and to, people; "It's a good thing to surprise," he said. I said he said such things of people's families to them. "That's a very good thing," he replied funnily, "I do that on purpose,

[1] Miss Martineau had published a short story in 1831, *Five Years of Youth*; but *Deerbrook*, published in 1839, was her first serious attempt at novel-writing. She declined a pension from Lord Melbourne in 1841, and again from Mr. Gladstone in 1873.

I think it right to warn people of the faults in their families"; and he turned to Lilford[1] and said, "Your family has always been reckoned very prosing, so I warn you of that," which made us laugh so. I said to Lord M. I had told Stockmar what Lord M. had said to me here and at Windsor, about those very high principles like A.'s not *holding* often, upon which Stockmar said, generally speaking that was true, but that he didn't think that would be A.'s case. Talked of C. Ponsonby[2] having, as Lord M. told us, a Black huntsman and a Black whipper-in; of looking over papers being such a fatigue; of a Swiss Clergyman who Lord De Grey[3] had got, disapproving of dancing; of a very pretty paper weight which Lord M. told me they had made for me at Birmingham, and which Mr. Scholefield was going to present me; he sent Lord M. one and a pair of razors. Talked of how George IV. came to have the names of Augustus Frederic besides; Lord M.'s being called William after the late Lord Fitz-William; I never liked the name William till I knew Lord M. and knew it was his; his brother Frederic

[1] Thomas Atherton, third Lord Lilford (1801–61).

[2] Charles Ponsonby (afterwards second Lord de Mauley). He had married in 1838 his cousin Maria Ponsonby, daughter of Lord Duncannon and granddaughter of the Earl of Bessborough.

[3] The titles in the Robinson family are intricate. Thomas Robinson, second Lord Grantham, married Mary, daughter of the second Earl of Hardwicke, heiress (under a special remainder) to her sister (Lady Lucas), who had been created Countess de Grey. The Lord de Grey mentioned in the text was the eldest son of this marriage, and became successively Lord Grantham and Earl de Grey; he was Lord Lieutenant of Ireland 1841–4. Dying without male issue, he was succeeded by his daughter in his barony of Lucas, and by his brother in the earldom. But that brother (the ex-Prime Minister) had already been successively created Viscount Goderich and Earl of Ripon. His son was long known as Earl de Grey and Ripon, before becoming Marquess of Ripon.

is called James also; the Duke of York and the late Lord Salisbury being his godfathers. Talked of the old Duchess of Brunswick and if Lord M. had known her.[1] "I've known so many old Duchesses," he said laughing. Talked of her brothers the Dukes of Cumberland[2] and Gloucester; of Prince Frederic[3] the youngest, whom Lord M. had never heard of; of the great Duke of Cumberland[4] and his being cruel, which Lord M. wouldn't allow, and said, "He was a fine man, not cruel, only to a few rebels."

Friday, 24th January.—Finished my letter to Albert. Wrote my journal. Received a letter from Louise with the delightful news that dearest Victoire's marriage with Nemours is arranged; dear, dear child, whom I love so dearly, whom I look upon as my sister. May she be happy; I'm sure she will be; how nice that we should *both* be *Brides* at the same time!

Saturday, 25th January.—Saw by the newspapers that we had *won Newark* by 9![5]

Sunday, 26th January.—Talked of the Duchess of Sutherland being at his sister's party, which I said was wrong of her as the Duke couldn't go. He said Fanny was very full of what he (Ld. M.) had said about the Pagets never learning anything, which he had said to George Byng here who told it Lady Agnes who wrote it to Lady Sydney who was very angry,

[1] Augusta, eldest child of Frederick, Prince of Wales, married Charles William, Duke of Brunswick.

[2] Henry Frederick, Duke of Cumberland, 1745–1790.

[3] Frederick William, died, aged 15, 1765.

[4] William Augustus, Duke of Cumberland, 1721–1765. Son of George II.

[5] The by-election was caused by the appointment of Sergeant Wilde to be Solicitor-General. He was afterwards Lord Chancellor Truro, and married Mdlle. d'Este. See Vol. I., p. 198, note.

and which Lady Cowper had been embellishing; Lord M. laughed very much, but I said I was sure he would get into great scrapes by saying things of people's families to them. "It's quite a right thing to do," he said laughing. I told him that he said such things of my family, which I didn't mind, but which I was sure he wouldn't like other people to say of his family to him. "Oh! yes, I would," he replied laughing. I said that I thought no Royal Princes *ought* to be in the House of Lords, which Lord M. does not agree in, but says they ought always to go with the Crown. "The Duke of York always went steadily with the Crown," Lord M. said, "except on the Regency, and then he went steadily with the Prince; when the King was gone he stood by the next person." . . .

Thursday, 30th January.—Talked of Miss Eden and her jumping into the river at Hampton Court and saving a child who fell in. "It was a courageous thing to do," he said. Of Lady Mayo,[1] and her being such a quiz. "Lady Mayo said to Lady Glengall,"[2] Lord M. continued, "'I understand you said I was the ugliest woman in the world'; so Lady Glengall, quite driven to the wall, said, 'Well, I must say, Lady Mayo, I think you are the most frightful woman I ever saw in my life.'" Talked of the Heralds' Office, and Sir Wm. Woods, and Lord M. said, "They were very foolish about those Arms" (A.'s) "when they had the precedent

[1] Arabella, wife of John, fourth Earl of Mayo, a Lady-in-Waiting to Queen Adelaide. She was daughter of William Mackworth-Praed. See Vol. I., p. 77.

[2] Margaret Lauretta, wife of Richard, second Earl of Glengall, and daughter and co-heiress of William Melhuish of Woodford, Essex.

under their very nose," which is quite true. "Old Lord Pembroke, who was then Lord Chamberlain," Lord M. continued, "said at the Coronation of George II., to Anstis,[1] who was Garter, 'Thou silly knave, that dost not even know thy silly work!'"

After dinner, when Lord Melbourne came in, the ladies were talking of colours being unlucky or lucky at a Wedding. "Yellow is the colour of Hymen," he said. I showed him Lord Wellesley's letter to Lord Anglesey, which Uxbridge gave me. "Humbug," Lord M. said as he took the letter, but as he went on reading it, he said, "That's right—that's right—good letter"; and when he returned it me he said, "Good letter." Lord M. sent me a letter from the Duke of Sussex before dinner, so delighted at giving me away, and I received one after dinner from him, which I gave Lord M., and he said in returning it, "He is very much pleased; I'm very glad."

We were seated as usual, Lord Melbourne sitting near me. He said he was quite well, but never *felt* quite well, which I said was the constant care and wear; and that he never felt quite free from some little ailing, nor did anybody; when he was young, he said, he never felt unwell, and used "only to live for my amusement," he said, and that if he were to begin life again he would do only that and not enter Politics at all. I said I thought people who only lived for their amusement bad, and that I was sure we should all be punished hereafter for living as we did without thinking at all of our future life. "That's not my case," Lord M. said; and we

[1] John Anstis, the elder, Garter 1718–44. Part of the time he was joint holder of the office with his son, who held it till 1754.

talked of living our life and beginning it again, and if it were possible, we agreed, we should try and correct ourselves. Talked of his having told me at Windsor that the young men in his day and he himself had been so very impudent; he said I must have misunderstood him, "for I was very shy; there never was a shyer man."

Friday, 31st January.—Then he showed me a note from Lady Burghersh saying she had seen the Duke, who would be anxious not to do anything to embarrass the Government, but that the Precedence lay rather on awkward ground; and that they wouldn't oppose the 2nd reading, but make alterations in the Committee. The remainder of the time that Lord M. was with me, we talked almost entirely about this ill-fated Precedence, and I fear I was violent and eager about it. I said to Lord M. he must fight it out. The House of Lords *might* sit next day, he said, in order to get on with it; and in answer to my saying it was so dreadful not to have the Power even to give my Husband rank, Lord M. said I couldn't, that that was "the law of the Country," and he thinks convenient at times. I declared if they didn't grant it to Albert for *his* life, I would give it all up and let him only have the rank Uncle Leopold had had. "Is that really your opinion?" Lord M. said, "for that would end it at once." I then hesitated, and said he must fight it out. "That's what I wish to know," Lord M. said. He told me, which I couldn't at first understand, that the Marriage couldn't take place until the Bill was passed, as the Bill would be void if it wasn't passed before. I showed him the Queen of the French's letter. I begged him to let me know, which he promised he would, and

I repeated it was necessary he should fight it out. "Very well, Ma'am," he replied; "if we *were* beat, if you wished it we might say, 'Well then, we'll follow the Precedent'"; I said I must reflect about it. I fear I vexed him, kind, good man, as he looked, I think, grieved at my pertinacity.

Saturday, 1st February.—I was awoke at a little past 8 by a box from Lord John, dated ½ p. 5, with the most welcome, most delightful news, that we had had a Majority of 21![1] How delightful! How happy and light this made me feel! (Lord M. sent me a letter in the morning from Duncannon, saying he hoped I would consent to the Limitation of Precedence for my Life, as many of our friends wished for it. I wrote to Lord M. I was much against it; Lord M. agreed in my feelings, but thought as they should certainly be beat we had better give it up. Talked of my not wishing now to go to the Whitehall Chapel, as I heard the Pew was so public. "You'd better go," Lord M. said; I resisted; "Nothing so good as going in the midst of a large congregation," he said. I really couldn't, I said. "You'd better go," he added, as he went out of the room. I said I had seen Chantrey, who said he would go to his house; and Lord M. promised to sit, and also to Hayter, *here*. I said I feared Lord M. thought me grown obstinate. "Rather," he replied, mildly and kindly. Why was he so particularly anxious I should go to church? I said. "It's a good thing before your marriage," Lord M. said. "I always wished you to go there." It was just that going before the marriage, so publicly, I said, which I disliked. "But it's of great import-

[1] On Sir John Yarde-Buller's motion of want of confidence.

ance that you should get over that dislike of going amongst everybody."[1]

Sunday, 2nd February.—After dinner when Lord Melbourne came in, he told me he was pretty well. I took him aside and talked to him about what had happened. They were to have a Cabinet at 12; I said I was sorry for my excited letter. "Oh! never mind that, don't think of that," he said so kindly. I said to him he was always so kind. "The Duke said, 'It's an injustice, and for God's sake don't let the House of Lords be guilty of an injustice,'" Lord M. said. "He's got that into his head." At this moment Lord M. received a note from the Duke, saying he was glad to see that Lord M. wished to settle this matter without any debate, and that he had requested Lord Lyndhurst to prepare two Amendments, which he said he would send to Lord M. as soon as he received them in the morning. Lord M. couldn't read from where he dated it. I asked Lord M. what he had written to the Duke. Lord M. said, "that nothing could give me more pleasure than to hear the tone in which he talked of his wish to settle this amicably, at the same time that it gave me great pain to see the wide difference which lay between us, and that I hoped therefore he would let us hear what he meant to do that we might deliberate upon it." "It's a very odd thing," Lord M. said, "the Duke of Wellington said to Clarendon, 'I like Lord Melbourne, I've a very good opinion of him, and I think he's the best Minister the Queen can have, and he has given her

[1] The Queen's shyness was very natural in so young a Princess. Greville says that when she announced her marriage to the Privy Council her hands trembled so that she could hardly read the Declaration.

very good advice I've no doubt; but I'm afraid he jokes too much with her, and makes her treat things too lightly, which are very serious.' Now there may be some truth in that," Lord Melbourne added. I said oh! no, but that perhaps as I often scolded him he jested a little about religion, which he denied. "It shows the shrewdness of the man," Lord M. said.[1]

Monday, 3rd February.—"I've got the Duke's ultimatum," Lord M. said, shaking his head, "it's what I thought";—adhering to the Precedent and giving Albert rank after all the Princes of the Blood, which I said was really a great deal too bad. "So we think," Lord M. said; "the best way will be to leave all Precedence out of the Bill, and say we'll settle it hereafter; then let it be settled as you like, partly by your prerogative and partly by Act of Parliament." This is much the best.[2] . . .

Thursday, 6th February.—Received a delightful letter from dearest Albert from Brussels dated 4th, with a very funny book of Caricatures. Wrote to Lord M. Received letters from Uncle and Louise. Saw a very funny little bluish grey Scotch Terrier, which I have bought, called Laddie, a dear little thing; it's gone down to Windsor. Lord Albemarle brought dear little Henry Byng[3] (George Byng's 2nd boy) to kiss hands as Page of Honour; he

[1] This passage illustrates not only the Duke's shrewdness, but Lord Melbourne's good-tempered readiness to accept criticism and even rebuke.

[2] This is how the Prince's precedence was ultimately settled. The attempt to put it into the Bill was a mistake. Lord Melbourne's Government mismanaged the House of Commons in everything connected with the Queen's marriage.

[3] He was Equerry to the Queen, and afterwards Earl of Strafford.

looked delightful in his costume. At 20 m. to 3 Lord Melbourne came to me and stayed with me till 25 m. p. Talked of my having too much to do. "You must have," he replied; and the Duke of Devonshire's not having been invited (to the wedding), which I said he had; of the Duke of Wellington's being asked. Talked of Miss Hope-Johnstone's marriage[1]; of Uncle's saying poor dear Albert was worried and pale. "Oh! it's very natural," Lord M. said. He said the Chancellor must come to A. as soon as he arrived to administer the Oaths of Allegiance and Supremacy, on account of being naturalized. Talked of its being a fine day for their crossing, and Clarence Paget's being at Calais. "Oh! they say he's a very handy fellow," Lord M. said, "he'll bring them over anyhow." I told Lord M. there would be a great piece of work, I feared, about the Duke of Sussex and Lady Cecilia,[2] for that he had insinuated, without mentioning the exact thing, that he would ask Lord M. to ask me something which he had very near at heart. "Oh! it'll never do," Lord M. said. Talked of Albert's Commission not being gazetted till after he had taken the Oaths. Talked of Lord M.'s staying Thursday at Windsor. "I'll try and manage it."

[1] Miss Mary Hope-Johnstone was married on 3rd February to the Right Rev. Hugh Percy, Bishop of Carlisle.

[2] After the death of Lady Augusta d'Ameland (formerly Lady Augusta Murray: see Vol. I., p. 197) the Duke of Sussex had contracted a marriage (void, like his former one, under the Royal Marriage Act) with Lady Cecilia Buggin, daughter of the second Earl of Arran, and widow of Sir George Buggin, a solicitor. She afterwards assumed the surname of Underwood. The Duke was probably asking that Lady Cecilia might be raised to the peerage; for on 10th April following she was created Duchess of Inverness.

Friday, 7th February.—Just before I went out I received a delightful letter from dearest Albert from Dover, written in the morning; he suffered most dreadfully coming over; he is much pleased with the very kind reception he met with at Dover. Talked to Lord M. of Albert's letter, and one from Torrington saying dearest Albert's reception had pleased him so, as A. feared he wouldn't be well received; but Lord M. agreed with me that a Vote of the H. of Commons had nothing whatever to do with that. At this moment I received a letter, and a dear one, from dearest Albert from Canterbury, where he had just arrived, and where he had also been very well received, as I told Lord M., who said, "I've no doubt; his reception has been such that he must take care not to be intoxicated by that," which I said I was quite sure he needn't fear. Talked of Soult and his reception here having made him so friendly to England; of Sebastiani's removal; of Guizot. "You can always tell him you have read his book," Lord M. said laughing. We were seated as usual, Lord Melbourne sitting near me. Talked of Bull-dogs; of the Marriage Ceremony; my being a little agitated and nervous; "Most natural," Lord M. replied warmly; "how could it be otherwise?" Lord M. was so warm, so kind, and so affectionate, the whole evening, and so much touched in speaking of me and my affairs. Talked of my former resolution of never marrying. "Depend upon it, it's right to marry," he said earnestly; "if ever there was a situation that formed an exception, it was yours; it's in human nature, it's natural to marry; the other is a very unnatural state of things; it's a great *change*—it has its inconveniences; everybody does their best, and depend upon it you've done well; difficulties may arise from it," as they do of course from everything. Talked of popular assemblies, of my having grown so thin. "You look very well," he said; "after all," he continued, much affected, "how anybody in your situation can have a moment's tranquillity!—a young person cast in this situation is very unnatural. There was a beautiful account in a Scotch paper," he said, "of your first going to prorogue Parliament; 'I stood close to her,' it says, 'to see a young person surrounded by Ministers and Judges and rendered prematurely grave was almost melancholy'; 'a large searching eye, an open anxious nostril, and a firm mouth,'" Lord M. repeated this several times, looking so kindly and affectionately at me; "A very true representation," he said, "can't be a finer physiognomy"—which made me smile, as he said it so earnestly. Talked of Albert's being a little like me; of the Addresses and dinners A. would be plagued with; of my taking him to the Play soon. "There'll be an immense flow of popularity now," Lord M. said. Talked of the difficulty of keeping quite free from all Politics. I begged Lord M. much to manage about Thursday, which he promised he would, as I said it always made me so happy to have him. "I am sure none of your friends are so fond of you as I am," I said. "I believe not," he replied, quite touched, and I added also he had been always so very kind to me I couldn't say *how* I felt it.

Saturday, 8th February.—At ½ p. 4 the Carriage and Escort appeared, drove through the centre gate, and up to the door; I stood at the very door; 1st stepped out Ernest, then Uncle Ernest, and then Albert, looking beautiful and so well; I embraced him and took him by the hand and led him up to

H. R. H. Prince Albert

from a portrait by Dalton after F. Winterhalter

my room; Mamma, Uncle Ernest, and Ernest following. After dinner Albert and Ernest shook hands with Lord Melbourne. "I think they look very well," Lord M. said when he came up to me; "I think he (A.) looks very well." Talked of their passage; Lord M. said it was such a very good thing that Albert attended service in the Cathedral at Canterbury. I sat on the sofa with my beloved Albert, Lord Melbourne sitting near me. Talked of the gentlemen that Uncle had with him. Lord M. admired the diamond Garter which Albert had on, and said "Very handsome." I told him it was my gift; I also gave him (all before dinner) a diamond star I had worn, and badge. Lord M. made us laugh excessively about his new Coat, which he said, "I expect it to be the thing most observed."

Sunday, 9th February.—Received a beautiful Prayer-book from Mamma; breakfasted at 10. Wrote to Lord M. Dearest Albert and Ernest came in, Albert looking so well, with a little of his blue ribbon showing.[1] He brought me 4 beautiful old Fans. At 12 I went down to Prayers with my beloved Albert, Mamma, Ernest, and my ladies and gentlemen. Mr. Vane read and the Bishop of London preached a very fine sermon. The Service was over at 5 m. p. 1. Talked of dearest Albert's being agitated. "That's very natural," Lord M. said, "I don't wonder at it." Lord M. promised to stay Thursday. I took his hand and pressed it, and thanked him for all his kindness, which I hoped he would continue. I couldn't believe what was to happen next day, I said. At a ¼ to 6 my

[1] The ribbon of the Garter was at this time worn by day. The Duke of Wellington constantly wore it, with a white waistcoat. The star was sometimes worn *without* the ribbon.

beloved Albert came to me and stayed with me till 20 m. to 7. We read over the Marriage Service together and tried how to manage the *ring*. Wrote my journal. At 8 we dined. The dinner was just the same as the day before with the exception of Lord Albemarle, Lord Erroll, Lord Byron, Col. Grey, and Stockmar; and with the addition of Lord Surrey and Col. Cavendish. Albert led me in and I sat between him and Uncle E. It was my last unmarried evening, which made me feel so odd. I sat on the sofa with dearest Albert, Lord Melbourne sitting near me. Talked of A.'s having talked to him (Ld. M.); of guessing words; the Lord's Prayer being almost entirely composed of Saxon words, all but 4; of the Cathedral at Canterbury and Bishop Chicheley[1] being buried there.

Monday, 10th February.—Got up at a ¼ to 9—well, and having slept well; and breakfasted at ½ p. 9. Mamma came before and brought me a Nosegay of orange flowers. My dearest kindest Lehzen gave me a dear little ring. Wrote my journal, and to Lord M. Had my hair dressed and the wreath of orange flowers put on. Saw Albert for the *last* time *alone*, as my *Bridegroom*. Dressed.

Saw Uncle, and Ernest whom dearest Albert brought up. At ½ p. 12 I set off, dearest Albert having gone before. I wore a white satin gown with a very deep flounce of Honiton lace, imitation of old. I wore my Turkish diamond necklace and earrings, and Albert's beautiful sapphire brooch.[2] Mamma

[1] Henry Chichele, or Chicheley, prelate and statesman. Archbishop of Canterbury and Founder of All Souls' College, Oxford. Died 1443.

[2] The diamond necklace was left by Queen Victoria to the Duke of Connaught, and the sapphire brooch to the Crown. The lace is in the possession of H.M. Queen Alexandra.

and the Duchess of Sutherland went in the carriage with me. I never saw such crowds of people as there were in the Park, and they cheered most enthusiastically. When I arrived at St. James's, I went into the dressing-room where my 12 young Train-bearers [1] were, dressed all in white with white roses, which had a beautiful effect. Here I waited a little till dearest Albert's Procession had moved into the Chapel. I then went with my Train-bearers and ladies into the Throne-room, where the Procession formed; Lord Melbourne in his fine new dress-coat, bearing the Sword of State, and Lord Uxbridge and Lord Belfast [2] on either side of him walked immediately before me. Queen Anne's room was full of people, ranged on seats one higher than the other, as also in the Guard room, and by the Staircase,—all very friendly; the Procession looked beautiful going downstairs. Part of the Colour Court was also covered in and full of people who were very civil. The Flourish of Trumpets ceased as I entered the Chapel, and the organ began to play, which had a beautiful effect. At the Altar, to my right, stood Albert; Mamma was on my left as also the Dukes of Sussex and Cambridge, and Aunt Augusta; and on Albert's right was the Queen Dowager, then Uncle Ernest, Ernest, the Duchess of Cambridge and little Mary,

[1] Lady Adelaide Paget, Lady Sarah Frederica Caroline Villiers, Lady Frances Elizabeth Cowper, Lady Elizabeth West, Lady Mary Augusta Frederica Grimston, Lady Eleanora Caroline Paget, Lady Caroline Amelia Gordon Lennox, Lady Elizabeth Anne Georgiana Dorothea Howard, Lady Ida Hay, Lady Catherine Lucy Wilhelmina Stanhope, Lady Jane Harriet Bouverie, and Lady Mary Charlotte Howard.

[2] Eldest son of the second Marquess of Donegall, an A.D.C. to the Queen and Captain of the Yeoman of the Guard. Sat about twenty years for different Irish boroughs. He was created Lord Ennishowen in 1841, and became Marquess of Donegall in 1844.

George, Augusta, and Princess Sophia Matilda. Lord Melbourne stood close to me with the Sword of State. The Ceremony was very imposing, and fine and simple, and I think OUGHT to make an everlasting impression on every one who promises at the Altar to *keep* what he or she promises. Dearest Albert repeated everything very distinctly. I felt so happy when the ring was put on, and by Albert. As soon as the Service was over, the Procession returned as it came, with the exception that my beloved Albert led me out. The applause was very great, in the Colour Court as we came through; Lord Melbourne, good man, was very much affected during the Ceremony and at the applause. We all returned to the Throne-room, where the Signing of the Register took place; it was first signed by the Archbishop, then by Albert and me, and all the Royal Family, and by: the Lord Chancellor, the Lord President, the Lord Privy Seal, the Duke of Norfolk (as Earl Marshal), the Archbishop of York, and Lord Melbourne. We then went into the Closet, and the Royal Family waited with me there till the ladies had got into their carriages. I gave all the Train-bearers as a brooch a small *eagle* of turquoise. I then returned to Buckingham Palace alone with Albert; they cheered us really most warmly and heartily; the crowd was immense; and the Hall at Buckingham Palace was full of people; they cheered us again and again. The great Drawing-room and Throne-room were full of people of rank, and numbers of children were there. Lord Melbourne and Lord Clarendon, who had arrived, stood at the door of the Throne-room when we came in. I went and sat on the sofa in my dressing-room with Albert; and we talked together there from 10 m. to 2 till 20 m. p. 2. Then we went downstairs where all the Company was assembled and went into the dining-room—dearest Albert leading me in, and my Train being borne by 3 Pages, Cowell, little Wemyss, and dear little Byng. I sat between dearest Albert and the Duke of Sussex. My health and dearest Albert's were drunk. The Duke was very kind and civil. Albert and I drank a glass of wine with Lord Melbourne, who seemed much affected by the whole. I talked to all after the breakfast, and to Lord Melbourne, whose fine coat I praised. Little Mary[1] behaved so well both at the Marriage and the breakfast. I went upstairs and undressed and put on a white silk gown trimmed with swansdown, and a bonnet with orange flowers. Albert went downstairs and undressed. At 20 m. to 4 Lord Melbourne came to me and stayed with me till 10 m. to 4. I shook hands with him and he kissed my hand. Talked of how well everything went off. "Nothing could have gone off better," he said, and of the people being in such good humour and having also received him well; of my receiving the Addresses from the House of Lords and Commons; of his coming down to Windsor in time for dinner. I begged him not to go to the party; he was a little tired; I would let him know when we arrived; I pressed his hand once more, and he said, "God bless you, Ma'am," most kindly, and with such a kind look. Dearest Albert came up and fetched me downstairs, where we took leave of Mamma and drove off at near 4; I and Albert alone.

[1] Princess Mary of Cambridge, Duchess of Teck, mother of Queen Mary.

APPENDIX

From Morley's "Life of Gladstone," vol. iii. p. 472.

"Mr. Gladstone wished we knew more of Melbourne. He was in many ways a very fine fellow. In two of the most important of all the relations of a Prime Minister he was perfect. I mean first, his relations to the Queen, second, to his colleagues."

The foregoing pages justify Mr. Gladstone's estimate of Lord Melbourne, but he might have added among Lord Melbourne's perfect relations as a Prime Minister, those to his political opponents

Lord Melbourne's Family

Peniston Lamb's elder brother was a solicitor at Southwell, who managed the affairs of the family of Coke of Melbourne Hall, co. Derby. This solicitor had two sons—Robert, who took orders and became Dean and subsequently Bishop of Peterborough; and Matthew, who followed his father's profession, and in 1740 married Miss Charlotte Coke. Her brother, Sir George Coke, died unmarried, and left all his property to his sister. Her husband, Matthew Lamb, succeeded to the large fortune of his uncle Peniston, mentioned in the text, and their son, Peniston, was bequeathed the whole of the fortune of his uncle the Bishop of Peterborough. Matthew, who was for many years M.P. and was made a baronet in 1755, purchased Brocket Hall, co. Herts, from the Winnington family.

His son, Sir Peniston, also M.P., purchased Melbourne House in Piccadilly, which stood on the site of the Albany. He was created Baron Melbourne in the Irish peerage in 1770 and Viscount Melbourne in 1815. He married the daughter of Sir Ralph Milbanke, who was the aunt of Lady Byron.

H. M. Queen Victoria

from a portrait by Dalton, after F. Winterhalter.

Sir T. Coke, *d.* 1727;
mar. i. Miss Mary Hale,
ii. Lady Mary Stanhope.

Sir George Coke,
d. unmarried
Aug. 1748, and left
Melbourne [1] and
all his property
to his sister
Charlotte.

Charlotte,
m. Matthew Lamb
in 1740.

Mr. Lamb,[2] solicitor, Southwell, Notts, the Cokes' lawyer.

Robert,
Dean and afterwards
Bishop of Peterborough,
left all his property
to his nephew
Peniston.

Matthew,
mar. Charlotte Coke, 1740;
M.P. Stockbridge, and
afterwards Peterborough;
purchased Brocket, 1746;
made Baronet, 1755.

Son, Peniston, *b.* 1748;
mar. dau. Sir Ralph Milbanke,[3] 1769;
bought Melbourne House,
Piccadilly, where Albany
now stands, from Sir
Stephen Fox;
M.P. Luggershall, 1770;
cr. Baron Melbourne, 1770,
Viscount M. 1815;
d. 1828.

Peniston Lamb,
b. 1770;
d. unmarried 1805.

William Lamb,
second Viscount Melbourne,
b. 1779; *d.* 1848.

Frederick James,
cr. Baron Beauvale, 1839;
suc. as third Viscount
Melbourne, 1848;
d. 1853.

George,
b. 1784;
d. 1834.

[1] Melbourne Hall, co. Derbyshire, in possession of Coke family from 13th century.
[2] His brother Peniston, a lawyer in London, made large fortune and left it to his nephew Matthew.
[3] This Sir Ralph Milbanke was the father of another Sir Ralph, whose daughter married Lord Byron. Lord Melbourne was therefore Byron's first cousin by marriage.

PEDIGREE No. 1.

ERNEST AUGUSTUS (Elector of Hanover) = SOP
1629–1698.

Frederick I., King of Prussia = Sophia Charlotte,
1657–1713. 1668–1705.

GEORGE I. = Sophia Dorothea of Zell,
1660–1727. 1666–1726.

Frederick William I. = Sophia Dorothea,
King of Prussia, 1685–1757.
1688–1740.

Frederick II., "the Great," 1712–1786.

Prince Augustus William, 1722–1758.

Philippina = Charles, Duke of Brunswick.

Anne = Prince of Orange,
1709–1759. great-great-grandfather of Queen Victoria's suitor.

Amelia, 1711–1786.

Caroline Elizabeth, 1713–1757.

Frederick William II., 1744–1797.

Charles William Frederick = Augusta,
Duke of Brunswick, 1735–1806. 1737–1813.

GEORGE III. = Charlotte Sophia of
1738–1820. Mecklenburg-Strelitz,
1744–1818.

Edward Augustus, Duke of York, 1739–1767 (*o.s.p.*).

Willia[m] Duke of Gl[oucester] 1743–1805.

Frederick William III., 1770–1840.

Charles George Augustus, 1766–1806 (*o.s.p.*).

Augusta = Frederick I.,
–1788. King of Württemberg, 1754–1816.

Frederick William = Duchess
1771–1815, Marie of
Duke of Brunswick. Baden.

Caroline = GEORGE IV.,
1768–1821. 1762–1830.

Frederick = Frederica,
Duke of York, 1763–1827 (*o.s.p.*). Princess Royal of Prussia, 1767–1820.

WILLIAM IV., 1765–1837. *m.* Adelaide of Saxe-Meiningen, 1792–1849.

Edward, Duke o[f] Kent, 1767–18[20] *m.* Mary Louis[a] Victoria, 1786–1861, of Saxe-Coburg-Saalfel[d] widow of Prin[ce] Emich Charles Leiningen.

Frederick William IV., 1795–1861.

William I., German Emperor, 1797–1888, *m.* Augusta of Saxe-Weimar, 1811–1890.

William I., 1781–1864.

Charles F. A. W., Duke of Brunswick, 1804–1873 (*o.s.p.*).

William, Duke of Brunswick, 1806–1884 (*o.s.p.*).

Charlotte = Leopold of Saxe-
1796–1817 Coburg-Saalfeld,
(*o.s.p.*). afterwards King of the Belgians, 1790–1865.

Charlotte, *b.* & *d.* 1819.

Elizabeth, 1820–1821.

VICTORIA, 1819–1901

Frederick III. = Victoria, Princess Royal of
1831–1888. Great Britain, 1840–1901.

William II., *b.* 1859.

Princess Thyra = Ernest Augustus,
of Denmark, Duke of Cumberland,
b. 1853. *b.* 1845.

Alphonse, Baron von = Frederica,
Pawel Rammingen, *b.* 1848.
b. 1843.

Victoria Georgina *b.* & *d.* 1881.

Mary, 1849–1904.

Christian Frederick, 1885–1901.

Maximilian = Mary Louisa,
Prince of Baden, *b.* 1879.
b. 1867.

George William, *b.* 1880.

Alexandra = Frederick Francis, Grand Duke
b. 1882. of Mecklenburg-Schwerin,
b. 1882.

Olga, *b.* 1884.

Ernest Augustus, *b.* 1887.

Elizabeth of Anh[alt] *b.* 1857.

Mary Alexandra, *b.* 1902.

Berthold Frederick, *b.* 1906.

THE HOU

lector of Hanover) = SOPHIA (Grand-daughter of JAMES I.)
8. 1630–1714.

of Zell,
6.

Ernest Augustus, Duke of York, Bishop of Osnaburg, 1674–1728.

GEORGE II. = Caroline of Anspach,
1683–1760. 1683–1737.

Caroline Elizabeth, 1713–1757.

Frederick Lewis, Prince of Wales = Augusta of Saxe-Gotha,
1707–1751. –1772.

George William, 1717–1718.

Louisa = Frederick V.,
1724–1751. King of Denmark. 1723–1766.

Mary = Frederick II., Landgrave
1723–1772. of Hesse-Cassel.

William Augustu
Duke of Cumbe
1721–1765
(*o.s.p.*).

tus,
rk,

William Henry = Maria, Countess-Dowager
Duke of Gloucester, Waldegrave,
1743–1805. *d.* 1807.

Henry Frederick,
Duke of Cumberland,
1745–1790, *m.* Lady
Ann Horton.

Frederick William, 1750–1765.

Caroline Matilda = Christian VII.,
1751–1775. 1749–1808.

Frederick VI., 1768–1839.

Landgrave Frederick = Caroline of Nassau
1747–1837. Usingen, 1762–1823.

Sophia Matilda, 1773–1844.

Caroline, 1774–1775.

M IV.,
837, *m.*
de of
Meiningen,
1849.

Elizabeth,
1820–1821.

Edward, Duke of Kent, 1767–1820, *m.* Mary Louisa Victoria, 1786–1861, of Saxe-Coburg-Saalfeld, widow of Prince Emich Charles of Leiningen.

VICTORIA, 1819–1901

Ernest Augustus, Duke of Cumberland, King of Hanover, 1771–1851, *m.* Frederica Caroline of Mecklenburg-Strelitz, 1778–1841.

Mary Alexandrina = George, King
of Saxe-Altenburg, of Hanover,
1818–1907. 1819–1878.

Augustus, Duke of Sussex, 1773–1843 (*o.s.p.*).

Adolphus, Duke of Cambridge, 1774–1850, *m.* Augusta of Hesse-Cassel, 1797–1889.

Octavius, 1779–1783.

Alfred, 1780–1782.

Mary = William Frederick,
1776–1857. Duke of Gloucester, 1776–1834 (*o.s.p.*).

Charlotte, 1766–1828, 2nd wife of Frederick I., King of Würtemberg (*o.s.p.*).

Augusta, 1768–1840.

Elizabeth, 1770–1840, *m.* Frederick, Landgrave of Hesse-Homburg, 1769–1829 (*o.s.p.*).

Sophia, 1777–1848.

Amelia, 1783–1810.

Landgrave William, 1787–1867, *m.* Charlotte of Denmark, 1789–1864.

Augusta, Duchess of Cambridge, 1797–1889.

Mary, 1849–1904.

George, Duke of Cambridge, 1819–1904 (*o.s.p.*).

Augusta = Frederick William, Grand
b. 1822. Duke of Mecklenburg Strelitz, 1819–1904.

Mary, 1833–1897 *m.* Francis, Duke of Teck, 1837–1900.

Louise = Christian
1817–1898. King of D
1818–

Elizabeth of Anhalt = George Adolphus Frederick,
b. 1857. *b.* 1848

Adolphus = Lady Margaret
Duke of Teck, Grosvenor,
b. 1868. *b.* 1873.

George, *b.* 1895.

Victoria, *b.* 1897.

Helena, *b.* 1899.

Victoria Mary, Princess of Wales, *b.* 1867.

Francis, *b.* 1870.

Alexander = Princess Alice
b. 1874. of Albany,
b. 1883.

Frederick VIII., *b.* 1843.

Queen Alexandra, *b.* 1844.

George, King of Greece, *b.* 1845.

THE HOUSE OF HANOVER.

f York, Bishop of Osnaburg,
'4–1728.

ouisa = Frederick V., King of Denmark, 1723–1766.
1751.

Mary = Frederick II., Landgrave of Hesse-Cassel.
1723–1772.

William Augustus, Duke of Cumberland, 1721–1765 (*o.s.p.*).

Caroline Matilda = Christian VII.,
1751–1775. 1749–1808.

Frederick VI., 1768–1839.

Landgrave Frederick = Caroline of Nassau
1747–1837. Usingen, 1762–1823.

Alfred, 1780–1782.

Mary = William Frederick, Duke of Gloucester, 1776–1834 (*o.s.p.*).
1776–1857.

Landgrave William, 1787–1867, *m.* Charlotte of Denmark, 1789–1864.

Augusta, Duchess of Cambridge, 1797–1889.

ta,
40.

Elizabeth, 1770–1840, *m.* Frederick, Landgrave of Hesse-Homburg, 1769–1829 (*o.s.p.*).

Sophia, 1777–1848.

Amelia, 1783–1810.

iam, Grand
klenburg
9–1904.

Mary, 1833–1897 *m.* Francis, Duke of Teck, 1837–1900.

Louise = Christian IX., King of Denmark, 1818–1906.
1817–1898.

Mary,
of Wales,
867.

Francis, *b.* 1870.

Alexander = Princess Alice of Albany,
b. 1874. *b.* 1883.

Frederick VIII., *b.* 1843.

Queen Alexandra, *b.* 1844.

George, King of Greece, *b.* 1845.

Dagmar, Empress-Dowager of Russia, *b.* 1847.

Thyra, Duchess of Cumberland, *b.* 1853.

Waldemar, *b.* 1858.

PEDIGREE No. 2.

Sophia = Emmanuel Count Mensdorff-Pouilly, 1777–1852.
1778–1835.

- Hugo, 1806–1847.
- Alphonse, 1810–1894.
- Alexander, 1813–1871, *m.* Alexandrine, Countess Dietrichstein, 1824–1906.
  - Hugo, Prince of Dietrichstein, *b.* 1858, *m.* Olga, Princess Dolgorouky, *b.* 1873.
  - Albert, *b.* 1861.
  - Clotilde, *b.* 1867, *m.* Albert, Count Apponyi.
- Arthur, 1817–1904.

Antoinette = Alexander, Duke of Würtemberg, 1771–1833.
1779–1824.

- Duke Friedrich Wilhelm Alexander, 1804–1881, *m.* Marie, 1813–1839.
  - Philippe = Marie Thérèse of Austria, *b.* 1845.
    b. 1838.
- Ernest, 1807–1868, *m.* (*morg.*) Natalie Mme. de Grunhof, *b.* 1836.

Grand Duke Constantine, 1779–1831. = Julia, 1781–1860.

(*2nd*) Princess Marie of Würtemberg, 1799–1860. = Ernest I., Duke of Saxe-Saalfeld-Coburg, 1784–1844 = (*1st*) Louise of Saxe-Gotha-Altenburg, 1800–1831.

- Ernest II., Duke of Saxe-Coburg and Gotha, 1818–1893, *m.* Grand Duchess Alexandrina of Baden, 1820–1904.
- Albert = QUEEN VICTORIA, 1819–1901.
  1819–1861.
  - EDWARD VII., *b.* 1841.
  - Alfred, 1844–1900, Duke of Saxe-Coburg and Gotha, *m.* Marie Alexandrovna, Grand Duchess of Russia, *b.* 1853.
    - Alfred, 1874–1899, (*o.s.p.*).
  - Arthur, *b.* 1850, Duke of Connaught, *m.* Princess Louise Margaret of Prussia, *b.* 1860.
    - Arthur, *b.* 1883.
  - Leopold, 1853–1884, Duke of Albany, *m.* Princess Hélène de Waldeck-Pyrmont, *b.* 1861.
    - Charles Edward, *b.* 1884, Duke of Saxe-Coburg and Gotha, *m.* Princess Victoria of Schleswig-Holstein-Sonderburg-Glücksburg, *b.* 1885.

(*2nd*) Edward Augustus = Duke of Kent 1767–1820.

- Ernest, 1830–1904, *m.* Marie, Princess of Baden, 1834–1899.
- Edward Freder *b.* 1833.

N.B.—Those underlined are children of King Louis Philippe.

ERNEST, the Pious,
1601–1679.

John Ernest,
1658–1729.

Franz Josias,
1697–1764.

Ernest Frederick = Sophia Antoinette of Brunswick-Wolfenbüttel.
1724–1800.

Francis Frederick of Saxe-Saalfeld-Coburg, 1750–1806. *m.* (*2nd*) Augusta Caroline Sophia of Reuss Ebersdorf, 1757–1831.

(*1st*) Louise of Saxe-Gotha-Altenburg, 1800–1831.

(*2nd*) Edward Augustus = Mary Louisa Victoria = (*1st*) Emich Charles, Prince of Leiningen,
Duke of Kent 1767–1820. | 1786–1861. | 1763–1814.

Ferdinand = Antoinette de Kohary,
1785–1851. | 1797–1862.

Princess Charlotte of Wales, 1796–1817. = LEOPOLD I. King of the Belgians, 1790–1865. = Louise Marie, 1812–1850.

QUEEN VICTORIA, 1819–1901.

Charles, 1804–1856, *m.* Marie, Countess of Klebelsberg. 1806–1880.

Feodore, 1807–1872, *m.* Ernest, Prince of Hohenlohe-Langenburg, 1794–1860.

Victoria, 1822–1857, *m.* Duc de Nemours, 1814–1896.

Ferdinand, 1816–1885, *m.* MARIA II. da Gloria, Queen of Portugal, 1819–1853.

Leopold, 1824–1884.

Augustus = Clémentine,
1818–1881. | 1817–1907.

Louis, 1833–1834.

Louise, *b.* 185[...] *m.* Philip of S[...] Coburg, *b.* 18[...]

[...]ld. [...]–1884, [...]e of [...]ny, [...]Princess [...]ne de [...]leck-[...]nont, [...]861.

Ernest, 1830–1904, *m.* Marie, Princess of Baden, 1834–1899.

Edward Frederick, *b.* 1833.

Charles, *b.* 1829.

Hermann, *b.* 1832, *m.* Leopoldine of Baden, 1837–1903.

Ernest, *b.* 1863, *m.* Alexandra, Princess of Saxe-Coburg-Gotha, *b.* 1878.

Victor, Count Gleichen, 1833–1891, *m.* Laura, daughter of Sir G. Seymour, *b.* 1833.

Albert Edward, Count Gleichen, *b.* 1863. | Feodore. | Victoria. | Helena.

Frederick = Adelaide,
Duke of Schleswig-Holstein, 1829–1880. | *b.* 1835.

PEDRO V. 1837–1861.

LUIS = Marie Pie of Savoy,
1838–1889. | *b.* 1847.

CARLOS = Amélie of Orleans Bourbon,
b. 1863. | *b.* 1865.

Louis Philippe, Duc de Bragance, *b.* 1887.

Manuel, Duc de Beja, *b.* 1889.

Augustus = Leopoldina, Princess of Brazil,
b. 1845. | 1847–1871.

Clotilde = Archduke Joseph of Austria,
b. 1846. | *b.* 1833.

Amélie = Duke Maximilian of Bavaria,
b. 1848. | *b.* 1849.

Philippe = Louise,
b. 1844. | *b.* 185[...]

Leopold, *b.* 1878. | Dorot[...] *b.* 18[...]

Prince Ferdinand of Bulgaria = Pri[...]
b. 1861.

Boris, *b.* 1894. | Cyril, *b.* 1895.

[...]s Edward, [...] 1884, [...]uke of Saxe-[...]oburg and [...]otha, [...] Princess [...]ictoria of [...]chleswig-[...]olstein-[...]onderburg-[...]lücksburg, [...] 1885.

THE ANCESTRY OF PRINCE ALBERT.

…arlotte = LEOPOLD I. = Louise Marie,
…ales, King of the Belgians, 1790–1865. 1812–1850.
…1817.

…old, …1884.

Augustus = Clémentine,
1818–1881. 1817–1907.

Louis,
1833–1834.

LEOPOLD II.,
b. 1835,
m. Marie Henriette of Austria,
1836–1902.

Philippe, Comte de Flandre, 1837–1905. = Marie, Princess de Hohenzollern, *b.* 1845.

Charlotte *b.* 1840 = Archduke Ferdinand, afterwards Emperor Maxmilian of Mexico, 1832–1867.

Louise, *b.* 1858, *m.* Philip of Saxe-Coburg, *b.* 1844.

Stéphanie, *b.* 1864, *m.* Rudolph, Crown Prince of Austria, 1858–1889.

Clementine, *b.* 1872.

…oldina, …incess …Brazil, …47–1871.

Clotilde *b.* 1846. = Archduke Joseph of Austria, *b.* 1833.

Amélie *b.* 1848. = Duke Maximilian of Bavaria, *b.* 1849.

Philippe *b.* 1844. = Louise, *b.* 1858.

Leopold, *b.* 1878.
Dorothea, *b.* 1881.

Prince Ferdinand of Bulgaria *b.* 1861. = Princess Marie Louise of Bourbon-Parma, 1870–1899.

Boris, *b.* 1894.
Cyril, *b.* 1895.
Eudoxie, *b.* 1898.
Nadejda, *b.* 1899.

Baldwin, 1869–1891.

Henrietta *b.* 1870. = Emmanuel, Prince of Orleans, *b.* 1872.

Josephine *b.* 1873. = Prince Charles Antoine of Hohenzollern, *b.* 1868.

Albert *b.* 1875. = Elizabeth, Duchess of Bavaria, *b.* 1876.

Leopold, *b.* 1901.
Charles, *b.* 1903.
Marie, *b.* 1906.

INDEX

(*The page references in italics refer to Introductory Notes or footnotes.*)

Printed by Hazell, Watson & Viney, Ld., London and Aylesbury.

847604

Printed in Great Britain by
Amazon.co.uk, Ltd.,
Marston Gate.